The New
Ad Media
Reality

THE NEW AD MEDIA REALITY

Electronic over Print

BARTON C. WHITE

QUORUM BOOKS
Westport, Connecticut • London

Library of Congress Cataloging-in-Publication Data

White, Barton.
    The new ad media reality : electronic over print / Barton C. White.
        p.   cm.
    Includes bibliographical references and index.
    ISBN 0-89930-795-7 (alk. paper)
    1. Broadcast advertising.   2. Advertising.   I. Title.
HF6146.B74W48   1993
659.14 – dc20   93 – 18242

British Library Cataloguing in Publication Data is available.

Library of Congress Catalog Card Number: 93–18242
ISBN: 0-89930-795-7

First published in 1993

Quorum Books, 88 Post Road West, Westport, CT 06881
An imprint of Greenwood Publishing Group, Inc.

Printed in the United States of America

The paper used in this book complies with the
Permanent Paper Standard issued by the National
Information Standards Organization (Z39.48–1984).

10 9 8 7 6 5 4 3 2 1

To my mother, Dorothy R. White,
who taught me the meaning of perseverance
by her own example

and

To Carol . . . and the memories we share

Contents

Illustrations

FIGURES

Preface

Bringing clarity to the main thesis of this book and dispelling traditional myths have been made easier for me through interaction with hundreds of media salespeople and business owners and managers over the past several years in seminar settings. My thanks to these many people who have willingly given me feedback on the varied topics discussed in the chapters that follow.

Naturally, nothing moves forward without an equal but opposite force. I am grateful to Cliff Dodge, former executive director of the Colorado Broadcasters Association and present executive director of the Colorado Motor Carriers Association, for providing just the right amount of encouragement to cause this project to gain momentum and roll on to completion.

I also extend sincere gratitude to graphic artist Kathy Barnes, whose cheerful attitude and professional skills ensured a better and more complete manuscript. Much thanks also goes to American Demographics Books of Ithaca, New York, who provided much needed and detailed demographic information that made Chapter 5 so complete.

Every writer also needs a publisher who is more human and understanding than the mold should allow. That person is Eric Valentine. He is a solid professional whose understanding and flexibility made writing the manuscript more joy than labor. He gave me a rope the length of Long Island and said, "Run with it," also knowing the precise time to reel it back in and say "Rewrite!" For this guidance, I am eternally grateful.

And finally, thanks to you, the reader, for caring enough to want additional information that may lead to heightened future success. This book, after all, is for you and the tomorrows you will create with newly acquired knowledge and the inspiration to change the paradigms of the past.

Introduction

This book must necessarily begin with an explanation, for it may not be what the reader expects. Many books are written about advertising and how to put advertising, promotion, and marketing to work in corporate America for maximum efficiency, but few present the various forms of mass media with concrete recommendations. This book will take such a stand and will make such a recommendation, simply due to the fact that all advertising is not created equal.

The explanation of this thesis, however, and the attendant marketing and advertising discussions supporting this reality will not be painted in such excruciating detail and complexity that the average reader would not be inclined to proceed further into the material. Education is most successful when it is broken down into simple, understandable components.

THE CHALLENGE TO ADVERTISERS

That the typical corporate and business advertiser today is facing an uncertain economic future within an increasingly competitive business environment unforeseen in past decades is an observation few would dispute. That this sprawling corporate landscape, cluttered with new businesses and retail arenas amid the carcasses of the old, also includes a fair number of radio and television stations, thrifty-nickel type papers, and more billboards and signs than the eye can behold is also an undeniable reality.

Competition is as rampant within the advertising industry as it is within the business community it seeks to serve. More media outlets can provide choices for the consumer, but such media clutter can also be a source of confusion for the corporate or business media planner who is genuinely perplexed about managing an advertising budget that will generate desired results while simultaneously reflecting the least amount of possible waste.

The challenge to business and corporate advertising managers is, of course, to minimize such advertising waste by efficiently reaching an identified demographic or market segment, by placing the right message on the right media at the right time. If this is not attended to, advertising waste is inevitable and budgets become inefficient.

Over time, since the message of the business is not reaching the proper market segment efficiently, business traffic declines, sales erode, and the corporation itself may teeter on the verge of bankruptcy. Those not able to reverse such a situation will become additional carcasses amid yet other new businesses, which enter the arena feeling they can do better. Indeed, the marketplace is at once complex and confusing to both consumers and advertisers.

THE COMPLEXITY OF THE 1990s

The marketplace of earlier decades, which may now appear so innocent and simplistic, has evolved into a complex matrix of consumer choices that are changing the way in which products and businesses are promoted and advertised.

When I was growing up, I wanted a 1957 Chevy. And a 1957 Chevy was just that—one model as easily identified then as now. The choice was the color that one model would be. Today's domestics, as well as imports, come in dozens of models that make shopping for and buying a new car an entirely different experience. That simple, uncomplicated marketplace for the 1957 Chevy also existed for just about every other product and service as well.

McDonald's opened up for business in 1955 and had all of us lined up to the street to buy a burger that was not nearly as good as we could get elsewhere but only cost fifteen cents. Fast food was McDonald's. Today the colorful marquees of fast food restaurants on crowded strips beacon customers like so many bug lights. Not only is the food served fast, but many now offer home delivery as well.

The experience of eating (no longer "dining") is quite different and more complex than it used to be, making the experience of today's consumer vastly different from that confronting consumers in the marketplace of the 1950s and 1960s. McDonald's, though, has managed to hold onto its "first and number one" position during the evolution of market change by cleverly adapting to customer needs and targeting its advertising to generations of younger children who find it difficult to believe other food exists outside of "McDonaldland."

The "Big Blue" of IBM once owned the computer marketplace. If consumers wanted a computer, they went to IBM. Today the selection is almost as vast as models in a new car lot, with most of them claiming to be "IBM compatible." A different playground today? You bet.

ADVERTISING BUDGETS THEN AND NOW

With fewer products in the pipeline and fewer stores selling them, the days of yore were indeed less complex. Shopping was done mostly downtown, with the large department stores (today in large part either in Chapter 11 or out of business completely) magnetically drawing consumers to midtown on crowded buses and, yes, in their 1957 Chevys! Advertisers promoted at will, with more margins available to them than today's competition affords, and if there was waste in this effort, well, so be it.

Today's advertisers cannot afford waste. The profit margins are not there as before. Micromanaging by defining an exact demographic for a precise marketing effort must exist if a store wishes to celebrate a new century by remaining in business. Catering to a specific market niche means that the days of mass marketing to an entire nation are virtually over. Products will begin to carve out local niches in various sections of the country in order to appeal to the more indigenous traits of that region.

NATIONAL IS OUT–LOCAL IS IN

While many of us think we are watching "national" commercials during the evening news or prime time television, several are actually commercials for a national product that are designed for the cluster or region in which we live. Good national commercials are developing a strong verbal and visual consistency tied to the local, cultural identity of the region in which they are aired. In a word, they are nationally consistent but consciously local.

Crest toothpaste, for example, does not try to get "everybody" to buy their toothpaste by using the same national commercial. They have different strategies designed for the youth market, for ethnic populations, and for middle-aged parents. Each segment can be micromanaged by using highly targeted media to accomplish campaign goals.

Budgets for the big companies are no longer national in nature. Campbell's Soups, for example, does not try to hit "everybody" by scheduling one national commercial. They have divided the country into twenty-one clusters with separate marketing strategies targeted to each unique area. "Local" is in. "National" is out.

Notwithstanding, some companies on the national/global scene whose products seem to cut across all cultures, regions, and demographics, have found target marketing surprisingly uncomplicated, simply because the world population is the intended target market. Such a homogenized view of all cultures can only be taken by companies whose product is the undisputed brand leader—companies like Coca-Cola, whose advertising has gone global and runs in over one hundred countries with the same basic message. That a "McWorld" sameness does exist, allowing a company like Coca-Cola to cut across cultural boundaries, cannot be denied. But within that world cocoon lies regional and cultural differences that most businesses cannot ignore.

Today's marketplace is also showing that it is no longer product-driven alone. Consumers are searching for experiences that go beyond merely identifying a "1957 Chevy" and buying it. The experience of "buying" itself and even of the post-buying period are significant parts of today's consumer experience.

REEVALUATING MEDIA AND ADVERTISING CHOICES

In the face of these changes, traditional forms of advertising via the local newspaper must be reevaluated, as the newspaper that once flourished as the main vehicle for delivering news and information to consumers in bygone days has also seen its marketplace radically change — just as the market has changed for the Chevy, for fast food restaurants, and for computers.

The newer kids on the block are the radio and television stations that have changed the way in which all consumers now receive their news, information, and entertainment. Because of this, the electronic media offer the opportunity for today's advertisers to target their defined market niche by surgically striking at that one defined group who can and will keep them in business for the long run. Such narrow target marketing is something that simply cannot be done with print media.

Advertisers must recognize this change as surely as they must recognize the changes that have occurred in the marketplace over the past three decades. Such a change in attitudes is what is termed a "paradigm shift" in thinking. As the rules change to fit a new game, advertisers must change with the times or go out of business altogether.

WHAT THIS BOOK IS NOT

This book is not a vain attempt to empirically validate data and conclusions. Much of the information discussed is, of course, validated by accepted research in the fields of consumer behavior, marketing psychology, and advertising, but the problem with any type of research is that it presents the majority conclusion based on the operating variables that exist with a particular market segment at the time of data collection. There is always a minority opinion and available counter-research to validate an opposite finding.

At some point, anecdotal evidence, common sense, and personal experience must inevitably enter the equation. No apology is made for that occurrence in this book. Attempting to present the thesis in any other way be would seeking to quantify that which is nonquantifiable. As Jeffrey Pfeffer correctly points out, there are limits to facts and analysis: "It is evident that analysis and outside expertise can be employed strategically to affect decisions and actions. . . . But this is not invariably the case. It turns out in organizational life, common sense and judgment are often more important than so-called facts and analysis."[1]

THAT UNPREDICTABLE CONSUMER

Most of us are inclined to put our own instincts and observations ahead of what is presented by available research. Do consumers really care what national trends say they ought to be thinking, doing, or eating, and why they are doing it?

Consumers make predictable as well as inexplicable buying decisions every day. The reasons for such behavior are presented, understanding that the consuming public is going to do what they are going to do. No amount of data crunching can explain why young adults continue to take up the habit of smoking in face of all the available health data on the subject, or why adults keep eating Frosted Flakes or Fruit Loops when they know they ought to be swallowing oat bran.

As your guide, I merely attempt to steer you through this maze of consumer behavior, marketing, advertising, and promotion in an attempt to discover what appears to be a solid working model for advertising success. Many may not accept my conclusions, but let them be the first to advance working models and ideas of their own that will result in increased market share and business-related goal achievement.

A DIFFERENT APPROACH

That I have chosen to defend one form of advertising over other possible forms does present a different approach from the traditional business book analysis, but for what I hope to be very logical reasons. As the reasons for this choice unfold, the reader will receive a large dose of the currently available advertising and market research. This information will be presented in ways that will be useful to the typical mid-sized corporation or business that plans and implements its own advertising strategy with the help of advertising sales representatives from the various mass media outlets or with the assistance of an advertising agency. Information is also presented in ways that are understandable and not encyclopedic in depth and volume.

Insofar as there will be no attempt to hide the point of view this book attempts to present, there will be no apologies. I am unabashedly pro-electronic media, favoring radio and television as the advertising outlets that will produce the best, most cost-efficient results for advertisers.

There are multiple reasons for this preference, which I will disclose in the following chapters, although the reader should note that one single method of advertisement for every situation is never recommended. A media mix appears to be the sane approach with newspaper, under certain defined conditions, a part of that mix. All advertising, print as well as electronic, is arguably effective; it is just that some forms of advertising are more efficient.

The rationale for my approach stems from what is known about the published research and writing in the areas of advertising and marketing over the years. More important, however, this approach comes from years of working with these businesses as an advertising sales representative and from my current consulting practice that puts me in touch with media salespeople and businesspeople from across the country on a monthly basis.

From interacting with these groups, I have developed an attitude and a perspective that I believe are defensible and will help all retail and consumer-oriented businesses survive a volatile decade that will surely see a "shake-out" of many as we prepare to enter a new century filled with economic and social insecurity.

Additionally, I am weary seeing corporations and businesses losing market share or eventually failing altogether, while directing a majority of their advertising budget toward the print media. I am tired of media planners putting thousands and thousands of dollars into advertising that they do not understand and of the knee-jerk reaction those who plan and work in advertising have toward solving real business problems.

As a result, I seek understanding and efficiency in the media planning process. I have yet to work with a retail group or professional media salespeople who really know what advertising can do. All businesspeople, understandably, want results today and uniformly advertise this week for results this weekend. Advertising does not work this way. It is not the panacea that people expect, especially when it is used incorrectly.

ADVERTISING WASTE

An important economic concern is that of waste in advertising or investing in advertising that does not produce an identifiable return. Advertising is produced and scheduled each day that is neither creative nor targeted toward the correct market segment or consumer group. It is bought and sold with no further thought than conforming to what had always been done before, and in light of personal relations developed within a marketplace "at the club."

What is bought is fraught with overexpectation—that "everyone" wants what is being advertised and that the entire populace is a viable market. Not much is understood about the very small market that is actually interested in anything any corporation or business does on a daily basis and how that small "bulls-eye" can be efficiently targeted. This book will address that issue for the reader in understandable terms.

Probably the world of advertising will not be greatly advanced or improved by another book on the topic, but it may be nudged onward by greater overall understanding at all levels.

THE ECONOMIC NECESSITY OF ADVERTISING

The overall need for advertising and its role in our competitive economic system is likely beyond dispute. Without advertising of all types, consumers would be ignorant of available products and their resultant advantages and/or disadvantages within the greater marketplace. Few consumers go into any store with no prior knowledge of the product or service for which they have a need.

Consumers know what is available in the marketplace and generally know the features they are looking for and can afford. What they fail to understand and maybe care less about is the complicated processes by which this knowledge becomes a part of their psyche. But a savvy advertiser who understands such a phenomenon will have a tremendous marketing advantage.

Since advertising, per se, can almost be considered an a priori necessity, what will not be attempted in the overall discourse is to somehow "prove" to the reader that advertising works. Volumes have been written on this issue and I have no desire to redo the wheel. The bottom line is that, yes, indeed, it is a necessity and it does work—but usually only if it is used correctly. Exactly how to engage in advertising that is fruitful is one of the goals of this book.

Such information is, of course, readily available to the business community, given the number of media and advertising salespeople the average retailer or businessperson may see in one week. Surely these professionals could instruct and educate the buyer. Some do, of course, but the truth is, most of them do not know how advertising works either.

THE COMPETITIVE ENVIRONMENT

If advertising planners desire to keep their jobs or corporations want to remain in business in a hotly competitive environment, they need to become as knowledgeable about the information in this book, and maybe even more so, as are the people whose job it is to sell advertising to them.

Make no mistake about it. Businesses today are engaged in heavy head-to-head competition and nobody has ever said that it is going to become easier. Look around you if you are a businessperson. How many direct competitors do you have? How many new competitors could enter your marketplace before the year 2000? Depending on market size, some of these businesses will not be here to ring in a new century.

And the competition is not just price competition, a mistake many businesses make. Consumers buy and become loyal customers because of many buying variables; price is only one of several discussed in this book.

Since head-to-head competition is a reality and not a myth, advertising presents a stage on which the positive and unique attributes of a business can be displayed to an audience who understands that "imitation" rather than uniqueness is the business buzzword of the 1990s. Helping a business discover its true uniqueness, so that more than its advertising can stand out in the cluttered marketplace, is also a goal of this book.

OTHER ROLES OF ADVERTISING

Advertising also serves the role of teacher and educator. Certainly there exists a bias toward the product or service being promoted, but most consumer groups (children would be the obvious exception) can be expected to know this and to be able to process the information in meaningful ways that will assist in the overall decision-making and buying process. This approach gives overall credit to the masses, who are generally able to distinguish advertising from other forms of programming and are not swept up in the "culture jammers" paranoia that sinister forces are at work in the marketplace and that media images erase critical thinking by becoming a cultural substitute for common sense and reason.

This book assumes that advertising greases the wheel of the local community's economic infrastructure, and that radio or television is the proper way to reach a mobile market of dual-income families that no longer have the time to get information from the printed source our parents had the leisure time to consume over breakfast or an evening meal.

That the electronic media dominate our society in ways earlier generations probably would never understand is beyond dispute. This book makes no moral argument that children should spend more time reading than watching television (which they understandably should), that teenagers ought to turn down the volume on their stereos or boomboxes, or that adults should spend more quality time with family or books at the expense of prime time television.

The point is, each of us will still remain loyal to our favorite radio stations and the prime time sitcoms will always draw millions of viewers, regardless of all the valid educational arguments made in favor of more reading and more quality family time. And all of us in the business – advertisers, media planners, consultants, and academics – know this. We know full well where all people spend a great portion of their day, and advertisers are going to attempt to get these audiences to attend to their message, regardless!

There exists a media culture whose values seem to place the commodity or advertised product above the human factor, but such commodities do not exist as a result of the media. They exist to meet the needs of and to serve the consumer, with advertising being the legitimate means by which to present the commodity to that individual.

ON BEING GREEN AND THE ENVIRONMENT

It would be irresponsible to address the issues in the following chapters without expressing deep sensitivity for existing global environmental concerns. A book on advertising certainly promotes consumption within highly developed societies that use up a disproportionate amount of the available natural resources.

Yet without consumption, jobs in the developed nations would not be available to support the populations of the developed countries, who would then not have the tax dollars to assist and educate developing countries as they struggle with a myriad of concerns, not the least of which are environmental.

Consumption of natural resources is not the issue anyway. It comes down to *responsible* consumption. The 1992 UN Earth Summit focused the attention of the world on environmental concerns when 110 global leaders met in Rio de Janeiro to discuss ways in which the environment can be protected.

The companies that truly learn the meaning of responsibility, which become "green" in their manufacturing, packaging, and distribution processes and not just in their advertising, will own the markets of the future. To advocate consumerism with such companies is responsible.

Consumers are not altogether naive about the environment. They will buy environmentally "safe" products if they are available and will shun those companies that pollute without conscience. By supporting those manufacturers and businesses that are efficient and verifiably green, a huge consumer statement can be made that will have a noted collective environmental impact.

THE DIRECTION OF THIS BOOK, CHAPTER BY CHAPTER

I have begun this odyssey by giving the reader a perspective on advertising, advertising waste, and the observation that all advertising is not created equal. After Chapter 1 gives the reader a brief historical tour that shows how print has become a part of the economic infrastructure for literally generations, it is not difficult to understand the knee-jerk reaction to making it a huge part of the advertising budget despite the lifestyle changes from a reading society to one dependent upon the electronic media for information and entertainment.

The evolution of the electronic media society in this century is also attended to, from David Sarnoff to modern-day consumer decisions and how they are made.

The second chapter will give the reader a more thorough understanding of consumer behavior and how advertising influences this behavior. Various consumer models will be discussed that will provide a more thorough understanding of the dynamics of the local marketplace as advertising decisions are made.

Chapter 3 will specifically get into areas that most businesspeople and media representatives are confused about: what advertising in general can and cannot do and what the specific limitations of all forms of advertising are.

Discussed will be exactly how the nonintrusive nature of print advertising works and how the intrusive nature of the electronic media affects consumer behavior. Why businesspeople need to look at advertising as a long-term proposition is also given the appropriate amount of attention.

Also addressed will be the specific variables that cause a potential consumer to become a loyal customer. Price is only one variable, advertising another.

Chapter 4 discusses learning behavior and the psychology behind how we are taught and how we learn new information. Educational psychology ties directly to the ways in which advertising and the various forms of mass media operate. Understanding these concepts can help the reader decide which media to buy for advertising purposes and why.

In Chapter 5 attention is turned to the important topic of market segmentation and target demographics. This can help corporate media planners and businesspeople better identify who their customers really are, something that must be precisely known before media can be purchased to reach those prospects and customers.

Chapter 6 details important concepts most advertisers do not understand: the percentage of consumers who are in the market at any given time for any given product. How to reach this segment with solid, creative copy is also attended to.

Chapter 7 delves into the minds of dozens of corporate media planners who have given their opinions about their advertising experiences with newspapers and with the electronic media. Their responses are revealing and insightful at best, naive and hopelessly traditional at worst. These candid interview responses are analyzed and commented upon in the attempt to further advance the understanding of how advertising works or should work in this last decade of the twentieth century.

Chapter 8 concerns itself with the new technologies that dance before all consumer groups and advertisers as we enter a new century.

NOTE

1. Jeffrey Pfeffer, *Managing With Power* (Boston: Harvard Business School Press, 1992), p. 254.

The New Ad Media Reality

CHAPTER 1

Advertising and Information

The enemies of advertising are the enemies of freedom.
— Enoch Powell, British Politician

ADVERTISING IS NOT CREATED EQUAL

All advertising is not created equal. There is no parity in the advertising game and there never was. There exist distinct and measurable differences in the forms of advertising available to America's corporations, businesses, and retailers, although one could have difficulty understanding such differences when presented with the lopsided advertising expenditures that have favored the newspaper industry over the electronic media in the past seven or eight decades.

Simply stated, these expenditures have been the decisions of well-meaning ad executives, retail budget managers, and agency media buyers who did not and still do not fully understand these differences. When decisions on which media should be used to accomplish advertising objectives are made with incomplete information, traditional notions begin to take the place of logic. The beneficiary of a thought process that does not contain complete information will naturally be the newspaper industry and print advertising, a part of the business infrastructure for generations.

The Language of Corporate America — Retailing

In the world of corporate affairs, invariably driven by management concern for a defensible return on investment capital, the better-than-average understanding of the advertising component looms more pivotal to business success than mere academic curiosity. Indeed, business competition in all markets seems to have gone awry, making marketplace survival a product of keen marketing, promotional, and advertising efforts.

However, the need to understand the essence of "what is" in advertising runs deeper than the need to preserve a set ideology or a firm set of principles. What is being protected by the better understanding of how advertising works in a consumer-oriented economy are the principles of business itself within a capitalistic, free-enterprise system. What drives corporate America and, hence, a large segment of the country's economy is not the high-tech industries of Silicon Valley, the emerging luster of biotechnology companies, or even the fiber-optic developments in new telecommunications technologies.

What pushes America forward is the developed system of moving goods and services to the ultimate end-user or consumer, or simply stated, the system of doing business vis-à-vis the retail marketplace. The business of retailing is the business of America, representing a sizable portion of the Gross National Product. Competition is high within the retail industry, as barriers to entry are few.

An enterprising company with a better idea and the capital to back it, can launch such an idea in the form of a product in whatever time it takes to manufacture, distribute, and stock the product on the appropriate retail shelves. The marketing, advertising, and selling of the product provide service sector jobs, the reordering of the product in demand retains manufacturing jobs, and the resultant profits provide investor returns, which can then be reinvested or used to buy other goods or services.

Without appropriate advertising designed to appeal to specifically identified target markets with the least amount of waste, this system of moving manufactured goods and professional services to consumers can break down. The result of a broken retail/business system is the reverse of a system running well: loss of manufacturing and service sector jobs and the eventual closing of once successful businesses. This phenomenon is already occurring; some of the more established retailers like Bloomingdale's and Macy's have reorganized under Chapter 11 bankruptcy protection.

However, corporate success stories in retailing are far more dramatic than the apparent doomsday scenarios. Arkansas-based Wal-Mart, once opening stores only in small towns across the South and Mid-America, is now setting its sights on metro markets in the more populated states and is predicted to become the nation's largest corporation, surpassing even General Motors, by the end of the decade. En route to this legendary success, Wal-Mart has provided better returns for its investors than any of the new high-tech companies, biotech stocks, or top Fortune 500 companies. When businesspeople talk retailing, whether on the local, regional or national level, they are talking big business collectively and the language of corporate America.

The oil that runs the machine of big business goes by the name of advertising and to not fully understand retail/corporate advertising in its widest and fullest sense is akin to starting a combustion engine with a gallon of milk. More than luck will be needed to produce results.

Advertising Waste

A major concern facing those who plan, purchase, and evaluate advertising space and media schedules is that of overall waste. That is, how much of the company's or store's advertising is going unnoticed, is not being consumed by the appropriate demographic group or intended target customer, or is not producing results even when it is placed or targeted correctly with the appropriate mass media, the correct schedule, or space allocation and at the right time for maximum results?

That waste does occur in all forms of advertising is beyond dispute. Waste occurs not only in the delivery of the message itself (being targeted to the wrong demographic or not being properly impressed upon a right demographic), but in the copy that is used to impress or reach the intended target group (the right message targeted to the right market segment is ineffective with the wrong copy).

Reducing Advertising Waste

Reducing actual waste inherent in the advertising process may be argued from many perspectives, but the corporate/business advertising budget itself may be a logical place to begin, simply because these budgets often finance other projects outside the realm of pure advertising, "pure" being that effort designed to elicit a direct consumer response to a product or a business.

As an example consumers certainly cannot respond to off-media promotions (below-the-line) costs such as trade shows, the cost of which is invariable borne by the advertising budget. Trade shows are designed to move merchandise from manufacturer to retailer, thus enabling stores to be stocked with goods that can then move with the assistance of advertising. If consumers are out of the loop, waste certainly does occur; in this case, however, it occurs because the budget was used improperly — not because what was done was improper. Separate promotional budgets to differentiate promotional efforts from advertising efforts may be advisable for companies that roll both off-media promotions like trade shows and direct retail advertising efforts into one.

And what about so-called above-the-line or pure budgetary costs? Of course waste does occur in the mass media advertising effort itself. Some convincingly argue that the real measurable effect of any advertising may be negligible under even the most ideal circumstances. However, certain above-the-line advertising expenditures, designed to elicit direct consumer response, are equally inefficient in delivering customers or in even making available an advertising message in any meaningful way.

The Yellow Pages is an example. As a reference medium, such a directory is referred to *after* the consumer's mind has been directed or franchised by traditional forms of the mass media. As such, Yellow Page "advertising" space for any business is mere courtesy display, not advertising.

If such an effort born from the advertising budget is not advertising, waste clearly exists as the expenditure is line-itemed under the advertising budget. Perhaps more businesses should consider the creation of a separate promotional budget apart from an advertising budget that is directed toward actual consumer-oriented retail advertising.

A Specific Approach to Waste

The concept of waste in this book will concern itself only with above-the-line media expenditures or those designed to produce direct retail results. One possible approach to the concept of "waste" in these types of advertising investments may be to actually confront the mindset of advertisers themselves, as well as the advertising agencies that place media buys. Optimism reigns supreme for those who place advertising, be they retail ad managers or media buyers for an advertising agency. No advertising of any type, however, is a panacea. Overexpectation of results can trigger increased buys, much the same as a hungry diner, optimistic about the amount of food that can be consumed from a limitless buffet, increases the amount of entrees on the plate, only to leave half uneaten. Targeted, well-planned advertising is not necessarily more effective if exposures are increased. A wear-out effect may be the result, with actual diminishing returns.

The vast amount of waste in corporate/business advertising actually occurs when advertising is placed with the least effective of the mass media (newspaper); inherent waste is minimized when advertising is placed on an educational/intrusive medium (radio or television) where consumers have no choice but to receive the impression. More simply stated, a one-time impression medium (newspaper) has little overall effect on cognition when compared to the intrusive nature of the electronic media where cognition is enhanced by the consumer receiving the message passively, that is, without choice. Waste is therefore minimized in cases where budgets favor the electronic media.

The evidence in this regard is compelling. To make a point, surely none of us consciously intends to memorize the many popular songs from past decades that are carried around for a lifetime inside of our heads. But those songs are there. Therein may lie some insight into how proper mass media selection may reduce advertising waste. Simply use the media whose function is unconsciously educational.

Advertising Waste in Perspective

All advertising managers and buyers fear great amounts of waste as a worst case scenario and, indeed, some waste is likely to occur with every buy. Maximum waste, however, can be avoided and, in fact, greatly minimized if the essence of advertising and what it can actually be expected to do for a company or product is fully understood before buying decisions are made.

Such understanding, however, does not seem to be apparent when one compares the total dollars spent on advertising and where these dollars are placed with the number of major retail businesses that lose significant market share to their competition each year or who file for Chapter 11 bankruptcy protection.

When market share erodes, what has happened is apparent: somewhere, somehow, the intended public did not respond. Lack of response certainly does correlate to advertising waste, even though numerous other variables are at play when market share is negatively impacted. These variables will be examined in Chapter 3, but one clear point can be made at this juncture. The companies whose stores are failing in the marketplace today are not necessarily new retail starts that have been in business for less than five years. The companies and the businesses failing today are established and respected retail leaders that have been in business in their respective fields for generations.

What these businesses failed to understand and what was partially responsible for market share loss was not their inability to grasp the changing nature of retailing or the intricacies of buying the right goods that the customer would demand in the consumer marketplace or even to present their goods properly in the retail environment.

What these businesses and companies did not understand and still do not is *how* to effectively reach a changing, mobile marketplace where over half of the women are in the workforce; where reading habits and the gathering of consumer information have dramatically changed; where large metro markets contain no majority group of consumers (the former "mass" market now composed of various minorities signifying a shrinking middle class); and where the mass media of radio and television have lost their essence of "mass" and are now narrowly targeting their intended markets.

When lack of understanding exists, decisions are made in a vacuum and knee-jerk reactions occur, leading to traditional decision making and the support of the status quo or what has always been. What has always been is the newspaper. What will not necessarily produce the results businesspeople expect today is this very same vehicle they have always used: the newspaper.

Such a recommendation, however, will be very difficult for many to comprehend and ultimately to do. Therefore, to understand the genesis of this phenomenon that has brought such favor to the newspaper industry, we need to backpedal for just a moment. Realizing how deeply ingrained newspaper is in the minds of the American psyche can help explain why newspaper advertising decisions are made today in such a knee-jerk, traditional manner. The decision to buy newspaper advertising is almost genetically ingrained and continued even after the more "glamorous" introduction of radio and then of television, as this quick but interesting step back in time will reveal.

A HISTORICAL PERSPECTIVE

A product of the age of mass production mothered by the Industrial Revolution, advertising grew up in the newspapers of Mother England and migrated to the eastern shores of America in the halcyon days of publishing when newspapers flourished in every city and town as essentially the only form of communication for both consumers and the advertising merchant class. The anticipated daily newspaper was a diversion from the pressures of urban life and, for many, the uncertainties of frontier existence.

As America developed a pioneer spirit and left the relative comforts of the larger cities to trek westward, the only established convenience that accompanied the wagon trains were the hand presses. Opening new frontiers was unarguably difficult. There were simply no guarantees, no certainties except the one provided by such presses — the daily newspaper.

Newspaper Growth

By the 1800s the newspaper industry had become a dominant cultural force. In New York City alone, there were forty-seven papers with a combined circulation of ninety thousand. Achieving greater influence and collective success than anything ever published in Europe, newspapers reached nine-tenths of the population. The American people, hard-working by nature and political by instinct, were ripe for all the information they could lay their eyes on.

Special interest papers grew up, pandering to the needs of certain prejudices and political groups, edited by those who wished to advance their own particular religious, mercantile, or political cause. Many, however, were respected for their high quality and established an early tradition for sound reporting and editorial standards. Hence, publications like the *Cleveland Plain Dealer,* the *Cincinnati Gazette,* the *New York Tribune,* and the *Philadelphia Ledger* became known for fairly explaining and interpreting local and national issues and justifiably enjoyed widespread circulation and notoriety.

Westward, Ho!

As the masses of European humanity pushed ever westward in search of their "manifest destiny," the towns and cities of the Plains and the American West grew to support their needs. Those thousands whose spirit of adventure or whose desire to discover wealth carried them across the Mississippi and the Missouri rivers had, of course, little interest in towns or cities. There were none to speak of, but there was an abundance of fertile agricultural land for a myriad of crops, grazing land for cattle, and panfuls of precious metal riches in the Rocky Mountain West if you could stake your claim before the next prospector.

After these settlers had established their niche in this new land of plentiful game, untamed beauty, and an indigenous people the white man and his government did not care to understand or tolerate, only then did the townsmen follow to make their living by providing the goods and services needed by such a rapidly expanding area. The entire land area west of the great rivers provided new expansion markets for these entrepreneurs, who built trading posts and city centers along the major trading routes established by the hunters, trappers, and early settlers.

The Press in the Developing West

Those who came to make their fortunes from their predecessors included the bankers, the merchants who ran the general stores, the bootmakers, the blacksmiths, the bakers, the doctors and lawyers, the barbers, the ministers, the sa-loonkeepers and brothel owners, and, of course, the newspaper editors with their hand presses. It was not unusual for a newspaper, usually a top priority in the establishment of a new town, to set up shop outdoors and publish a daily paper until a building was built or became available.

"Frequently, a newspaper preceded the town itself. William H. Adams, editor of the *Kansas Weekly Herald* of Leavenworth, printed his first issue on a river-bank in 1854 and wrote that 'All the type in the present number has been set under an elm tree.' When the first house in town was built, the paper moved in."[1]

One of the jobs of an early editor was to promote the community of which he was a part. Attracting prospective residents was a priority if these new towns were to survive. If an editor did not do an adequate job, according to the stan-dards of the citizenry, he could literally be run out of town. The story is told that in 1878, the editor of the Medicine Lodge Kansas paper, the *Barber County Mail,* printed an edition with broken type that was so hard to read "dissatisfied residents invaded the editor's premises and seized him with the intention of tar-ring and feathering him. No tar was available and no one was willing to contrib-ute the contents of a precious feather bed, but a way was found. The editor's critics coated him with sorghum molasses and feathered him with sand burrs, both of which were in abundant local supply. Then they capped the punishment by riding him around town on a wooden rail. The editor sold the paper shortly and left for parts unknown."

It is evident that newspapers have been a part of the infrastructure of America from colonial times through the development of the American West, but they have often been *the* infrastructure. Newspapers, saloons, and hotels seemed to appear overnight and with them, printed stories of untold commodity and mineral riches that could be found in the Rockies. Thousands of gold seekers with their families and possessions piled high on ox wagons invaded cities like Denver to pan the riches of Cherry Creek and Clear Creek, usually only to find disappoint-ment and starvation. Many people seemed to be trekking eastward, going back home with bitter thoughts of "hoax" on their weary minds; but many were still coming westward to find their fortune.

As soon as many would get halfway home, other stories of mining claims yielding unimagined riches would circulate via publications like Horace Gree-ley's *New York Tribune.* Many would then turn around to once again seek their future in the streams of the Rockies, much like a gambler often succumbs to the temptation of putting just one more dollar into the slot machine before retiring for the night.

The Press as Purveyor of Mythology

All during this time, newspapers in their role as trumpeters of a new way of life in the American West were building a mythology for readers in the populated and sometimes overly crowded cities of the industrial North and the Eastern Sea-board. This mythology had less to do with the reality of settling a rugged and

untamed wilderness than it did with building the notion of a Wild West complete
with a stage full of heroic characters.

Without a native mythology, America had to manufacture its heroes. A nation turning one
hundred years old had no *Odyssey*. . . . So the mythmaking machinery of nineteenth-
century American media created a suitably heroic archetype in the cowboys of the Wild
West. The image was of the undaunted cattle drivers living a life of reckless individualism,
braving the elements, staving off brutal Indian attacks. Or of heroic lawmen dueling with
sixguns in the streets at high noon. This artificial Wild West became America's *Iliad*. It
was an image so powerful, appearing first in the newspapers and reinforced in dime novels
and later through countless Hollywood movies, television series and cigarette commercials that it entered the American political mentality. This code of the cowboy shaped
policy and Presidents, perhaps most notably Teddy Roosevelt, Lyndon Johnson and
Ronald Reagan.[2]

The Newspaper as Advertising Vehicle

Ever since *The City Mercury* of 1620 England made itself available to the public free of charge, supported by advertising revenue only, the courtship of the
mercantile or business community by the newspaper industry was not to be re-
buked. As newspapers developed reputations and readers, so the developing merchant class was determined to reach this large class of reader-consumers through
advertising. Advertising supported both the publishers (through ad revenues) and
the merchants (by increasing awareness and, hence, retail or direct sales), therefore early solidifying a symbiotic relationship that exists to this day. In fact, many
local newspapers and the businesses that first supported them are today owned by
the same families that have done business together for generations.

That partnership between newspapers and the greater business community has
taken on even greater significance in the modern era of media advertising choice
where the traditional decision to buy newspaper as the main advertising vehicle
remains dominant despite logical arguments to the contrary.

Newspapers and the American Psyche

It is apparent that America's relationship with its many daily and weekly newspapers is deeply rooted and goes far beyond the cavalier attitude assumed by dis-
posing of the household newspaper on a daily basis. The newspaper has
historically been a part of American culture and, in fact, has *created* that culture
in many instances.

The newspaper industry itself represents American rugged individualism at its
best, its presses churning on river banks unsheltered as new towns grew before
them. Existence in a developing America was arguably a day-to-day, life-and-
death struggle.

Newspapers as Comfort Zone

Newspapers carved their niche as America's comfort zone with every fallen timber and every seed sown west of the Appalachian Trail, much as they had earlier established themselves as part of the Eastern infrastructure in cities like Philadelphia, New York, and Boston. Regardless of the politics, the economics, or the elements, the newspaper would publish. Day to day, week to week, and month to month, it was the one constant in an uncertain environment that populations everywhere could anticipate with regularity. And, as such, it has become ingrained in the American psyche—a permanent fixture that is a part of our consciousness, the definition of who we are as a people.

The Growth of Newspaper Advertising

The rise of the newspaper industry in America was exponential to the advertising support given it by the merchants who were eagerly touting their goods and services to a growing and equally eager populace. Newspaper ads for the barbershop services of shaving, shampooing, and haircutting "in the latest fashion" were common, along with ads for saloons, general merchandise, boots, firearms, and family provisions like groceries, blankets, and hats. With newspaper penetration (percentage of circulation within the general population) never higher, consumers seemed willing to read and believe most of what was in print—from editorials and editorial cartoons to the text of the many advertisements sprinkled throughout each daily or weekly edition of their local community newspaper.

This love affair with the American newspaper continued quite some time. In 1914 the number of newspapers publishing on a daily or weekly basis peaked with 2,250 individual papers and reached the ebb after World War II with 1,749 papers.[3]

The affair was certainly more than overnight and it was not until the advent of an even more appealing force that the luster of what was once considered the "mother's milk to an infant town" began to fade. This new force was an offspring of the age of the telegraph, only this new medium did not need wires. It was wireless communication, the most powerful advertising force ever unleashed, and it went by the name of "Radio."

THE GROWTH OF RADIO, TELEVISION, AND CABLE

As interesting as the development of the newspaper infrastructure in America, is the development of what seemed to be a magical technology in its day. Radio captivated the imagination and the attention of consumers of all ages and, of course, of corporate America who early on understood the power of using the latest in technologies to reach eager groups of consumers. However, even in the early years of wonderment, few totally understood how powerful this new elec-

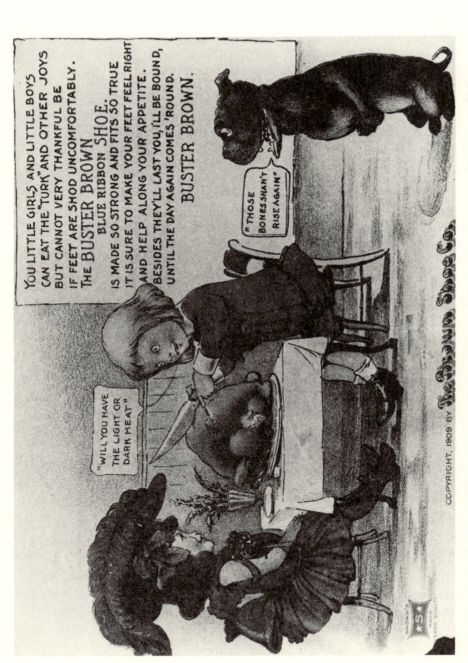

Buster Brown advertisement, 1909. Creativity took the form of poetry and a canine commentator. (Department of Library Special Collections, Western Kentucky University)

tronic medium would be as an advertising vehicle and how efficient it would be in the franchising of the consumer mind, something no newspaper could ever do then or now.

The Early Pioneers

The 1920s ushered in not only an era of "roaring" good times and a sense of the "high life," but also an era of uncontrolled growth within a new industry the Navy dubbed "broadcasting." During the time that the press was establishing itself within the political, economic, and social infrastructure of America, scientists worldwide like Hertz, Volta, Ampere, and Maxwell were experimenting with the basic nature of electricity.

Not only is this early history more interesting, it is important in documenting the central role of radio as an informational and entertainment medium more significant and relevant to the American public than newspaper ever was, even in the salad days of the developing Eastern Seaboard cities and the westward migration of frontier settlers.

Guglielmo Marconi

It was Guglielmo Marconi, an Italian working in Britain because his native country had snubbed his ideas, whom historians credit for developing the wireless telegraph. His new device could send Morse code dots and dashes up to a mile by utilizing radio or Hertzian waves, thus developing what was to be known as long-range communication or, simply, radio.

The British actually awarded Marconi the first patent ever issued for wireless telegraphy in 1896, and by 1899 his newly developed Marconi Wireless Telegraph Company was sending messages a distance of thirty-six miles. In 1901 he sent his famous dot-dot-dot or the Morse code letter "S" across the Atlantic from Cornwall to Newfoundland and a new era had begun. However, this new era would not be without its colorful characters and patent confusions over an emerging technology.

Nathan Stubblefield

In all fairness to broadcast history, it should be noted that Murray, Kentucky native Nathan Stubblefield claims to have invented the "radio-telephone" that led to the actual development of radio several years before Marconi sent his letter "S" across the Atlantic. An obscure and neglected figure of this era, Stubblefield actually transmitted his voice a distance of three miles in 1892 near his home in Murray and again in 1902, a feat far superior to Marconi's crude transmission of Morse code signals. Records seem to substantiate this claim. In fact, a photograph taken on the Potomac River, March 20, 1902, documents the first marine demonstration of "wireless telephony" using Stubblefield's voice-transmission invention.

Even before this photograph and wireless demonstration, a reporter from the

Broadcasting and receiving messages on the Potomac River, March 20, 1902. This was the first marine demonstration of "wireless telephony." Nathan Stubblefield is pictured third from the left. (Department of Library Special Collections, Western Kentucky University)

St. Louis Post-Dispatch, in a full-page article on January 12, 1902, wrote, "However underdeveloped his system may be, Nathan B. Stubblefield, the farmer inventor of Kentucky, has already discovered the principle of telephoning without wires. Today, he gave the Sunday Post-Dispatch a practical demonstration of his ability to do this and discussed his discovery as frankly as his own interest and self-protection would permit."

However, in this developing era of new technologies, it was not who was first with the new technology; it was who was first at the patent office. The U.S. Patent Office did issue Stubblefield a patent on May 12, 1908, but it came too late. Not only did Marconi have prior patents, but a research engineer, Dr. Lee DeForest, had received a patent in January 1907 for his audion tube, enabling radio or voice transmission as we know it today to come of age. DeForest filed over thirty patents from 1902 to 1906, setting the stage for radio patent wars on newly developed technologies that would last for decades.

DeForest himself would have difficulty with his patent rights, as his audion tube was an improvement of the Ambrose Fleming (a Marconi researcher) valve patent held by American Marconi. Since DeForest received the first patent and Stubblefield did not, history remembers DeForest and his professional heirs.

No one at this time seemed to be able to advance this new communication form without infringing on the rights of some other person or company — an understandable situation when dozens of scientists were working on the same new technology at the same time.

Nathan Stubblefield eventually died a historically forgotten man on March 28, 1928. Some poetic justice was served when the New York Supreme Court ruled in 1930 that his heirs had proven every detail in their claim for patent rights on radio transmitting and receiving equipment, but that the Statute of Limitations made void any claims to royalties.

Reginald Fessenden

With the technology for a new communications system apparent, improving upon it was the next step. Reginald Fessenden was able to develop an apparatus, similar to Stubblefield's, which would carry voice and music as well as the basic Morse code. In fact, General Electric built a high-frequency alternator in 1906 from Fessenden's original design.

Since Alexander Graham Bell had patented the telephone in 1876, Fessenden's wireless device was called the radiotelephone. It would change the American social and business landscape in a way unimagined until the advent of television some forty years later.

Fessenden unveiled his device on Christmas Eve of 1906 by first explaining what he was going to do and then playing phonograph music, playing a violin solo, and finally reading from the Bible and giving Christmas greetings. He later developed what was actually a radio set or receiver, the heterodyne receiver, which detected and decoded continuous wave signals. Because he was ahead of his time commercially, there was no market for what only worked in a laboratory setting and his inventions brought him no financial success.

Wartime and Technology

It is interesting to note that in times of war and pressing military needs, technological advancement often accelerates beyond the achievement level it could realize in peacetime. Such was the case with radio.

The need for improved communications systems in World War I brought funds and manpower to the development of this new laboratory technology, with the federal government taking control of the infant industry and suspending all patent restrictions and litigations. This allowed the new medium to develop unhampered, but operating control on the part of the government did not extend beyond the war. As the federal government had years earlier allowed private ownership and control of the telegraph industry, "it similarly handed over this important new medium of public communication to new interests. Radio was defined by this act as an arena of business competition as opposed to a public medium of communication to be operated by organizations of the government."[4]

This philosophy of private ownership of the airwaves obviously sets the American system of telecommunications apart from other countries like Great Britain and the former Soviet Union, where governmental control is the norm. It also sets the stage for our capitalistic indulgence in electronic media advertising to support the concept of private ownership.

David Sarnoff

Ever since a young man named David Sarnoff sat at his telegraph key and monitored the wireless distress signals being sent from the doomed *Titanic* that had rammed an iceberg in 1912, the commercial potential of this new wireless medium was apparent if not yet recognized. Sarnoff kept the American public aware of this historical tragedy for three days and nights, thus escalating the worldwide importance of a wireless form of communication.

As if by prophecy, Sarnoff would be the one to identify the commercial potential of wireless by later sending a memo to his superiors at his telegraph company predicting that a "radio music box" could be an economically profitable venture and could be placed in all American homes much as the piano or phonograph had been. It comes then as no surprise that when the Radio Corporation of America (RCA) consolidated a number of conflicting patent interests in 1919 to begin a commercial venture supported by stockholders, David Sarnoff was appointed the first president. He later founded NBC.

Chaos in the 1920s

It did not take long for this new "music box" medium to take hold with the American public, as dozens of stations seemingly sprang up overnight while manufacturers worked to produce these wondrous music boxes that could receive fascinating new signals. Not until 1927, with the frustrated assistance of Com-

David Sarnoff (left), the founder of NBC, and Guglielmo Marconi, the inventor of the radio, are shown during a visit to the RCA Communications transmitting center in Rocky Point, Long Island (N.Y.), in 1933. Sarnoff started his career at age 15 as an office boy for Marconi. (Courtesy, NBC-TV/Globe Photos, © National Broadcasting Company)

merce Secretary Herbert Hoover, did the Radio Act form the Federal Radio Commission (the forerunner of the FCC) to untie the frequency logjam by abolishing all existing radio licenses (thus forcing all to reapply), defining the AM broadcast band at 550–1500 kilohertz, and assigning spectrum space to stations applying for new licenses based on power, frequency, and times of operation. The new FRC also developed a plan that classified certain frequencies or channels as clear, regional, or local.*

However bad the logistical and technical nightmare of the 1920s seemed, it did nothing to dampen the spirit of the public who demanded more and more entertainment programming from this new music box companion that everyone had in their homes by the end of the decade and the beginning of the Great Depression.

Had newspapers been forgotten? Hardly. But nothing in print could captivate attention like the human voice in dramatic situations (soap operas), in concert (Kate Smith), or as an informational medium giving up-to-date news bulletins. Clearly, the American mood was beginning to shift toward the electronic media as the main informational source and away from the newspaper as early as the 1930s.

Early Radio Advertising

Businesses almost immediately recognized the commercial potential of radio as an exciting alternative to newspapers. This feeling was certainly actualized in the 1920s but never materialized on a grand scale, probably due to the recalcitrant nature of Herbert Hoover, who was adamant in his attempt to prevent what he saw as a public service medium from becoming a commercial medium. If Hoover would have had his way, the broadcast system in the United States would have developed along the lines of the British system, which did not allow advertising on radio.

Although David Sarnoff had forecast the radio music box several years earlier, it was the decision of Harry P. Davis, vice-president of the Westinghouse Electric and Manufacturing Company, which concretely gave birth to commercial household radio. He declared that a regular transmitting station, operated by the manufacturer of receivers, would create enough interest in the sale of sets to justify the expense of operating the station. Although this financial basis for broadcasting has long been replaced by the sale of air time for advertising, it was sufficiently practical at the time to get radio started as a medium for home use.[5]

WEAF Starts It All

With the technical interference problems of the 1920s creating enough problems for a fledgling industry, most of the stations on the air at the time were

* Joseph Dominick, Barry L. Sherman, and Gary Copeland, *Broadcasting/Cable and Beyond* (New York: McGraw-Hill, 1990). Used with permission of McGraw-Hill.

awash with red ink. Many were going out of business as any advertising dollars available at the time were flowing either to the newspaper or the magazine industries. Radio, basically being used as a public service, had limited income derived from those who wished to pay to get themselves on the air as singers or readers of poetry. It was apparent that unless some form of financial underwriting could be found, radio as a new service to America's households had no future.

Westinghouse's WEAF radio in New York was one of the company's so-called toll-stations, as it charged a "toll" to those who wished to put themselves on the air as entertainers. This was common practice for an industry with no developed programs or program sources. One interested party in paying this toll was the Queensboro Real Estate Corporation of Long Island, which in 1922 wished to advertise its new Jackson Heights suburban tracts for sale. After one ten-minute broadcast, all of its lots were sold. Soon after, department stores and tobacco companies began to sponsor programs and the rest, as we say, is history.

Media Growth Since the 1920s

Radio, the first national advertising and entertainment medium in the electronic field, grew from being a novelty to being the centerpiece of home entertainment. The 1930s and 1940s, the Golden Age of radio, saw an unprecedented growth in the new electronic medium despite the Depression years. Radio sets were financed, paid for, and repaired as a priority, sometimes even before rent or other pressing bills were paid. Its role in the family then was every bit as important as the role of television seems to be today. Programs featured top performers and commentary on the news issues of the day, all sponsored by the big national advertisers.

By the early 1950s the newer medium of television was flexing its muscles and had lured many of radio's national network shows and personalities to the developing medium. This, of course, meant that along with the shows and the personalities went the national advertisers.

When television actually became this commercial competitor to the radio and newspaper industries in the late 1940s, the American family's financial priority was to finance a television set, which soon became the electronic hearth, replacing not only newspapers and radio in terms of total time spent but the time families used to spend talking with one another around a stove or fireplace. Indeed, our entire social structure as a family-oriented society has changed drastically since Hertz's waves were harnessed as a viable commercial medium.

The Golden Age of Television

The decade of the 1950s became the Golden Age of television, a time when more Americans could tell you what time Jack Benny or Milton Berle or Amos 'n Andy came on than could tell you who was president. Commercials drove the medium as consumerism was unabashed in a seeming era of plenty that was a result of pent-up demand spawned by a wartime economy.

After the war, companies happily churned out advertised product after advertised product. As Tom Peters and Bob Waterman have ably pointed out, most were bought, not because of quality but because Americans, experiencing their first real rise in income in years and revelling in high postwar employment, would simply buy anything.

But the new found love-affair was here to stay. Americans would never abandon their television sets, but neither would they abandon radio. Radio, prematurely predicted by many to be dead during television's Golden Age, was able to change. As the national programs and advertisers defected to television, radio changed its format to offer music, news, and information programming to local audiences, selling its advertising time to local businesses. National advertising revenue was thus replaced by local revenue, actually greatly increasing the amount of advertising dollars for radio as a whole.

Radio thus changed from a predominantly national advertising medium to a predominantly local advertising medium during the 1950s, but it did take a baby boom generation to once again breathe life back into radio and to make it the local economic competitor it still remains today. Radio's strength then, as now, lies in the daytime programming period. The nighttime is reserved for television.

That television has established itself as in indispensable part of the lives of most Americans is beyond argument. The technical advances in the industry since it began spreading nationwide in the late 1940s and early 1950s have been staggering.

From black and white pictures of live performances, to color, to videotape that replaced the inconvenience of film processing, to smaller camcorders (a unit with both camera and videotape recorder) and portable videocassette recorders, to microwave antennas allowing live transmission of pictures and fiber optics to satellite transmission of events from anywhere on the globe, television has become a dominant part of American and global culture.

We need look no further than the live coverage of the 1991 Persian Gulf War when both our State Department and the government of Saddam Hussein, as well as the people of the world, watched CNN around the clock for live updates and coverage of unfolding events, to tell us of the importance and power of television within the greater world culture.

Embracing New Technologies, Abandoning the Old

A pattern emerging in the discussion of first newspaper, then radio, and finally television reveals the consumer's willingness to embrace the newest communication form. While not abandoning earlier established habits, the newest media seem to receive a disproportionate share of the consumer's attention.

This is not surprising. Consumers have always wanted, in fact demanded, what is "newest." Certainly "no one knew that electric lights were needed before they were invented, yet Edison did not create the need for electric lights. Anyone who had suffered through the poor light of oil burning in shallow vessels, candles, kerosene lamps or gas jets already had a need for better light. Each of these light-producing devices had come along to satisfy that need better than did its predecessor."[6]

In a similar fashion, the need for automobiles was not realized before they were invented. But the need for faster, more convenient transportation did exist. Hence, the public embraced Henry Ford's Model T over horse-drawn carriages. No one said, "What we need is a telegraph to produce faster communication" until Samuel Morse invented such a device. Each invention improved upon its predecessor — from town criers to newspapers, from newspapers to instant, electronic forms of communication both wired and unwired, from the telephone to wireless cellular phones, from radio to television.

In an electronic age, is it any wonder that the majority of people in the civilized world receive virtually all of their information from the electronic media?

Newspaper Infrastructure Remains Intact

There remains, though, one curious fact. During the time of unprecedented electronic media growth that spawned the two Golden Ages, newspaper was essentially relegated to the role of favorite son. But even in this new role cast in the minds of consumer America, the newspaper industry lost none of its power base as an integral part of the community infrastructure.

Even though circulation began to decline as a direct result of changing consumer habits (the switch to radio and then to television), Table 1.1 shows that newspaper has traditionally been the preferred medium for America's advertisers and, from the Depression years until the 1980s, has continued to enjoy generous revenues and profit margins far greater than its electronic cousins. This may partly be due to the fact that the cost of production (paper, ink, press maintenance, and, in most cases, union labor) that is needed to publish a daily newspaper in any given market is higher than the cost of producing and delivering a radio message, and, in most markets, even the cost of producing and delivering a television commercial. But, even so, the fact remains that over one-quarter of the total ad dollar has been budgeted for and, in many cases, still continues to go to the newspaper industry despite market erosion and changing lifestyles.

Print Domination Declines in the 1980s

This period of print domination, lasting from 1935 until 1980, began to reverse in the decade of the 1980s, as newspapers' share of total advertising expenditures began to decline in response to stagnant circulation and figures showing nearly one-half of the adult population not reading a daily newspaper.

Table 1.2 shows that the new advertising paradigm favors the electronic media as the preferred buy. The purpose of this book is to explain exactly why this

Table 1.1
Estimated Annual U.S. Ad Expenditures (in Millions of Dollars, Selected Years)

Media	1935	1945	1955	1965	1975	1980
Newspapers	761	919	3,077	4,426	8,442	15,541
National	148	203	712	784	1,221	2,353
Local	613	716	2,365	3,642	7,221	13,188
Magazines	130	344	691	1,161	1,465	3,149
Weeklies	54	188	397	610	612	1,418
Women's	51	97	161	269	368	782
Monthlies	25	59	133	282	485	949
Farm Publications	10	32	72	71	74	130
Television	-	-	1,035	2,515	5,263	11,366
Network	-	-	550	1,237	2,306	5,130
Spot	-	-	260	892	1,623	3,269
Local	-	-	225	386	1,334	2,967
Radio	113	424	545	917	1,980	3,702
Network	63	198	84	60	83	183
Spot	15	92	134	275	436	779
Local	35	134	327	582	1,461	2,740
Direct Mail	282	290	1,299	2,324	4,124	7,596
Business Papers	51	204	446	671	919	1,674
Outdoor	31	72	192	180	335	578
National	23	50	130	120	220	364
Local	8	22	62	60	115	214
Miscellaneous	342	555	1,793	2,985	5,571	10,744
National	168	327	1,002	1,745	2,882	5,663
Local	174	228	791	1,240	2,689	5,081
Total National	890	1,740	5,380	9,340	15,340	30,290
Total Local	830	1,100	3,770	5,910	12,820	24,190
Grand Total	1,720	2,840	9,150	15.250	28,160	54,480

Source: Advertising Age, July 18, 1977, and March 22, 1982.

should also be the thinking of corporate executives, advertisers, and media planners who still rely on the print media as their main conduit for getting an advertising message to the public.

Newspaper Advertising—The National Choice

Many of America's larger corporate entities have, indeed, begun to realize the importance of the electronic media in their media planning efforts. However, these larger corporate advertisers, whose efforts and examples are commonly imitated by smaller regional or local entities, do not seem to be setting examples for spending in the electronic media. Regional and local companies seem to be placing millions of advertising dollars into the print media (newspapers, direct mail, and magazines), just as they always have. Collectively, these thousands of

Table 1.2

Top Ten Companies by Ad Spending, Top Ten Product Categories in Ad Spending, and Measured Media Spending, 1991

Top 10 companies by 1991 ad spending

		Total measured ad spending			Top 200 brands			Number
Rank	Company	1991	1990	% chg	1991	1990	% chg	of Brands
1	Procter & Gamble Co.	$1,166.5	$1,236.1	-5.6	$360.1	$389.0	-7.4	8
2	Phillip Morris Cos.	1,110.4	1,203.7	-7.8	719.9	729.0	-1.2	7
3	General Motors Corp.	1,056.5	1,101.2	-4.1	1,032.1	1,073.1	-3.8	8
4	PepsiCo	542.0	547.2	-0.9	470.2	462.6	1.7	4
5	Ford Motor Co.	517.7	470.6	10.0	491.6	436.6	12.6	3
6	Sears Roebuck & Co.	462.3	591.1	-21.8	421.6	534.2	-21.1	3
7	Toyota Motor Corp.	442.5	406.5	8.8	441.3	405.2	8.9	2
8	General Mills	419.1	406.6	3.1	207.3	221.9	-6.6	4
9	Chrysler Corp.	414.8	412.8	0.5	388.6	376.5	3.2	4
10	AT&T Co.	391.7	506.8	-22.7	388.9	463.8	-16.2	1

Notes: Dollars are in millions   Source: LNA Arbitron Multi-Media Service

Top 10 categories among top 200 brands in 1991 spending

		Measured ad spending			Ad spending by media			Number
Rank	Category	1991	1990	% chg	Print	Broadcast	Outdoor	of Brands
1	Automotive	$3,587.7	$3,711.8	-3.3	$1,056.0	$2,515.4	$16.3	32
2	Retail	1,740.8	1,902.4	-8.5	834.2	902.7	3.8	25
3	Food	1,413.4	1,517.7	-6.9	168.9	1,243.2	1.3	19
4	Restaurants	1,224.3	1,258.6	-2.7	9.1	1,200.9	14.3	11
5	Entertainment & media	1,064.8	1,060.3	0.4	348.4	710.6	5.9	13
6	Telephone	632.1	653.5	-3.3	109.8	519.8	2.5	5
7	Beverages	629.1	718.6	-12.5	34.5	591.3	3.3	10
8	Drugs & Remedies	553.2	423.6	30.6	49.1	504.1	0.0	11
9	Beer, wine, liquor	552.5	470.0	17.6	26.0	509.7	16.9	3
10	Toiletries & cosmetics	478.6	460.2	4.0	154.5	324.0	0.0	11

Notes: Dollars are in millions   Totals include only brands from within the Top 200   Source: LNA Arbitron Multi-Media Service

Measured media spending for 1991

		All measured brands			Top 200 brands		
Rank	Media	1991	1990	% chg	1991	1990	% chg
1	Network TV	$9,456.2	$10,132.3	-6.7	$5,770.7	$6,147.3	-6.1
2	Spot TV	8,751.2	9,293.3	-5.8	3,130.5	3,104.2	0.3
3	Newspaper*	7,631.3	9,679.1	-21.2	1,749.4	1,877.6	-6.8
4	Magazine	6,515.2	6,737.7	-3.3	2,066.1	1,997.9	3.4
5	Syndicated TV	1,850.4	1,587.6	16.6	979.2	833.0	17.5
6	Cable TV networks	1,211.6	1,110.2	9.1	512.7	431.0	19.0
7	National spot radio	1,141.6	1,143.3	-0.1	356.5	347.7	2.5
8	Outdoor	684.0	688.8	-0.7	197.1	161.2	22.2
9	Network radio	578.7	766.4	NA	304.2	349.6	NA
	Subtotal print	14,146.5	16,416.7	-13.8	3,815.5	3,875.5	-1.5
	Subtotal broadcast	22,989.7	24,032.9	-4.3	11,053.7	11,212.8	-1.4
							-1.2
	Total	37,820.2	41,138.5	-8.1	15,066.3	15,249.6	

Notes: Dollars are in millions   * includes newspaper, distributed Sunday magazines   Source: LNA Arbitron Multi-Media Service

local and regional businesses will spend millions in the print-oriented media, far surpassing the combined revenues for radio and television. By so doing, such businesses are also setting themselves up for ultimate loss of market share due to the waste involved in buying advertising media that cannot efficiently target a defined demographic.

Figure 1.1 shows that as a percentage of total dollars spent, the local dollar favors newspaper advertising, an unfortunate statistic as subsequent chapters will show. Although this is also beginning to show signs of change in the 1990s, chalk up a bottom-line victory for the local newspaper in large metro markets as well as in smaller towns as we churn our way into the last decade of the twentieth century.

Newspapers—Out of Business

Despite being favored with regional and local advertising dollars, in recent years the increasing costs of operation and flat circulation figures that had been looming on the horizon of the 1980s have forced many newspapers to halt their presses forever. Although high-profile papers like the *Dallas Times Herald* have

Figure 1.1
Advertising Volume of Major Media, Local versus National

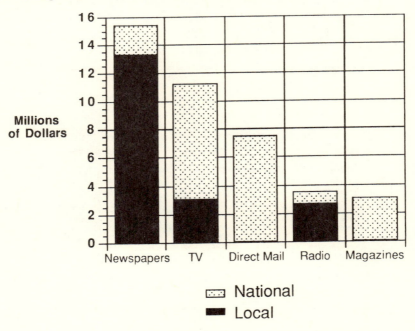

Source: *Advertising Age*, January 5, 1981.

drawn the most public attention, nearly 700 newspaper operations have folded over the past 40 years (134 since 1980) and many others in cities like Philadelphia have formed joint operating agreements (JOAs) to help keep each other in business.

The relationships, though, between business and newspaper have been established and continue intact today within the complex matrix of each community's infrastructure. It was and still is a good marriage, if for no other reason than for the old adage that "love is blind" and likely will always remain so unless a deeper understanding of the intricacies of advertising is developed by those whose responsibility it is to make advertising buying decisions.

Cross-Ownership—Protecting the Turf

Of all the variables involved in the discussion of newspaper and its dominant positioning throughout the decades, perhaps the most telling is the issue of radio and television ownership during these Golden Eras. Early on, realizing the potential threat of radio to an already established national, regional, and local revenue base, many newspaper companies in markets of all sizes simply decided that the solution was to own the competition. Hence the following marriages, only a few examples of many: the *Chicago Tribune* and WGN (World's Greatest Newspaper); the *Milwaukee Journal* and WTMJ; the *Wisconsin News,* purchased by the *Milwaukee Sentinel* and WISN (Wisconsin News); the *Daily News* of Bowling Green, Kentucky, and WDNS (Daily News Service); and the *South Bend Tribune* and WSBT. The print industry did not neglect television either, with WTMJ-TV in Milwaukee applying for the first commercial television license in 1939, the year television was first unveiled to the public at the New York World's Fair.

The late 1940s and early 1950s found newspapers protecting their interests in the television arena as well. Many newspapers established television stations under their ownership, fearing an exodus of readers to this new in-home theater. One anonymous newspaper executive of the time commented that the newspapers "named the most incompetent on the newspaper to run the television station, because even they could only be successful in this new field."

Newspapers early on recognized the public clamor for the new medium and the network revenue immediately available to a station as soon as it could get on the air and the coaxial cable could connect it to the network. Television investment also protected newspapers from any revenue loss their radio stations might have incurred from audience exodus to television.

The phrase, "If you can't beat 'em, join 'em," must have been coined by the newspaper industry protecting its financial infrastructure!

Of course, many other industries invested in the new communications medium of radio as well: the insurance industry's WSM (We Shelter Millions) in Nashville, Tennessee, and WTIC (Travelers Insurance Company) licensed in Hartford, Connecticut; WCFL (Chicago Federation of Labor); WOC (World of

Chiropractors) in Davenport, Iowa; and of course the retailers wanted to promote their establishments whenever they could, with stations like the Sears-owned WLS radio in Chicago (World's Largest Store).

But whenever possible, based on perceived competitive conditions and available capital, the newspaper industry entered the broadcasting arena in many markets, which served to increase their already dominant sphere of influence and to guarantee the publishing company a share in the revenues of the new and hotly competitive media.

It thus becomes apparent that when licenses for broadcast properties are issued to newspaper publishers, diversification of media ownership within a given market is reduced. Net revenues for the newspaper are increased while competition from different companies, with possible differences in operating philosophies and community service standards, is decreased.

The FCC realized its conflict between First Amendment obligations and allowing the newspaper publishers to dominate broadcasting in many markets, but no action was taken until 1975 when the Department of Justice pressed the FCC to take action. The new rules avoided confrontation by grandfathering cross-ownership that already existed, but no future combinations would be allowed. Existing combinations would eventually break apart when changes in ownership occurred. These new FCC rules were appealed, but the Supreme Court concurred with the commission.[7]

OUR CHANGING LIFESTYLES

In the 1990s, with a more mobile population boasting high percentages of working women and a diverse ethnic mix, individuals are spending more time with the electronic media than with any print form of communication. Most of us average seven hours a day in front of the television set and three and a half hours a day with radio, much of that radio being listened to as we sit in our cars trapped by urban gridlock, a motorist's nightmare but a boon to radio advertisers.

Indeed, our changing lifestyles, complete with a fair dose of daily stress, give us far less time to read newspapers or magazines. Reading demands active involvement, which means that the consumer must exert an effort to be exposed to the advertising or the articles. Radio and television are classified as passive media, as the consumer is required to do little—if anything—to absorb the advertising or the programming other than turning the set on. The commercials and the programming are absorbed with no effort by the consumer other than remaining alert. This is a concept that will be revisited throughout this book and one that should not be lost on corporate media planners, businesses, and advertising agencies.

Radio and Television as Social and Economic Infrastructure

During the Golden Age of radio and television, and continuing into the consumer-oriented decade of the 1990s, these "new" entertainment and advertising media may have been the darlings of the American public, but neither really was able to ride in the front seat of the economic limousine. As we have seen, newspapers were, and to a large extent remain, the principal medium for local advertising in all markets regardless of size. With newspaper infrastructure intact, the print industry occupies a position similar to that of the anchor store in a mall—it is the nucleus that draws consumer attention and around which smaller, satellite competitors revolve.

Television as Local Community Infrastructure

Many consumers would logically believe that the glamour medium of television would generate the highest revenues. It does—on the national level. Of the total television advertising seen by consumers, most is "national" in nature, placed by ad agencies buying for multimillion dollar corporations like Procter & Gamble, General Motors, or AT & T.

Traditionally the largest television buyer overall (network, cable, and syndicated), with budgets reaching over $500 million annually (Table 1.3), Procter & Gamble's monies are used to tout their line of household products like Head & Shoulders, Cheer, Tide, Pampers, Crest, and Gleem. The third largest television advertiser, the Philip Morris Company, now a consumer products company since shrinking tobacco markets forced diversification, spends nearly $400 million annually to promote their product line, which includes Jell-O, Miller Beer, and Maxim Coffee.

Radio as Local Community Infrastructure

Radio, arguably the strongest potential force for advertising effectiveness, due to its affordability, seems to be a minor player when pitted against newspaper in the advertising decisions of major corporations, regional companies, and local businesses. Yet radio, while affordable to local businesses, is not understood by those who make advertising buying decisions. Seventy-eight percent of radio dollars are local, and collectively these local dollars total nearly $8 billion. But, again, the collective advantage in terms of dollars spent goes to newspaper, a $16 billion local industry, as dollars will always flow to the traditional medium in lieu of one that is difficult to understand from a buyer's point of view. Naturally, more radio dollars will be spent in the larger markets of New York or Los Angeles than in the smaller cities like Des Moines, Peoria, and Lexington, simply because more dollars are available. Radio, though, is just as misunderstood in New York as it is in Des Moines and it is the intent of this book to assist all advertisers and media buyers to understand the uniqueness of radio and also television in relation to the traditional vehicle of newspaper that now survives, certainly not on performance or ability to deliver results, but rather on traditional reputation alone.

The Affordability of Newspaper to Regional/Local Advertisers

As our figures have shown, total television dollars spent flow more generously to the national networks than they collectively do to individual markets, both

Table 1.3
Leading Advertisers on Network Television (in Millions of Dollars)

	1991	1990	% change
1. General Motors Corp.	$ 527.8	$ 598.4	-11.8 %
2. Procter & Gamble Co.	515.7	557.6	-7.5
3. Philip Morris Cos.	389.5	402.2	-3.2
4. Johnson & Johnson	239.8	211.4	13.4
5. Kellogg Co.	236.6	301.3	-21.5
6. Ford Motor Co.	217.5	196.9	10.5
7. PepsiCo	204.6	193.4	5.8
8. Sears Roebuck & Co.	187.9	253.8	-26.0
9. Chrysler Corp.	176.2	190.0	-7.3
10. Toyota Motor Sales USA	173.7	170.9	1.6
11. American Home Products Corp.	173.3	150.5	15.1
12. AT&T Co.	172.0	244.9	-29.8
13. McDonald's Corp.	171.8	231.0	-25.6
14. Unilever U.S.	154.6	162.8	-5.0
15. General Mills	151.4	142.9	5.9
16. Anheuser-Busch Cos.	122.9	129.0	-4.7
17. American Honda Motor Co.	117.0	119.0	-1.7
18. RJR Nabisco	112.7	133.6	-15.6
19. Nestle Foods Corp.	109.0	145.6	-25.1
20. Eastman Kodak Co.	105.6	116.5	-9.4
21. Grand Metropolitan	103.3	183.1	-43.6
22. Bristol-Myers Squibb Co.	95.4	124.3	-23.3
23. Coca-Cola Co.	95.2	88.9	7.1
24. Walt Disney Co.	93.8	62.9	49.1
25. Warner-Lambert Co.	84.1	91.1	-7.7
26. MCI Communications Corp.	76.4	33.1	130.8
27. Clorox Co.	72.5	58.0	25.0
28. Thompson Medical Co.	71.6	75.5	-5.2
29. Mazda Motor of America	68.8	76.1	-9.6
30. Nissan Motor Corp. USA	66.4	125.8	-47.2
Total network TV spending	$9,456.2	$10,132.3	-6.7 %

Source: Advertising Age, May 11, 1992.

metro and nonmetro, leaving newspaper the top billing local advertising source in most cities and towns in America. To further underscore this point, Figure 1.2 shows the difference in television dollars flowing to the national level, the total dollars allocated to spot or random regional buys, and the dollars that flow to local television stations.

Television receives fewer local dollars while newspaper receives a higher percentage of local dollars simply because the number of local businesses that can afford television is far fewer than the number that can buy local newspaper space. Hence, the collective advantage, in terms of total dollars generated annually on the local level, again goes to newspaper.

Figure 1.2
Station Time Sales (in Millions of Dollars)

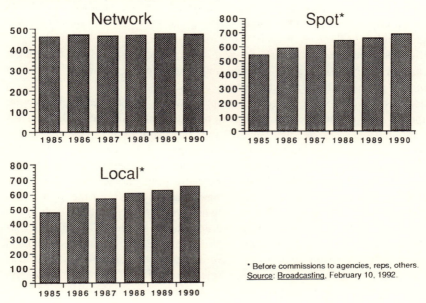

* Before commissions to agencies, reps, others.
Source: Broadcasting, February 10, 1992.

Newspapers have been and continue to be the big winners on the local level. Understand, though, that when the word "local" is used, small town America is not the intended definition. "Local," as in non-national, includes the largest of the media markets to the smallest. Advertisers in these 210 or so rated markets and thousands of smaller cities and towns collectively spend over $30 billion annually in nearly 18,000 newspapers, a figure that is close to $6 billion more than the total annual expenditure in television, including network revenues. Of that $30 billion, over $16 billion is spent by local businesses, the remainder coming from national and regional budgets buying placements such as full-color freestanding inserts (FSIs) for their area retail outlets.

The glamour image of the television medium, or even the radio industry, and the personality status afforded its on-air people certainly have made both radio and television a part of the local infrastructure, but not a part of the historic and traditional framework that was built decades ago by a savvy newspaper industry.

Even though the total number of advertising dollars given to newspaper has been declining since 1975 as a result of flat circulation and the closing of many daily newspaper operations, the position of respected elder in this local economic and social infrastructure will likely continue to be occupied by newspaper—unless greater understanding and education can be generated within each indigenous business community.

Advertising Agencies and Buying Decisions

Many corporate media buying decisions are, of course, handled by full-service, limited service, or in-house advertising agencies. Most of these agencies understand fully the role of each of the mass media in terms of their ability to deliver planned and intended results within the marketplace. Media are bought with specific campaign goals in mind and postcampaign follow-up is done to compare actual results with intended objectives.

However, many of these agencies, especially the full-service agencies with large art departments, tend to favor print or eye-oriented media for their clients for rational and justified advertising reasons, but also for one obvious reason: to keep the art department busy and, hence, employed. Art directors are not needed for radio and storyboards for television do not need a full-service art department. Thus, the electronic media may not received a proportionate buy from many agencies, even though their executives may be acutely aware of the tremendous advantages such media offer advertisers when compared to the limited ability of print advertisements to deliver intended advertising results. This thinking has helped solidify the position of newspaper in the larger metro markets populated by dozens of advertising agencies that favor print as the traditional buy, as well as in the smaller markets in which there is one or a handful of agencies whose buyers do not fully understand the electronic media.

One other factor may also be at play here. Agencies are driven to spend simply because all media buys are commissionable. Thus, advertising may or may not be bought with total end results as the operative motivator.

Newspaper's Economic Clout

Since newspaper has never lost its economic clout and has had a well-documented relationship with the business community since the days of the Revolution, its place within the community infrastructure has practically been guaranteed. In a word, newspaper has positioned itself strategically ahead of radio and television by claiming its rights of passage. It was here first with the most money and always has and always will want the "first and last dance."

CONSUMER BEHAVIOR THROUGH THE DECADES

An understanding of consumer behavior is paramount to an understanding of how consumers relate to advertising of any kind, whether print or electronic. If corporations and businesses can first understand human behavior, they will then be able to understand how consumers relate to, consume, and understand the advertising that is intended for them.

Although the fundamentals of consumer buying behavior were not generally known or researched in eighteenth- and nineteenth-century America, it would be fair to state that the motivators of our ancestors were similar to the motivators present in our population today. That is, each generation has wished and does wish a "better" life for its offspring. The cornerstone of a so-called better life rests in financial security, as access to capital gives access to the goods and services needed to survive in a modern, technological society.

Although the goods and services in nineteenth-century society were not as plentiful or widely distributed as goods and services today, they were nevertheless in demand. Demand spiraled in an era of industrialization and mass production, spurred on by the widely read but nevertheless irresponsible advertising of first the penny presses and then the "tabloid" approach of the big city dailies. Demands for more and better products drove the merchants and business class of early America, just as the demands for more and better goods drove the seafaring traders of the ancient world to develop and expand their markets.

A Model of Consumer Behavior

Consumer behavior exhibited by people as they plan their purchases has always been a combination of group, individual, and cultural factors. Consumer models presenting the factors that affect consumer buying behavior will be presented and discussed in the next chapter. Regardless, though, of which consumer model is chosen, "all models have one thing in common: they describe some basic behaviors, needs or situations and make the assumption that 'this is really what man is like.' "[8]

Changing Lifestyles and Consumer Demand

Through the decades of the twentieth century, the lifestyle of the average American has most certainly improved in response to rising wages and the availability of goods and services on a widely distributed basis, made possible by the development of nationwide transportation systems and of the rural free delivery (RFD) concept that, in 1896, opened up all of America to the letter and package service of the U.S. Post Office.

With RFD, goods could be ordered by mail-order catalogs (which would fit neatly into a shirt or suit pocket) and delivered directly to the home. Such a concept literally helped turn the country into a nation of consumers, as companies like the Chicago-based Montgomery Ward & Co., self-proclaimed as the "most complete store on earth," could ship to any address. Its chief competitor, Sears Roebuck and Company remained solely a catalog retailer until 1924, achieving gross revenues that year of $220 million with no retail outlets and using only the U.S. mail and railroad express for delivery.

The Advertising Choice

With rising real incomes from good wages in the industrial sector and an affluence not afforded earlier generations, manufacturers and retailers were determined to spread the message about their services in an escalating effort to increase product demand. The only question was, "By what means?" The obvious choice was the traditional choice and the only choice until the 1920s: newspaper. Print advertising became the choice most often made due to the time-honored relationships that had grown up over the decades between retailers and newspapermen who had carved out their niche side by side in a developing country that had given proper respect to a free press.

The question for corporate America in the 1990s concerns the traditional decision that gave the majority of a business' advertising budget to the print media. Will such an approach serve corporate America and the merchant class of this decade leading to the twenty-first century? Does such decision making continue to make sense as a new era filled with yet undiscovered electronic wonders awaits succeeding generations of consumers who have been reared with color television sets and Sony "Walkman" headsets tuned in to their favorite stereo rock stations?

As many popular culture prophets have warned, "The future isn't what it used to be."

SUMMARY

The importance of fully understanding advertising cannot be understated due to the strong correlation between the retail sector of the economy and the overall economic health of that economy and the nation. Corporate America understands that the production, consumption, and reordering of available goods and services is the key to maintaining service and manufacturing sector jobs. Advertising is a key ingredient to this complex matrix.

Reducing overall advertising waste is a prime concern for both the business and/or the agency planning such advertising. Waste is inherent in all forms of advertising, but can be minimized by the use of the intrusive forms of either radio or television that cause advertising impressions to be registered passively, without consumer consent. The one-time impression of newspaper that requires active cognition maximizes overall waste.

Understanding advertising necessarily means understanding the historical relationship between the newspaper publishers and America's merchant class, as well as the growth of the electronic media.

The genesis of the symbiotic relationship between America's newspapers and the business/retail community it serves can be traced to colonial America (with roots extending back to Cromwell's England of the 1600s). Playing a major role in the expansion and settlement of each region in America, the presses followed the early settlers westward, often "setting up shop" and publishing before a particular town was even built.

Relying on advertiser support to generate the revenue to publish, the newspapers needed the business community every bit as much as that community needed the public exposure to sell its products or services.

Hence, the concept of the print media as community infrastructure. No towns or cities could survive without offering citizens the services of hotels, banks, mercantile stores, or a local newspaper. These entities, in essence, built America. With a historical tradition three hundred years in the making, the decision of today's corporate decision makers and retail communities to use newspaper advertising as the main source of advertising and promotion is understandable. Such a decision may be argued to be genetically programmed, a decision of tradition.

Even the development of radio and television and their total acceptance by the American public did nothing to change the positive revenue picture for newspapers. Newspaper publishers concerned about profit erosion simply bought the competition; they either applied for a license to begin a new station or bought an existing station, thus protecting their profit picture and keeping the traditional infrastructure intact. Since 1975, however, this practice of cross-ownership has been disallowed (although certain "combos" may still exist due to grandfathering).

The way consumers respond to both print and electronic media advertising based on a lifetime of exposure is part of the study of consumer behavior. Consumers behave in a variety of predictable ways and respond to the advertising message to help them make choices in a marketplace abounding with competitive products in every conceivable product category. Retailers certainly understand this.

What retailers do not understand is the way in which the print media and the electronic media work as advertising vehicles. If they did understand such variables, more would change their media planning from a print-dominated orientation to one that generously includes the electronic media.

To understand why such a suggestion, which flies in the face of generational tradition, to switch from heavy print and light radio or television to heavy radio or television and light print, is desirable, we must first understand more about the basics of consumer behavior or what it is that motivates consumers to act as they do in the marketplace.

NOTES

1. From *The Old West: The Townsmen,* by the editors of Time-Life Books, with text by Keith Wheeler, © 1975 Time-Life Books.

2. Kenneth C. Davis, *Don't Know Much About History* (New York: Crown, 1990), p. 197.

3. Lynne Schafer Gross, *The New Television Technologies* (Dubuque, Iowa: Wm. C. Brown, 1990), p. 207.

4. Melvin L. DeFleur and Sandra Ball-Rokeach, *Theories of Mass Communication* (New York: David McKay, 1975), p. 83.

5. Ibid.

6. Barton C. White and N. Doyle Satterthwaite, *But First These Messages . . . The Selling of Broadcast Advertising* (Boston: Allyn and Bacon, 1989), p. 16.

7. Sydney W. Head with Christopher H. Sterling, *Broadcasting in America* (Boston: Houghton Mifflin, 1982), p. 486.

8. A. J. Kover, "Models of Men as Defined by Marketing Research," *Journal of Marketing Research* 4 (1967): 129.

CHAPTER 2

Consumer Behavior in the 1990s

Know then thyself. . . . The proper study of mankind is man.
                                                              —Alexander Pope

FAMILIARITY AND CREDIBILITY

Consumer behavior and the planning of corporate and business advertising may seem to be polar entities, but they are intricately linked to the greater understanding of how and why consumers make buying decisions and to the psychology of consumer behavior that drives those decisions. Since buying decisions are directly impacted by advertising, media buyers and planners on the corporate and retail levels must necessarily understand consumer behavior if they are to make appropriate long-range buying decisions that will positively impact market shares not only for the immediate quarter but for months and years into the future. One of the first rules of advertising is to "Know Thy Consumer." Although the pattern of consumer behavior can be viewed as unpredictable, consumers are human beings driven by predictable common needs: food, clothing, shelter, personal wants and satisfactions, and a secure environment in which to pursue the dreams and desires of being human.

There remains little doubt that consumers follow predictable patterns of behavior during the buying process, regardless of the time they are actually in the market before making a purchase or the length of time between purchases (the buying cycle) of the same or similar product or service. No matter which subconscious behavioral pattern or model of consumer behavior is followed, the consumer always progresses through a series of mental steps that ultimately cause him or her to make a buying decision in favor of one product or another or one brand over another, after choosing to enter one particular store or business over another to buy that product.

The reasons for such consumer choices appear complex, but consumers, as a general rule, do not buy products with which they are not familiar, do not normally shop in places that are unfamiliar, and will never buy a product or a service from any store without the question of credibility being answered in the potential buyer's mind. In other words, "is this store credible?" "Will they give me good service?" "Will they effectively handle any complaints I might have?" "Do I generally feel good about doing business with this store or with this salesperson?"

The answers to these questions have as much to do with image and perception as they do with consciously garnering hard answers to premeditated questions. Consumer models show that we all learn from and are influenced by our friends and family, as well as our teachers and societal role-models such as ministers, successful businesspeople, and media celebrities who can run the gamut from athletic heroes to rock stars. But we also form lifetime perceptions and images from years of advertising consumption—images that stay with us longer than even the names of friends and relatives, images that are indelible and are stored in our long-term memory as a permanent part of our knowledge base.

HOW ADVERTISING INFLUENCES CONSUMER BEHAVIOR

There remains little doubt that persons living in an advanced, technological society dominated by an advertising-driven economy are greatly influenced by the multiple forms of mass media that pervade modern culture. Of course, one may ask how such a general statement can be made with any degree of certainty. With over 5,200 advertising impressions (*New York Times* estimate) bombarding each consumer on a daily basis from all forms of advertising including print, electronic media, outdoor advertising, transit advertising, and even storefront neon signs (which can surely be considered advertising), how can any *one* have a dominant effect on consumer behavior?

Brand Leaders Since the Depression Years

One logical place to start would be to look at the various brand categories that are recognizable to each of us as consumers, but limit that list to *only* those brands that have maintained a dominant or leadership position in the national market for more than six decades.*

When this is done, a listing very familiar to most consumers emerges:

Goodyear	Prince Albert pipe tobacco
Swift bacon	Gillette razors
Eveready batteries	Singer sewing machines

*Reprinted, with permission of the publisher, from ROMANCING THE BRAND, © 1989 David N. Martin. Published by AMACOM, a division of the American Management Association. All rights reserved.

Nabisco biscuits	Crisco
Kellogg breakfast cereal	Ivory soap
Kodak cameras	Coca-Cola
Del Monte	Campbell's soup
Wrigley chewing gum	Lipton tea
Gold Medal flour	Life Savers
Sherwin-Williams paint	

The importance of this listing is illustrative of the way we act as consumers. The reason consumers have continued to purchase these familiar brands is simply because they always have. Consumers buy Gold Medal flour because they always have. Shoppers prefer Coca-Cola because they always have.

Simply stated, established brands have market value. When consumers find brands that are satisfying to them, they will stick with those brands. Consumers buy what is familiar to them, not because of an emotional or nostalgic attachment to that brand, but due to the confidence they have in what is viewed as a competent product.[1]

Another factor also begins to emerge as we examine this list of successful brand leaders. Each of these brands has also been advertised for six decades. Their corporate names are as familiar to us as our own names and are a permanent part of our knowledge base. Consumers buy what they are satisfied with, but what they are satisfied with is what they have always known. The reason they know what they know (the factors that led them to try the product for the first time) is the result of well-planned and consistent advertising throughout the decades.

Such advertising recognizes that we are products of our culture. We consume and engage in what is familiar. Many Southerners in smaller, rural markets enjoy country music because they were exposed to it at a very early age. Suburbanites in larger metropolitan areas may prefer rock music or jazz, again because that is what they have always known. But as the popularity of something increases, it becomes more accepted because it is more familiar. Hence, country music has caught on with the suburban crowd and rock concerts featuring popular groups draw well from rural communities.

Consumers react to what they know and to what they understand. Top 40 radio programmers in America have always known this. Play over and over again what is familiar by groups that are known and you will do well in the ratings as listeners prefer to hear songs that are familiar.

The Media and Culture

If advertising over time can be said to have played a significant role in the development of consumer brand awareness, the intricacies involved in the matrix of advertising, culture, and learning ought to be examined.

As Brian Mullen and Craig Johnson point out in *The Psychology of Consumer Behavior,* the overall effects of culture occur as a result of learning. In other words, we are who we are in our culture as a result of having learned about that culture as we developed. We learn to behave in certain ways through the classical conditioning of emotional responses to certain situations and certain people in our culture.

This learning process occurs as the consumer is exposed to observational learning stimuli. We observe certain behaviors; these behaviors are reinforced and become a part of who we are within our culture. Mullen and Johnson correctly point out that such exposure to a way of behaving within our culture becomes more likely within cultures that have more television sets.

Add to that radios and VCRs and we have three to four generations whose behavior has been and is being determined, to a large part, on the basis of behavior they see reinforced in the electronic media and, to some extent, in the newspapers if they choose to read them.

Shaping Our View of the World Through Mass Media

Our most influential teacher in modern culture may indeed be the mass media, the one dominant force outside of the immediate family (other than the school system) that is directly responsible for shaping our values, behaviors, and lifestyles. "Given the enormous amount of time most children spend with television, this means that broadcasting has become a major agent of socialization—that all important process which turns a squalling infant into a functioning member of society."[2]

Although advertising and media images through entertainment programming in radio and television do not create culture per se, they certainly act on that culture by helping consumers define their roles within that culture.

For example, the changing roles of women in our society over the past few decades are not a result of media or advertising, but these roles are reinforced by what is seen, heard, or read in the media. Culture comes first, media reinforcement second.

Hence, consumers will behave in the marketplace according to the established norms of behavior known as culture. But, as William Bolen points out, nothing will change the culture of the target market in the short run, including advertising: "due to its cultural background, a particular target market may feel that a woman's place is in the home. An advertising campaign for a product that depicts a different role for women will run into problems in terms of that market. A different market . . . may have no problem . . . because of a different cultural background."[3]

Cognition and Belief

The result of advertising and media images within a culture is what is termed cognition, or what is known or thought. Our collective beliefs as consumers about advertised products or even about complex social issues result from behaviors that involve perception, memory, and learning. Using this general model of consumer behavior (Figure 2.1), it can be seen how the media ultimately shape and reinforce social and cultural behavior within our advanced, technological society. The end result is that we are influenced by the mass media and media images, with the electronic media (radio and television) having the most dominant effect due to the time spent with that media compared to time spent with newspaper or print in general.

To underscore this factor, in 1992 the Nielsen ratings company reported that Americans over age 18 watch over four and a half hours of television per day. The time spent viewing television per television home per day, a much different figure, is even greater (Figure 2.2). Compare this with the average daily viewing (Figure 2.3), and the overall impact of the $10 billion per year television industry on ultimate consumer behavior cannot be underestimated.

The perspective that the media shape consumer behavior is not new. Researchers have noted that the more often a consumer is exposed to any category of social information, "the more established the category becomes in long-term memory and the more likely it is to be used to interpret social reality."[4]

Whatever model of consumer behavior is used, however, it must be remembered that the end result is always the same: moving the consumer from the "first glimmer of awareness of the need, to heightened interest, to conscious desire and finally to action."[5]

Influences of Mass Media Advertising

America's retailers and business communities certainly know from their own experiences that there is a correlation between mass media advertising and the

Figure 2.1
A General Model of Consumer Behavior

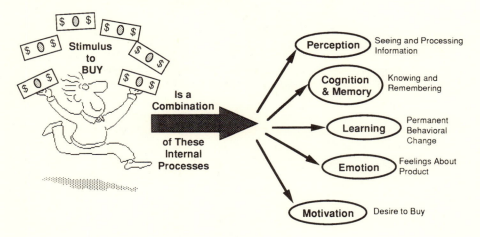

Figure 2.2
Time Spent Viewing Television per Television Home per Day

Source: Television Bureau of Advertising from A. C. Nielson Co.,
Broadcasting, March 2 1992.

effects or influences such advertising has on ultimate consumer behavior. As pervasive a force as newspapers and the electronic media have proven to be, it is necessary to discuss this area of "influences" more closely before investigating the ultimate question of which medium is likely to have the most direct impact on consumer buying behavior in the 1990s and beyond.

Figure 2.3
Television Information, Fall 1991

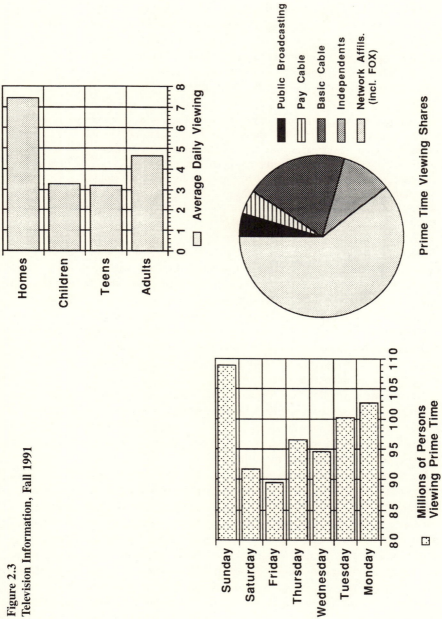

Average Daily Viewing

Homes
Children
Teens
Adults

0 1 2 3 4 5 6 7 8

■ Public Broadcasting
▯ Pay Cable
▨ Basic Cable
▨ Independents
▯ Network Affils.
   (incl. FOX)

Prime Time Viewing Shares

Millions of Persons
Viewing Prime Time

Sunday
Saturday
Friday
Thursday
Wednesday
Tuesday
Monday

80 85 90 95 100 105 110

No Pied Piper

In the overall discussion of consumer behavior and how such behavior is played out in the marketplace via the influence of advertising or any type of media promotion, it becomes apparent that no mass media can influence or convince consumers to buy what they otherwise would not have bought. Nor will any type of media imaging cause consumers to engage in any type of activity that otherwise would not have been done. The various forms of mass media and the far-reaching cultural influences of that media are no Pied Piper.

The real limitations to the persuasive powers of the mass media become apparent [with] attempts to change well-established attitudes, beliefs or habits of the public. . . . For example, anti-smoking messages have had minimal effect on the smoking habits of consumers. . . . Well-established advertisements for wearing seat belts . . . have been largely ignored. . . . Business promotion often has the same discouraging results. . . . The failure of the Edsel cost Ford over $250,000,000. . . . In cosmetics, food, soap and other consumer-oriented industries, the failure rate remains high in spite of . . . sophisticated research . . . and promotional efforts.[6]

Indeed, there are limits to the pervasive and persuasive powers of the mass media. The public simply will not buy what it does not wish to buy. Putting it another way, consumers will buy no products before their time. Diet drinks and light beer were soft sellers at the beginning of the fitness craze, but they were introduced at the right time. When the craze kicked in and people began running six miles a day, joining health clubs, and sweating off the pounds, sales set new records—not because of some slick Madison Avenue campaign convincing them to buy something they did not want or need but because the idea, the need for diet-oriented products, had come.

Markets are normally ready for the products that develop to fill those needs far in advance of the advertising that hails those products. In other words, there first exists a need; then, a smart businessperson fills that need through offering a new product or service; the businessperson then buys advertising to inform others that a new product is available to meet that need.

We are not manipulated into buying foods with less sodium, less fat, and fewer calories. Due to advances in medical research, we now know these types of foods are harmful to long-term health. So we look for these "lite" foods that advertisers are happy to tell us exist. If it were not for medical research and a more informed public, you would not be able to give these low-calorie food alternatives away! Why? Because they do not taste as good as the fat-crammed, high-calorie foods we would rather be consuming. So we look for and buy the "lite" products because of need, not because we were duped into it by an ad campaign.

Promotional messages of any type can only motivate the consuming public to buy or to do what it wants to buy or wants to do. Period. As the reader will see in Chapter 3, mass media advertising does not "make or break" any product or business. Consumer preferences are based on individual acceptance or rejection of the product or the business that is advertising, not on the advertising or promotion itself.

Internal and External Motivators

Ultimate consumer behavior is the end result of first becoming aware of a potential product or service and ultimately deciding to become a first-time consumer of that product or service. Making the initial decision to become a first-time consumer (when either acceptance or rejection occurs independent of the advertising) is a combination of various internal as well as external influences that spark the buying impulse.

The internal motivators that cause potential consumers to become customers are a combination of personal values, needs, wants, or desires combined with the economic wherewithal to pursue such needs or wants. Wanting to be socially accepted, to be attractive, or be considered a "winner" may be perceived needs, wants, or desires that are tied to a personal value system as opposed to the "real" needs of being a consumer of food, clothing, or shelter.

The external or social factors that influence decision making in the marketplace can be seen in one other model of consumer buying behavior (Figure 2.4). These factors include the influences of family and friends (social influences), opinion/role-model influences, and social class/cultural influences.

Figure 2.4
Factors Affecting Consumer Buying Behavior

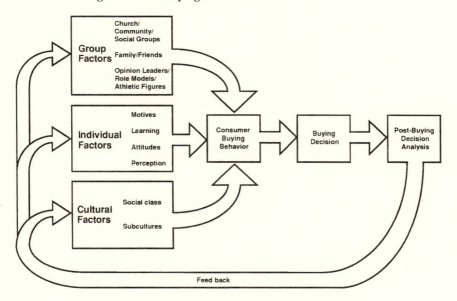

Source: Based on Figure 4.2. p. 87. in William Bolen's Advertising (New York: John Wiley & Sons. 1984).

The desire to please and to be accepted within the social circle of friends and family is characteristic of human nature. Family and friends are included in the same grouping, simply because as adolescents, our friends are as important as family and sometimes become a working part of the family unit; most of us probably spent more time with friends during our maturing years than with our own family, hence, "family-friends" can be considered as one external unit influencing consumer behavior.

Even though all members of a family-friend unit are themselves individuals, they listen to and rely on the opinions of other members of the unit. Our families and friends are more like us than any other grouping, and the desire to be accepted within that group is strong. Therefore, what they think and feel will influence how we think and vice versa.

Since we do not collectively agree all the time on how much should be spent or what style or model should be purchased, we learn to compromise with others and the results of informal family-friend agreements determine which movie will be seen, which outfit of clothing will be purchased, and even what make and model of family car sits in the driveway.

Identifying just who the decision maker is in this complex matrix of friends and family is oftentimes difficult for advertisers to define, but one thing can be stated with certainty: the family unit is changing. Out of economic necessity and from expanding opportunities, working women comprise over half of the labor force; the divorce rate has created more single parents than ever before; and people are living longer.

Advertisers need to make changes, to abandon their traditional ways of thinking in order to reach a new, mobile market where the conventional role of the woman has drastically changed.

Throughout our lives, people from outside the personal inner circle of family and friends also exert tremendous influence on the way we behave as individuals and as consumers. Such role-model influences include teachers, ministers, and professional people we may know on a personal basis and who are in a position to influence our behavior.

Other role-models, who also influence us greatly, are those we do not know personally — sports celebrities like Michael Jordan, Joe Montana, and Bo Jackson; media and movie stars like Peter Jennings and Tom Cruise. Those who endorse products (usually the sports celebrities) for a particular market group will influence many in that target group to desire that product.

Many local celebrities, such as disc jockeys or corporation presidents, can influence us indirectly when we see them driving certain cars, dining in certain restaurants, or behaving in certain ways that we admire or aspire to. This group is considered a secondary group but is nevertheless influential on ultimate consumer behavior.

Culture is generally agreed to include the complex matrix of social influences — values, morals, beliefs, and customs — which shape human behavior in any defined society. How we behave and how we expect others to behave toward us is a process of culture. Culture, in a word, defines behavior. We become a part of our culture through socialization into that arena by our families and friends, as previously discussed. "Cultural influences thus have a tremendous influence on the effectiveness of advertising. . . . A person's socializing process gives him or her guidance as to which products, services, ideas, people and causes are acceptable and which are not."[7]

Since the United States is composed of many subcultures, such as minority groups, religious groups, suburbanites and farmers, the Southern gentleman and the urban socialite, advertisers and marketers must learn that each group responds according to its own cultural bias and that the right group needs to be targeted with the right message on the right medium. Allowing for regional and lifestyle differences can make a big difference in the success of any particular advertising campaign.

What has been defined as culture and subculture can be categorized further into social classes within those cultures. Simply stated, we are all familiar with the terms "upper," "middle," and "lower" classes; essentially, these terms use economic and status symbols to define differences among people within any given society. Income and position, however, are themselves inadequate descriptors when attempting to define a social hierarchy for advertisers or marketers.

Indeed, there are sociological and psychological differences among the various classes that define how they will respond in the marketplace as consumers. Retail outlets themselves already cater to different status groups and locate themselves geographically to reach those groups. Restaurants, auto dealers, and furniture stores either define their target market or are chosen by a particular status group or social class that will comprise the largest percentage of their retail business.

Each consumer can subjectively define his or her position within a particular social class. We tend to view ourselves somewhere along the class continuum from lower to upper based upon our educational level, income, occupation, or neighborhood in which we live. Others tend to use these more objective measures to categorize us, much as we use these criteria to categorize them.

However, the most widely accepted standard that distinguishes the so-called middle class from lower status groups, even more than income, is occupation. Teachers, for example, are generally thought of as being "middle class" even though their incomes may be considerable less than many blue-collar workers who may often be labeled "lower status."

Regardless of income, how that income is actually spent may also assist in defining class membership. As Pierre Martineau discovered in a 1958 study, differing values among members of each status group dictate consumption patterns; what one consumes or owns can define social class.[8]

Middle Class	*Lower Status*
1. Pointed to the future.	1. Pointed to the present and past.
2. Viewpoint embraces a long expanse of time.	2. Lives and thinks in a short expanse of time.
3. More urban identification.	3. More rural identification.

4. Stresses rationality.	4. Essentially nonrational.
5. Well-structured sense of the universe.	5. Vague and unclear structuring of the world.
6. Horizons vastly extended; not limited.	6. Horizons sharply defined and limited.
7. Greater sense of choice making.	7. Limited sense of choice making.
8. Self-confident, willing to take risks.	8. Concerned with security and insecurity.
9. Immaterial and abstract in thinking.	9. Concrete and perceptive in thinking.
10. Tied to national happenings.	10. World revolves around family and body.

From analyzing these beliefs and motivators, it can be generally assumed that those of middle-class persuasion would be more inclined to purchase brand name items of long-lasting quality on more of a planned rather than an impulse basis; that spending and investing in general, even though tending to be more lavish, would reflect a conservative nature; and that the general appeal would be to status and trend (country club living) as opposed to a more home-oriented lifestyle (relatives coming over for meals/socialization).

Other Methods of Categorizing Consumers

The search to discover exactly who we are as a mass market of consumers is not new. Over the years, Americans have been categorized by psychologists, sociologists, and market researchers to help companies develop appropriate marketing strategies.

Here is a brief sampling of the many ways consumers have been categorized.[9]

Social Typologies
- Poor, middle-income, rich
- Lower-class, middle-class, upper-class
- Conservative, moderate, liberal
- Traditionalist, anarchist, liberated reformer, counterculturalist
- Innovator, early adopter, early majority, late majority, laggard
- Mover, maker, preserver, taker, changer, escaper, seeker

Market Typologies
- Bachelor, newlywed, full nest I, full nest II, empty nest, solitary survivor
- Active achiever, pleasure-seeker, traditional homebody, blue-collar outdoorsman, business leader, successful traditionalist

- Worrier, sociable, independent, sensory
- Push-button woman, identity seeker, weight-watching worrier, body acher, affluent hedonist, aromatic male, soother
- Outgoing, optimist, conscientious vigilant, apathetic, indifferent, self-indulgent, contented cow, worrier
- Traditionalist, new conformist, forerunner, autonomous, retreater
- Younger singles, younger couples, younger parents, midlife families, older households

Developmental Typologies

- Survival and security, belonging, esteem, self-actualizing
- Aggressive and animalistic, belonging and ordered existence, materialist, personalistic and being-motivated
- Impulse-ridden, conformist, autonomous, integrated
- Amoral and expedient, conforming, irrational-conscientious, rational-altruistic
- Security, social, esteem and autonomy, self-actualizing
- Inner-directed, tradition-directed, outer-directed, autonomous

Skills and Interests Typologies

- Realistics, investigative, conventional, artistic enterprising, social
- Athletic/mechanical, observing/analyzing, detail-oriented, artistic/intuitive, persuading, communicating/serving

How helpful these categories are to national, regional, and local advertisers is a matter of conjecture, but one factor can be counted on for the rest of this decade and into the twenty-first century: these categories will not be static. The operative word describing American culture will be "diversity" with the continuing rise in divorce rates and the resulting remarriages and single-parent homes, with the high number of working women, many of whom choose to remain childless, and the huge wave of aging baby boomers who can potentially be a moving and effective political force for positive change.

By 1999 nearly 59 million "boomers" will have turned forty and by 2005, the majority of all baby boomers will indeed be grey foxes over age 50. Targeting boomer business will still be profitable for many more years to come.

Consumer Confidence in the Mass Media

All things being equal, consumers tend to place a great deal of confidence in the mass media even though they often are very critical of the manner in which the press reports certain stories or of the types of news and entertainment programming that are available. Most of us have come a long way from Sinclair Lewis' Babbitt, who could not form an original opinion until the local newspaper had run an editorial on the matter. But the fact remains that we do rely almost exclusively on the mass media to supply us with our news and information on a daily basis. To what extent relying on the media for information as well as entertainment correlates to consumer confidence is questionable, but there is no doubt about the "love-affair" between mass media and the consumer. Criticize we may, but love that media, we do. What? Unplug the television, the radio, not subscribe to the evening paper? Surely, you jest!

SUMMARY

The proper understanding of advertising and how it works to the advantage of a corporation in a complex marketplace begins with the understanding of consumer behavior and how television influences such behavior. From total unawareness of a business or product to actually becoming a customer, consumer, or potential customer, behavior can be traced.

Consumers seem to follow predictable patterns of behavior during the buying process, rejecting that which is not familiar or that which they would not consider credible. Advertising plays a major role in the process of actually determining what is familiar and what is credible. Once a brand is established in the mind of the consumer, it is likely to be the brand of choice simply because it always has been.

Culture and learning play a major role in the maturation process. We learn how to behave within our culture as a result of the reinforcement of certain values, mores, or standards; such reinforcement emanates from our families, friends, churches, societal role-models, and even mass communication systems.

The media play an educational role in the cultural process as they help to reinforce certain behaviors, but it remains clear that consumers will not accept media messages that are not congruent with their cultural upbringing. Nor will they buy an advertised product if they neither need nor want it, merely because that product is advertised. There is no media manipulation of consumers that would otherwise cause inferior or questionable products to fail miserably in the marketplace.

Consumers make buying decisions, in part, due to a complex matrix of internal and external influences that reflect not only culture, but the social class that one is thought to be a part of.

With mass media and its role within our modern culture defined, we can now look at advertising per se and then at each of the mass media separately in order to understand exactly what it is that each of these can and cannot do in the marketplace of media images.

NOTES

1. David Martin, *Romancing the Brand* (New York: AMACOM, 1989), p. 15.

2. Sydney W. Head with Christopher H. Sterling, *Broadcasting in America* (Boston: Houghton Mifflin, 1982), p. 526.

3. William Bolen, *Advertising* (New York: John Wiley and Sons, 1984), p. 99.

4. Christine Hall Hansen and Ronald D. Hansen, "Constructing Personality and Social Reality Through Music: Individual Differences Among Fans of Punk and Heavy Metal Music," *Journal of Broadcasting and Electronic Media* 35/3 (Summer 1991): 337.

5. Martin, *Romancing the Brand,* p. 131.

6. William G. Nickels, *Marketing Communication and Promotion* (New York: John Wiley and Sons, 1984), p. 57.

7. Ibid., p. 59.

8. Pierre Martineau, "Social Classes and Spending Behavior," *Journal of Marketing* 23/2 (October 1958): 130.

9. Edward Cornish, ed., *The 1990's & Beyond* (Bethesda, Md.: World Future Society, 1990), p. 21.

OTHER WORKS CITED

Barge, J. A., R. N. Bond, W. J. Lombardi, and M. E. Tota. "The Additive Nature of Chronic and Temporary Sources of Construct Accessibility." *Journal of Personality and Social Psychology* 50 (1986): 869–878.

Hansen, C. H. "Priming Sex-role Stereotypic Event Schemas with Rock Music Videos: Effect on Impression Favorability, Trait Inferences and Recall of a Subsequent Male-Female Interaction." *Basic and Applied Social Psychology* 10 (1989): 371–391.

Mullen, Brian and Craig Johnson. *The Psychology of Consumer Behavior.* Hillsdale, N.J.: Lawrence Erlbaum Associates, 1990.

CHAPTER 3

Telling It Like It Is

The Expectations and Limits of Advertising

> There are things which we come to know so well . . . that we do not know how we know them. Perhaps we live best when we are not too conscious of how and why we do them.
>
> — Albert Einstein

THE CHALLENGE TO CORPORATE AND BUSINESS AD EXECUTIVES

Corporations and businesses that want to maximize advertising impact and minimize overall waste in their media planning efforts are now positioned to understand the intricacies of how advertising works in relation to the variables that affect consumer buying behavior. Building a base of general understanding regarding consumer and human behavior gives the necessary perspective to effectively relate the expectations of corporate and business advertising.

Well-meaning media planners and advertising executives, who spend a good deal of their professional careers planning and executing media buys, are prone to expecting too much from the advertising they buy. This occurs partly due to the need for personal justification of what decisions are made since such decisions will ultimately have to be defended if wrong and, of course, replicated with successive buys if right.

However, overexpectation in advertising is most often born from not understanding how advertising works, what it is supposed to do or actually can do in relation to overall corporate and business-related short- and long-term goals, and the relationship between advertising and other consumer buying variables.

This chapter should be of immense help to those in the planning process who

feel they possess an average or a better than average working knowledge of advertising, but would like to become even more effective in such efforts. Increased effectiveness in advertising decision making can give a company or a retail group the competitive edge that might make the difference between making margins or losing overall market share.

NEVER OVERPROMISE END RESULTS

One of the biggest mistakes made in the advertising industry by those selling advertising to advertisers is to overpromise end result to the client. Clients, whether on the corporate or retail level, expect end-result best-case scenarios.

Painting the silver lining to a potential customer may be the natural inclination of a media salesperson who understands the power of what he or she is selling, but it does not serve the industry or the client well. What does serve both constituents is an educated media buyer on the corporate level and an equally educated sales representative who understands advertising and can explain how it actually works to a potential customer without falling prey to the temptation of making exaggerated claims that may not live up to promise.

When end results are overpromised or overexpected, another potential consistent advertiser turns sour on advertising when those results are not actualized. If the corporate or business advertising planner or media buyer does not have the professional expertise to assist in making buying decisions, failing to understand how advertising works, he or she may waste a significant portion of the budget in a futile attempt to discover "what works and what doesn't work."

WHAT ADVERTISING CAN AND CANNOT DO

Very few media salespeople and even fewer businesspeople who make advertising buying decisions understand how the advertising they are selling or the advertising they are buying actually works. The situation is similar to a person who understands very little about an automobile selling that automobile to a consumer who knows nothing about cars. A sale may be made, but the transaction occurs in a vacuum of little to no understanding; hence, if there is a later problem, the buyer will blame the seller for hawking an inferior product and the seller will blame the buyer for not using it properly. It is a lose-lose situation, but one that happens daily all across America as well-meaning media representatives sell retail advertising to well-meaning business clients in a vacuum of little to no understanding. What will, can, and must change these daily scenarios is proper education and the knowledge that will lead to understanding. So advertising sales representatives need to stop overselling and those on the corporate levels who make the buying decisions need to stop overexpecting. In a word, both groups need to engage in the learning process.

The Lowest Common Denominator

Ask any group of media professionals or retail clients to define the one thing that advertising can do, if it could theoretically be broken down to a lowest common denominator, and you will receive multiple answers: "create awareness," "stimulate demand," "enhance overall image." Each answer, of course, contains a bit of truth about how advertising functions in our society, but it is rare that the one "correct" answer (the lowest common denominator) ever surfaces.

Yes, advertising can create images, motivate consumers, create desire, or do any number of things claimed by advertising people, but Hank Seiden was absolutely correct when he observed that advertising can only do one thing: convince a logical prospect to try a product or a service *one* time. From that point on, of course, the product or service stands on its own. Advertising has done all it can do. It convinced someone to try. Advertising does not make customers. Only products make customers.*

The understanding of this basic concept should prevent overzealous salespeople from promising something that cannot be delivered and advertisers, filled with expectation, from blaming their lack of success on any advertising they may be doing. Advertising does not sell; it does not convince people to buy. It can only cause a logical prospect or a potential customer to come to the door of a business one time only and no more. If the store or business is rejected at that point, such rejection has nothing to do with advertising but with the store or business itself. This concept will be developed shortly, but we must first understand just *who* a logical prospect or potential customer of any business engaged in advertising is, in order to expand the customer base of that business.

Logical Prospects/Potential Customers

A logical prospect for any corporation, business, or retail group must meet certain criteria; such criteria must be understood by advertisers who often tend to believe that "everyone" in their marketing area desires what they have to sell or what they are advertising on any given media. In fact, very few people in any given market are potential customers for any products or services being offered by any retail establishment during a typical business day. A person who does enter a store and agrees to make or does make a purchase is one who is in the market for that product or service and can afford the product or service being advertised.

Advertising, in and of itself, cannot sell a product or service to someone who has no need for such, is out of the market for any reason (someone who buys a new car today will be out of the automotive market for an average of three to five years), or who cannot afford it. Further, advertising does not make a satisfied customer; only good products create customer satisfaction. And, certainly, advertising a product that is perceived by the consuming public to be inferior in some way or promoting a business that is thought to have poor management does not save that product or business from market extinction.

Advertising encourages more first-time customers to try the product or the business being advertised; the ultimate consumer dissatisfaction with the resultant purchase causes rejection, giving no repeat business – the secret to long-term success in retailing. Business failure that results from consumer dissatisfaction will have nothing to do with the quality of the advertising, but everything to do with the perceived quality of the product or the business advertised.

Advertising is intended to get the logical prospect to the front door of the business. From that point on, advertising has little influence on customer behavior; the end result of consumer behavior has always been and always will be the responsibility of the store or the business on whose doorstep the potential customer is now standing.

Variables Influencing Buying Behavior

Advertising is only one variable of many that influence consumer buying behavior. It does not ultimately cause or actually initiate buying behavior. Advertising triggers the response needed to motivate the consumer to go into a particular store or place of business to look at and consider the purchase of a product or service. Since the product or service will be accepted or rejected on its own merits, advertising plays no role in ultimate consumer behavior other than that of reinforcement.

Once in a store, a consumer who has a favorable predisposition toward a particular product may be more inclined to buy than a consumer whose attitude is neutral. But certainly people do not enter a store and buy what they do not want merely because "the advertising is good."

What does trigger the buying decision on the part of the consumer is a complex matrix of variables, including advertising. But since advertising is perhaps the most noticeable of the variables, it is the one that usually receives the "blame" when corporations and businesses fail in their sales efforts.

How often do media salespeople hear from their clients, "Well, I didn't sell as many units as I had planned, so I guess not many people listen to your radio station. We better cancel that schedule." Retailers are notorious for blaming others when their efforts do not live up to expectation. They would do better to understand other variables that directly influence the buying behavior of their target market.

The Sales Wheel shown in Figure 3.1 graphically depicts the many variables that influence customer buying behavior in the marketplace. These are the criteria that will determine whether or not a potential customer becomes a consumer, apart from any advertising (although advertising must be considered as one of these marketing variables).

Figure 3.1
The Sales Wheel

The consumer may seem to be a complex organism at large in an unpredictable world, but marketplace behavior is neither complex nor unpredictable. Consumerism is driven by a large dose of common sense sprinkled with rational behavior. What consumers ultimately want can be given labels like value, convenience, or service. They want to feel good about doing business at a particular store or with a particular person; hence, the many factors on the Sales Wheel that influence sales emanate from that rational part of our being that tells us that what we want is little different from what others desire: to have our needs filled in the environment of our choice, making our buying decisions based on what *we* believe to be important to us whether that variable be price, service, or parking.

For purposes of discussion, we can divide the marketing variables on the Sales Wheel into two groups: external variables (those factors that exist in the environment outside of the immediate store or business) and internal variables (those factors that are part of the interior environment within the store or business). Both may be influenced either directly or indirectly by store management, but both most certainly contribute to consumer behavior within the complex marketplace of choice.

Simply stated, all things being equal, potential customers will usually not shop in a store they feel uncomfortable entering, which they feel looks shabby or "outdated," where they may have to walk a considerable distance, or where they perceive the store's reputation within the community is questionable for whatever reason. These are examples of external variables that may work for or against a particular business regardless of the advertising done.

Once in the store itself, budding consumers will not become customers if they are not treated well or are overly pressured by floor salespeople, if the price of the item sought is not within their budget or can be purchased for less elsewhere (price related to benefit/competition), if the item desired is not presented well (packaging/floor display), if there is disappointment with product quality or features, or if the business is perceived as being unhygienic (restrooms). Consumers are creatures of fashion and trend. They enjoy having what others desire or covet, so likely will not seek to own what is out of the mainstream of consumer taste.

These are examples of internal variables over which the retailer has more direct control since the consumer is actually in the store and can be spoken with one-on-one about product price and quality, benefits from paying that price, product features that set the product apart from its competition, delivery schedule, or service after the sale.

If each variable that ultimately influences consumer decision making could be run through a grinder and rolled into one overall variable that would stand out among all others, it would likely be the variable of service—total quality service or TQS, as Karl Albrecht of the TQS Group calls it.

Why is a total quality service approach critically important for business today? The most basic reason is that it's becoming virtually impossible to create a sustainable competitive advantage through a tangible product alone. Whether it's a computer, a new type of insurance, a new investment concept, or a new fast-food item, the time span from innovation to imitation by a competitor is becoming shorter and shorter. Tangibles alone can seldom contribute a permanent or even long-lasting competitive edge.[1]

Service must be more than rhetoric. Albrecht points to the 1988 survey of 3,375 executives in North America, Europe, and Japan conducted by Management Center Europe in conjunction with the American Management Association and the Japanese Management Association that concluded service should indeed be the highest of all organizational priorities:

- Over 90 percent of the respondents saw service to the customer as "more important" or "much more important" in the next five years.
- Nearly 80 percent rated improving quality and service to customers as the key to competitive success in their future.
- Ninety-two percent recognized that one of their key responsibilities, regardless of organizational position, was ensuring superior service.

Ironically, these same executives viewed their current customer service as inadequate, with little measuring or reporting of customer satisfaction, little to no training given employees in service skills, and limited analysis of competitors' services and products in comparison to their own. Albrecht correctly concludes that "At this point in the progress of the service revolution, it seems fair to say that rhetoric and reality are running neck and neck, with rhetoric slightly out in front."[2]

Advertising and Sales

As a variable, advertising should be looked at as an external force whose role is played out over the long run. That advertising is a force whose results are seen over an expanding period of time, as opposed to an entity that brings in immediate results, is a concept shared by many who study advertising. David A. Aaker and John G. Myers conclude that "a convenient and enticing advertising objective involves a construct like immediate sales or market share. The ultimate aim of advertising is often . . . immediate sales. . . . [Such] objectives that involve an increase in immediate sales [are misguided because] 1) advertising is only one of many factors influencing sales, and 2) the contributory role of advertising often occurs primarily over the long run."[3]

The relationship is not well understood by many retailers and businesspeople. There is no direct correlation between immediate sales and advertising expenditures. Advertising is one variable on the Sales Wheel but its purpose is to educate consumers over a period of time so that they will become logical prospects, come into a store, and become customers, possibly for years.

Advertising as Planning for the Long Term

When done correctly, advertising is a courting ritual that courts with intended long-term results. Checking how much advertising was done for this weekend's sale with the actual sales volume for the weekend is myopic management at best. The general influence of this weekend's advertising may not be felt for weeks; no correlation exists between short-term sales volume and current advertising. Today's customers providing those immediate sales are consumers who have been educated over the past several months or longer by the store's advertising.

This point is also well made in advertising journal research. Anthony I. Morgan, senior vice president and research director at Backer & Spielvogel, Inc., observes that

almost no one would deny that advertising's role is to help sell the product, but this is hardly the whole story, especially when time and/or media weight are viewed as significant variables. Most testing systems evaluate a commercial's worth on the basis of a single exposure's ability to do the job immediately, to sell today. I think this may be a vast oversimplification of advertising's role. The path to greater sales is not always a simple Hear-Understand-Do taking place in 24 hours.[4]

Added Value and Long-Term Effects

Of course, some immediate results can be expected from any advertising, but the majority of customers are built over a time period exceeding several months up to a year. Expecting immediate sales from advertising should not be the goal of a businessperson who understands that such promotion is one variable of many that influence retail sales and that the more immediate factors influencing sales are the external and internal variables of added value.

This has been noted by Syracuse University's John Philip Jones: "The long-term effect [of advertising] is the result of advertising working in conjunction with the added values of the brand. . . . The reason why . . . advertising has a long-term effect different from the short-term effect is repeat purchase, to which the added values make a major contribution. . . . Larger sales results accrue to brands with more added values."[5]

The Advertising Investment Return Curve

If the true effect of advertising is primarily seen over the long run, it would make sense to believe that there would be a "lag" between the time of the initial advertising investment and the actual results seen from that investment, especially if those dollars are placed in the electronic media of radio or television. The electronic media, as explained in the rest of this chapter, educate consumers over time via intrusive repetition.

This "lag time" concept, in fact, seems to be the case as shown from research done by Coleman and the Radio Advertising Bureau (Figure 3.2). Initially, most advertising investments will cost more than the sales they are able to produce, which is why measuring sales results the day after a store event is not indicative of the real value of advertising. After a period of time, however, sales and profits that are the direct result of the earlier advertising will flow to the business.

Retailers often become impatient with what they feel to be advertising that is not working properly and cancel a schedule of commercials right before the time that such advertising would begin to produce an investment return for them. This impatience stems from a lack of knowledge of how advertising works and of the research graphically depicted in the Advertising Investment Return Curve.

As Jones has noted, "It is more economic to spend more on advertising than the brand [or business] can immediately afford than to spend what the brand [or business] can afford in the certain knowledge that this will be too little to be effective."[6]

Exactly how many weeks are needed to produce a noticeable return is, of course, a function of the advertiser's sales and marketing objectives, the size of the advertising schedule, the specifics of what is being advertised, and the economic, social, and political conditions existing within the marketplace at the time of advertising. However, thirteen weeks is usually a reasonable amount of time for measurable results provided that the advertiser has attended to the variables

Figure 3.2
Advertisement Investment Return Curve

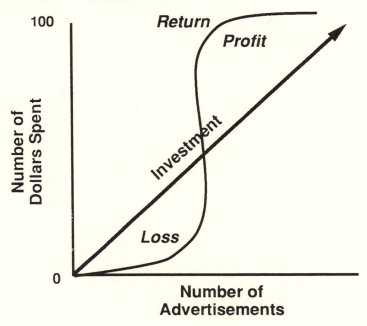

on the Sales Wheel and does not expect advertising to do more than bring a logical prospect to the front door of the business for the first time.

This being understood, it becomes easier to look at advertising as a long-term investment and not something done exclusively for short-term results. Such desired long-term goals, however, can only be accomplished by properly budgeting appropriate media that are designed to accomplish long-term results.

The question is, of the two distinct types of media, print media (newspaper, magazines, billboards, flyers, etc.) and electronic media (radio and television), which type is designed to produce consumer results for the long term, in addition to providing some short-term success for today that all merchants expect?

This brings us to the discussion of newspaper and of radio/television, as there are distinct differences between the two that merchants usually do not understand. Lack of understanding means a great amount of waste in the allocation of advertising budgets and the execution of the promotion purchased by these budgets.

THE NEWSPAPER

Newspaper, a traditional part of American culture and the infrastructure that grew with each community, is the form of advertising turned to by most corporations when making media recommendations to their retail outlets or to the businesses that stock and sell their merchandise. It is also the option preferred by most advertising managers at the store level. Print advertisement to these decision makers represents the conventional way to promote a business and is mostly purchased out of habit, with little thought given to consumer psychology in relation to the manner in which the medium works as an advertising vehicle.

The key point here is "advertising vehicle." The powerful effect and integrity of newspapers as an editorial and news force are beyond question. What needs to be looked at is the effectiveness of this print medium as a purveyor of the advertiser's message to the consumer.

Frequency and Repetition

Two concepts addressed throughout this book are deeply embedded in our heritage and culture, and are dominant within our educational, religious, and social institutions. Their focus defines who we are as a people and who we are as individuals.

These concepts are repetition and frequency. We are who we are within our culture because of repeated exposure to certain values, standards, and mores. In the first and second chapters, we discussed how and why consumers buy what is familiar. What is familiar is so because of repeated exposure at an early age to certain ideas, concepts, or even advertised products.

People learn tastes for food, cultural events, furniture styles, paintings and other goods and services. . . . The question of most concern is how and why do people learn such tastes? One rather simple answer is exposure. You learn to like goods and services as they become common, more accepted more familiar. The most obvious example of the learning of taste is in food among young children. Children in some countries learn to like rice or cow's blood or beetles. Early exposure to such foods creates a preference that is hard to alter.[7]

We are what we are because we learn what we learn through repetition of concepts in our immediate cultural environment. The frequency of these exposures produces a behavioral pattern that stays with us for a lifetime.

How, then, do we tie the medium of newspaper into the concepts of frequency and repetition and ultimately advertising effectiveness? This question is answered by applying the concepts of frequency and repetition to the newspaper as an advertising vehicle.

A One-Time Impression Medium

Any advertisement placed anywhere within a newspaper is, by definition, a one-time impression. Further, that one-time impression is made only if the reader chooses to look at or actually read the ad. Newspaper readers are directed to that medium for in-depth news, sports, editorials, television listings, or the comics, spending an average of twenty to twenty-five minutes doing so. Since the main motivation for reading the newspaper is to obtain information of local or national interest, this leaves little time for reading the majority of the contents of most newspapers, which are the column inches devoted to advertisements.

Even if the reader chooses to look at the ad, the problem with one-time impression viewing is that learning involves repetition, a concept thoroughly discussed in the next chapter. One-time impressions are stored in the short-term memory bank of the brain and will fade within twenty to thirty seconds. With no reinforcement or carry-over effect, the impression will not be lasting and will never become a permanent part of the knowledge base.

Because the time lapse between newspaper ads is close to one day or twenty-four hours, assuming ads are run on daily basis, the mind has discarded most if not all of the ad seen the day before and must start the information-processing stage all over again.

Additionally, yesterday's newspapers have no audience, giving the many advertisements in each edition a limited time value. Once newspapers have been read within a given household, they are neither kept nor passed along to others, as magazines often are. A written record with no audience but the recycling bin does little to enhance long-term customer awareness.

To aid recall of newspaper or any type of print ad, the same message must be reinforced by the electronic media. Even the one-time impression Pepsi ad from Ray Charles would not be remembered in print—but everybody sings the media message "uh huh" when they see the print ad in magazines or on billboards.

When Newspaper Ads Are Actually Read

Newspaper ads are essentially viewed on a "pass-over" basis. The ads are noted, but the reader is not motivated to devote time to them unless two specific consumer situations are in play:

1. The reader is in a "high-involvement" state, in the market for a particular item or service. The desire to buy "today" is extremely high.
2. The reader, being in a high-involvement state, is motivated by the price of the product or service in the newspaper ad.

To put it in story form, if a man is experiencing no problems with his lawn-mower today, he will not take time away from his newspaper reading to read an advertisement about a product he has no interest in. He is out of the market and is not a logical prospect. Advertising cannot sell something to someone who has no need; this man is out of the market because his mower is working properly. He will therefore pass over the ad as if it were never printed in the first place.

Now let us take this same man working in his yard a week later. His lawnmower experiences a transmission failure that is beyond reasonable expense to repair. Suddenly, he is in the market for a new lawnmower and his motivators change. Reading the newspaper that evening, he will be looking for lawnmower ads because he is now a logical prospect who has a need, is in the market, and will be motivated by the prices offered through newspaper advertising.

A more complete discussion of the percentage of logical prospects who are in the market at any given moment can be found in Chapter 6, but the unmistakable point is clear: a small minority of the total universe reading a newspaper on any given day is actually in the market for any advertised product or service and will be motivated enough to actually read any particular newspaper ad.

Newspaper advertising is viewed by choice; the consumer makes the decision to read the ad or pass over the ad based on immediate need. There is nothing "intrusive" about print advertising that will cause the ad to be noted if the reader does not choose to note it. This is in stark contrast to the highly intrusive nature of the electronic media, whose ads are seen and heard without choice by the consumer. This "intrusive" concept can be highly advantageous to a businessperson interested in minimizing advertising waste, as will be discussed at the end of the chapter.

Advertising research seems to bear this out. Herbert E. Krugman (1965) notes that the reading of printed words is a demanding cognitive task requiring active participation; most consumers attempt to avoid this and are therefore unlikely to read anything that is of no interest to them. The idea that passive consumers of the media will not become involved in reading what does not interest them is also advanced by the findings of A. G. Greenwald and C. Leavitt (1984). Such findings are in contrast to what the electronic media can do: cause advertising consumption to occur even when no interest exists.

Coupon-Clippers

Before we leave the discussion of the print media, it should be noted that there exists a population of "coupon-clippers" who are less interested in newspapers for the information value they hold than for the ads and coupons that can be found throughout each edition. These people, usually frugal housewives who are competent budget managers, are in the market for anything that will give them savings, not necessarily for any identified product. Coupons, of course, limit themselves to the food items, restaurants, or retail stores that stock household consumer goods or soft goods that are the fare of coupon mongers. Naturally excluded are the larger retail categories like furniture stores, automobile dealerships, home-remodeling centers, and up-scale stores that do not depend on coupons for additional traffic flow.

Are Newspapers Worried?

Clearly, as we prepare to enter a new century of technological wonders, the newspaper industry is more than concerned. The May 5, 1992 edition of *USA*

Today noted that "While the USA added 12 million households in the 1980's, daily newspaper circulation stayed virtually flat. The percentage of adults who read a newspaper every day—73 percent in 1967—has been threatening to dip below 50 percent since the late 1980's. Newspaper's share of advertising expenditures has fallen 4.4 percentage points—to 25 percent—since 1975. . . . The USA began the 1980's with 1,745 daily newspapers and ended the decade with 1,611."

In addition, *USA Today* writes, nonclassified local retail advertising that accounts for 52 percent of a newspaper's ad revenue comes mostly from department stores. Twenty-four percent of all department store space is in Chapter 11 bankruptcy proceedings. To stay in business in the latter part of this decade, many publishers will have to accept 5 percent to 6 percent profit margins instead of the traditional 20 percent to 40 percent.

Evidently, the newspaper industry has not well served the many department stores experiencing declining sales and going through the pain of Chapter 11. Bloomingdale's in the East, Macy's in the East and the Midwest, and Frederick-Nelson in the Northwest, now totally liquidated and bankrupt altogether, are but three examples of empires devoted to newspaper that are either reorganizing or out of business due to declining traffic, sales, and gross revenues. Of course, economic, social, and cultural conditions contributed partly to the revenue decline in the retail industry, but it is also evident that changing consumer lifestyles meant that newspapers were no longer efficiently impacting large numbers of consumers as they had done for decades in the twentieth century.

OTHER PRINT MEDIA

Direct Mail

Advertising should be looked at as long-term rather than short-term. Immediate sales returns are fine and desirable, but should not be the overall goal of well-planned media campaigns.

Of course, we do not live in a world of absolutes and there will always be some type of exception. Direct mail seems to be one of these exceptions where the measurement of immediate response is the only valid standard by which to gauge the success of that form of advertising. Direct mail is really an "either-or" proposition. Consumers either throw it away or they act on it. There is no carry-over effect. Direct mail does not, however, work for everyone.

When measuring direct-mail response, one must assume the role of consumer and ask why some pieces will be tossed in the wastebasket and why other pieces will be kept for potential follow-up. The answer lies in the concept of familiarity discussed in Chapter 2. Consumers basically toss direct mail pieces from stores or about products with which they are not familiar or for which they have no need (they are out of the market). If they are in the market, they will keep the piece and may act on it in the future.

This is why the most successful direct mail campaigns are done by stores with current customer lists. That takes care of the familiarity issue, as long as the mailer also advertises familiar products. To insure a higher percentage of response, businesses must advertise established brand names that will be immediately recognized by the consumer. New product lines or unfamiliar items cannot be established in the mind of the consumer via direct mail.

Even if these steps are taken, remember that the customer must still be in the market and motivated by the offer on the mailer in order to keep it out of the wastebasket. Response can be measured and immediate results can be expected from this type of advertising. However, the market is limited to those who are logical prospects. The national response rate to direct mail is in the neighborhood of 2 percent to 4 percent. Merchants considering this form of print advertising, still a one-time impression at best, must seriously weigh the costs of producing a quality piece that will attract consumer attention with the potential return from their planned campaign area.

Outdoor or Billboard Advertising

A popular form of advertising for businesses within close proximity to freeways, billboards have the advantage of directing consumers to specific store locations or areas. They are large, and contain short messages that are easy to read. Outdoor displays are best used in urban areas with large traffic counts. They are especially logical for the medium of radio since billboards are targeted to a mobile population stuck in gridlock a large portion of the morning and evening hours. Television stations plugging their evening news team, beer distributors, and cigarette companies are heavy users of outdoor advertising.

Weather, environmental clutter, and not being able to afford expensive nighttime lighting curb the number of potential viewers and, again, each time a board sighting is made by a motorist, it is still only a one-time impression. Although some billboard one-time impressions can be quite memorable, these expensive creations, seen along Santa Monica Boulevard in Los Angeles or adjacent to major freeways in all markets, cannot be worked into the budgets of local merchants whose main interest is getting the biggest possible "bang" from their ad dollar.

The Yellow Pages

Yellow Page directories are not an advertising medium. The Yellow Pages even admit to not being an advertising but a *reference* medium.

The Yellow Pages publication, *Yellow Pages Update,* writes that the Yellow Pages acts as "a source of information on suppliers of particular goods and services that the consumer already has decided to purchase. . . . The Yellow Pages . . . can be said to be the final link in a chain. While the other media—TV, radio, magazines, newspapers and direct mail—create demand and awareness, the Yellow Pages completes the buying cycle by directing the consumer to a place where the desired purchase can be made."[8]

Hence, the Yellow Pages serves as a dictionary of sorts. It is referred to by consumers only after they have decided what they want to purchase; they may need a telephone number or an address, so they can let their "fingers do the walking" to the appropriate place on the page. But the pages themselves play no role in the production of retail sales through consumer education, frequency, or repetition. "Since it reaches consumers when they already have made their decision to buy, it need not convince, only point the consumer in a direction."[9]

The concern about this form of retail or business promotion is the high cost involved, taken from the advertising budget itself, in placing a courtesy message in a reference medium that has no correlation with the creation of either demand or consumer awareness.

Granted, merchants need to list their places of business in a Yellow Page directory, but in many markets multiple directories exist. This forces retailers to feel the necessity of placing messages of courtesy in each directory, the result being unnecessary duplication and wasted funds that could have been used more wisely. Retailers would do better by sticking with the standard Bell directory, if they choose to run a display message, and placing only the store name, address, and phone number in any other Yellow Page supplemental edition distributed within the market.

Magazines

Although an obvious form of print advertising, magazines offer some distinct advantages over their less distinguished cousins, the newspapers. Magazines today have permeated our culture, catering to special interest groups of every sort. There are magazines for political liberals as well as conservatives, for runners and dieters, computer buffs and crossword puzzle enthusiasts, cat, dog, and horse fanciers, health food nuts, and the gay population. These tabloids have become the print industry's version of narrowcasting and are probably the least expensive way for national and regional advertisers to reach large audiences in print.

Their overall quality and ability to offer photo-quality color set them apart from the less sophisticated black and white so familiar to newspaper readers. Unlike newspapers, magazines are kept around the house for future reference and "pass along value" to other readers. Good magazine ads, also unlike most colorless newspaper advertisements, have what is called "stopping power." "Stopping power" is the ability to immediately focus a reader's attention on an advertisement containing, for example, unusual or eye-catching photography. Regional editions of national magazines make it possible for mid-sized companies to become a part of well-known weekly or monthly editions. Magazines also have the advantage of being subscribed to and purchased over-the-counter by above average wage earners, who are usually the better educated and more sophisticated consumers.

However, magazines remain a one-time impression medium by strict definition. Waste is apparent, as ads run in national, general-appeal magazines such as *Time* or *Newsweek* are less efficient than those appearing in specialty magazines where demographics and advertisements can be more effectively matched. Magazines, too, tend to be associated with the larger companies whose budgets lend themselves to a wider than regional coverage. Companies and businesses whose scope is either regional/local or national in nature with a local/regional emphasis in various segments of the country need to understand how the electronic media can place them in the minds of potential consumers more efficiently than can even the strongest of the print media.

THE ELECTRONIC MEDIA

The electronic media, defined simply as either the medium of radio or of television and its many systems of delivery, are as different from print in their ability to deliver advertising messages to potential consumers as the invisible carrier wave that delivers the electronic signal is from its tangible cousin, the printed page. Understanding these differences can have a profound impact on the longevity of a business and the way in which it chooses to invest its advertising dollars.

Radio and Television—The Intrusive Media

The argument that entertainment programs on both radio and television exist only as vehicles to deliver commercial messages to large numbers of potential consumers has been advanced by numerous media critics over the years; it would be hard to argue against such a point, for it is precisely that commercial system, self-supporting as it is, which gives us a government-free information and entertainment system whose only cost to the consumer is the price of a receiver set and the electricity to run it.

The concept of programming, then, is to run the information and/or the entertainment alongside the commercials that make such programming possible. They are interwoven together in a tapestry of entertainment programs, news, sports, weather, public service announcements, and commercials—a mosaic where all becomes one and the consumption of the advertising is as natural as consuming the program, be it radio or television.

Commercials *are* a part of the programming and listeners or viewers consume them whether they want to or not because they are one with the program. Unlike the active medium of newspaper that requires attentive involvement, the consumer of radio or television has no choice but to attend to the advertisements (or, of course, leave the room or engage in other activities). There is no "pass-over" choice to be made with a medium whose advertisements are intrusive by nature and viewed or heard with no effort on the part of the consumer other than to turn the set on.

Industry Research on Passive Media

These distinctions have been noted in advertising research. In 1984 David W. Finn noted that "Print is a passive medium requiring an active audience. That is, the audience can selectively 'sit through' or 'pass over' different content. . . . [Thus] the content of the message will remain unseen and no opportunity for learning it exists."[10]

His research further notes that television (radio could also be included) is a medium that allows the viewer little freedom to "pass over" low- or no-interest advertisements with the end result being that the consumer will get something from the message. Thus, any advertisement that is at least "noted" will influence cognition. Two of Finn's propositions are that television has a higher probability of influencing awareness than print advertising, and that the repetitive nature of television will lead to more learning of brand claims than print advertising.[11]

Krugman (1965) noted the differences in the consumer's processing of print versus broadcast advertising and the demanding cognitive task required to consume the print media. Low-involvement consumers simply will not read printed material, but will be exposed to the intrusiveness of radio or television advertisements.

A developing theme in this chapter, noted by researchers like Morris Holbrook (1984) and Greenwald and Leavitt (1984), essentially marks the inability of the print media to elicit a response from uninvolved readers (those who are not logical customers or who are not in the market) who are not motivated to note or read the message. The very nature of the broadcast media makes it ideally suited to influence passive consumers, as the verbal information is noted with no effort and no consumer choice since it is intrusive.

Other studies (Murdock 1967; Edell and Keller 1989) reiterate how consumers extract more information and exhibit heightened retention from radio and television than from printed media. It should also be noted that the more the consumer is involved, the more attentive he or she will be to the radio or television message. In other words, a logical prospect will pay attention at a heightened level. As noted by Laura M. Buchholz and Robert E. Smith, "the level of consumer involvement played a significant role in determining the number of personal connections and subsequent recognition of brand and copy points."[12]

Despite the greater attentiveness given to media messages by those in a state of high involvement, the message here is that the intrusive nature of the electronic media affects cognition and produces consumer responses, even when the consumer is not in the market and in a "no"- or "low"-involvement state.

The "Zap" Factor

Of course, with the modern conveniences of television remote control or the scan features of radio, one can always "zap" from a commercial to another station; however, the chances of "zapping" into another commercial are quite good, so consumers have learned to become content with their favorite music station or their favorite television programming, accepting the intruding advertising messages that register with them, even if they are not logical prospects for what is being advertised and would otherwise choose to ignore such messages.

The advertising agency, J. Walter Thompson, has also noted that although zapping does occur, commercial audiences or those who actually do sit through a given television commercial are only 6 percent smaller than program audiences.

Repetition, Reach, and Frequency

Commercial messages intrude into the lives of consumers not once or twice, but multiple times over the lifecycle of a commercial campaign. Such multiplicity provides *repetition,* a key ingredient in the psychology of learning as we will see in the next chapter. Such repeated or successive exposures seem to be valuable in media planning, as multiple exposures over time are desirable in the awareness process.

In recent years advertisers on both the local and national levels have become increasingly concerned about the concepts of repetition, reach, and frequency. Reach and frequency have recently been studied by George Murray and John Jenkins, among others, who conclude that this increasing level of sophistication is due to several factors:[13]

- Clients and agencies becoming more professional and sophisticated
- The dramatic escalation in North American media costs (air time and production costs) during the past fifteen years or so
- The effect of technology on the electronic media, with cable systems fragmenting television audiences by offering many new stations created exclusively for cable (like CNN and ESPN)
- The commercial clutter brought about by the almost complete replacement of sixty-second commercials by fifteen- and thirty-second ones
- An increasingly competitive marketplace forcing advertisers to place emphasis on short-term sales promotions

All of these factors combine to constrict advertising budgets even further, thus making it mandatory to maximize the effectiveness of each advertising effort. The search for advertising effectiveness, Murray and Jenkins conclude, proceeds on three levels:

- Maximizing the advertising weight each campaign will deliver for a given number of dollars
- Improving the caliber of creative strategies and executions to ensure maximum effectiveness of advertising efforts
- Making sure that advertising campaigns have effective reach

Frequency

Moving beyond mere repetition is the media term "frequency," or the average number of times a target audience or an average person is exposed to an advertising message during a given media schedule. Frequency is the preferred term of media planners when discussing "repetition," and, as we will see, is necessary to keep awareness levels high within a desired demographic. Frequency is the ultimate marketing goal after general awareness or reach has been established within a population group; that desired target group can then be educated by repetitive messages programmed with little waste on the stations those people spend most of their time with.

Reach

Reach, or the total number of different listeners or viewers who tune in to a given program or station at least once during a specified time period, is also a useful measure in achieving marketing goals. However, it should be pointed out that although reach and frequency occur simultaneously, they occur at different rates. Together they measure the combined number of people who are exposed once, twice, or more times to media commercials. Depending on campaign goals, an advertiser may wish to develop a large reach, that is, expose a great number of potential customers to an advertising message. A new strip mall just opening, for example, may desire to inform as many people in a market area as possible that it is now open for business. Informing as many as possible (reach) is a more desirable goal at this point than repeated exposure (frequency).

Effective reach can be achieved most efficiently with the electronic media (due to their intrusive nature) than the print media, which are largely ignored by all except those in the immediate market (logical prospects). The strip mall management could sponsor a one-time television event, such as a movie or sporting event, to achieve effective reach. If frequency were desired, the management could sponsor a recurring program such as the evening news, a soap opera, or a daily program on either radio or television that would provide repeated exposures or frequency.

The Inverse Relationship Between Reach and Frequency

It is interesting to note the inverse relationship between reach and frequency. If a program (like a movie or football game) has a large reach, it likely will deliver little frequency, as the advertiser will be one of many sponsors. Conversely, if a program such as a recurring drama on television or a daily radio format delivers large frequency, the reach will likely be smaller as each radio station or program is one among many with a defined (smaller) percentage of the larger available audience. To put it another way, each television program or radio format has its own defined audience; they are extremely loyal and will listen or view more frequently. However, while a Super Bowl is watched only once, it will provide tremendous reach.

High reach and high frequency simply do not occur simultaneously, but neither is probable without the intrusive nature of the electronic media providing exposures on an "unannounced" basis. If reach or frequency is attempted by the newspaper, the ad placed will only be referred to by consumer choice and will enter the soon-to-be-forgotten short-term memory.

Repeated impressions provided by the electronic media begin to implant themselves in the long-term memory of the brain to become a permanent part of the knowledge base. Future consumer action can then be correlated to the education received about the product, at an earlier time, via repeated media advertising. (Remember the importance of repetition and culture discussed in the previous chapter.)

Research Findings

Research into the concepts of reach and frequency has supported common-sense and anecdotal observations that the more concentrated or intensive an advertising schedule is, the more effective it is in generating consumer response and/or awareness. As well, a correlation exists between the amount spent on advertising, as a percentage of sales, and the likely purchase possibilities of the consumer.

Advertisers, then, must be concerned with the total amount spent as a percentage of sales and even further, as a percentage of margin or profit they can expect from their investments.

To illustrate, the following table presents a few examples of typical consumer industries and the amount of advertising spent as a percentage of total sales and as a percentage of margin. Also included is the annual growth rate of the industry. Figures are from the July 13, 1992 issue of *Advertising Age* magazine.

Industry	Ad $ as a % of Sales	Ad $ as a % of Margin	Annual Growth Rate
Shoe Stores	4.0	10.8	7.7
Department Stores	2.8	14.3	4.0
Eating Places	3.4	17.4	6.2
Family Clothing Stores	2.3	6.7	11.5
Jewelry Stores	3.2	11.3	12.4
Lawn, Garden, Tractor Equipment	1.3	4.9	8.5
Retail Stores	5.9	26.4	7.2
Videotape Rental	4.2	8.3	31.2

The up side appears to be that there is, indeed, an annual growth rate in each of these industries. Advertising dollars as a percentage of overall sales runs less than 6 percent, but as a percentage of margin can exceed 25 percent, depending on the business category. Clearly, the more efficiently advertising dollars are spent, the higher the margins or profits. Effective advertising, targeted efficiently, will produce fewer ad dollars spent as a percentage of margin.

Reach and frequency are indicators of advertising efficiency and can best be accomplished via the intrusive nature of radio or television, but there are problems with the concepts of reach and frequency.

The Problem with Reach and Frequency Measurements

Certainly, a dilemma has been presented to the media planner or the advertiser. Which is more important? Reach or frequency? As was shown, it depends on the marketing or promotional goals of the advertiser; but what clouds the discussion is the fact that if reach is the desired goal, frequency must be sacrificed. If frequency needs to be raised, a corresponding loss in reach is the result.

Steve Marx and Pierre Bouvard have tackled this issue.[14] Addressing the issue of radio buying, where these figures most often come into play, they explain that media planners and buyers use the terms "total reach" (how many different people are exposed to a message) and "average frequency" (how many times the average person is exposed). These figures do not lead to effective schedules. Two stories make the point that the concepts of reach and frequency ought to be rethought.

The authors invite us to look into a skillet where some eggs have been burnt to a crisp and others are raw and runny. One could say that "on average" the omelette has been prepared well, but who would want to eat it?

Their second example is a story of two statisticians who go hunting. Upon seeing a deer in a forest clearing, the first one fires but misses; the bullet soars past the deer, right in front of its nose. The second hunter then fires but also misses, the bullet zooming past the deer's tail. The two then begin cheering and hugging each other because, on average, they killed the deer.

The point is that media schedules based on averages miss the intended target audience. Marx and Bouvard recommend discarding the discussion of reach and frequency and replacing the two concepts with one new term: effective frequency.

Effective frequency draws reach and frequency together by providing a hard number that tells an advertiser the exact number of listeners who have been exposed to a commercial at least three times in a given week. Such a concept focuses on results rather than theory.

These two concepts still remain at the heart of electronic media discussions of the battle to dominate consumers' minds. If businesses want to remain in business in the competitive economic environment of the 1990s, using the electronic media to achieve repetition, reach, frequency, or effective reach will provide the surest way to touch potential consumers with the least amount of waste.

But a central question remains: If one remains interested in using the traditional concepts of reach and frequency, which many advertisers and planners still do, how much reach and how much frequency are necessary? Such discussions are still helpful, even if the concept of effective reach is endorsed, as the information presented is generally helpful to a more complete understanding of how the media and the advertising industry operate in a competitive media environment.

Reach and Frequency—When Is Enough Enough?

Generally speaking, the newer or the more unfamiliar a business is to the general public, the more important the concept of reach becomes. Building brand or store awareness is the operating goal. Once the store name becomes better known, a good media planner would put additional dollars into building frequency or what could be termed unaided brand or store awareness within that segment of the community defined as the target customer of the store or business that is advertising. This is because it becomes too costly, at a certain point, to effectively reach everyone in a given market area; so one must concentrate on the heavy user/consumer to maximize the ad dollars that are available. An advertising rule of thumb indicates that if a business can reach 70 percent of its marketing area, it should then turn to building frequency; attempting further reach would only waste the ad dollars spent.

Ideal Reach

Advertisers and media planners are both on a constant search for the ideal schedule — one where the maximum number of commercials are run for optimum effectiveness, but not so many as to cause a decline in effectiveness. This point, if and when it is achieved, can be considered in the traditional sense as the point of ideal reach. Since most consumers are not logical prospects or in the market for the advertised product at any given time, this threshold should be maintained on a consistent basis, as it is not known exactly when a "warm" prospect will become a "hot" prospect and be ready to buy.

(Consistency can also address the marketing concern of memory lapse that occurs after being exposed to a media schedule; with continual, consistent reminding, it is more difficult to forget. This concept of memory lapse and how to keep consumers from forgetting your advertising message is fully developed in the next chapter.)

When the consumer enters a high-involvement state and is ready to purchase, the advertiser will desire brand or store awareness to be such that the now logical prospect will enter the business to (hopefully) become a loyal customer.

This point of ideal reach will likely differ from brand to brand and from store to store within any given market, but such ideal reach is generally considered to fall within the area of three to ten exposures (Figure 3.3). Most research shows that at least three exposures to a target group over a defined period of time are necessary to maintain awareness at an acceptable level.

Reach generally varies from medium to medium, with radio and television recognized as being able to generate exposures and frequency more rapidly than other advertising forms, with measurable results often occurring within a four-week time period.

Although researchers claim that print (newspapers and billboards) are high-frequency media that can produce results within that same four-week period, forgotten is the fact that the nonintrusive nature of those advertising forms precludes large numbers of exposures that the intrusive nature of radio and television can provide.

Individual advertisers, however, must establish their own budgets to determine overall awareness needed and then, after awareness/reach is established, determine how much frequency will be necessary to maintain top-of-mind awareness that will result in unaided store or brand awareness.

Figure 3.3
Effective Reach

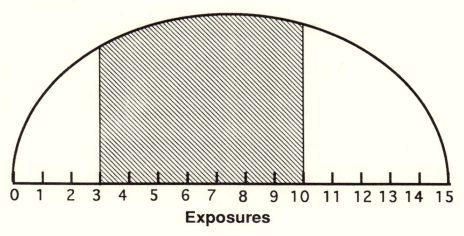

Exposures

Frequency—How much Repetition Is Needed?

To maintain a high level of awareness among a defined target or demographic group depends on several variables:

- uniqueness of store or product
- competitive pressures—how much competition there is and how they are advertising, marketing, and promoting
- medium selected to build and maintain frequency
- creative nature of advertising campaign

If a given store or product with a market is so unique that general awareness provides a great deal of word-of-mouth advertising, then less frequency directed toward the target market of that store or product will be necessary to maintain an already established level of awareness. Most businesses, however, do not have this unique advantage.

If there were only one fast food outlet in every market or one soft drink available at the grocery store, word-of-mouth would maintain awareness at a high enough level to maintain consistent business without having to build frequency through advertising. But since there are multiple fast food restaurants from which consumers can choose and many different brands of soft drinks available in all grocery stores, advertisers face the challenge of keeping their brand or their store at the top of the consumer's mind so a buying decision in their favor can be made when the consumer takes action.

Keeping awareness high means greater and more consistent frequency through proper media planning, meaning running the right message with the right media at the right times to penetrate the defined target market.

Since marketplace competition is a fact of life for most businesspeople, frequency is often determined by how often the "other guy" is promoting or advertising. Matching the frequency of a competitor may or may not be advisable, especially if that competitor has a larger store or presence in the market and a larger market share.

Frequency can be built to offset competitor advantages by selecting a radio station that specifically targets the defined demographic the store is attempting to reach. Going head-to-head by attempting to build frequency through expensive newspaper advertising will quickly drain the budget, in addition to creating a great deal of waste, as only those in the "now" market will ever know the newspaper ad has been placed.

Aside from what has just been mentioned about building frequency through the electronic media as opposed to the expense of a one-time impression print medium, other considerations enter into the discussion of how much frequency is enough to establish top-of-mind awareness.

Media selection will depend, in part, on the advertiser's need for flexibility. Marketing situations created by buying opportunities, seasonal weather conditions, or unexpected demand (thus depleting stock) can change planned advertising directions. A flexible medium such as radio or television can respond immediately by providing necessary copy changes. Inflexible media that require lead time for layout and printing cannot accommodate an advertiser's need for flexibility.

A second consideration that may affect media selection is the season of the year. With daylight savings and warm temperatures from April through October, more people spend a majority of time outdoors rather than indoors. To reach an active outdoor population will mean utilizing the most mobile of all media, radio, and perhaps the most permanently placed of all advertising forms, billboards.

Winter months, when people spend most of their time indoors, may be the best time to consider building frequency through television. Consumers will read more, so newspapers and magazines will come into play more during this season. Since the same number of people drive to work in the winter as in the summer, radio is a frequency player during all seasons of the year. Each advertiser, though, must necessarily respond to his or her indigenous market. In Phoenix, for example, temperatures are so hot during the summer that most people tend to spend the days indoors and venture outside to become consumers in the evening hours.

A final consideration in the selection of the appropriate media to establish frequency is the creative nature of the advertising or the manner in which the advertising draws consumer attention to the advertised product or store. All of us can remember highly creative ad campaigns, many of them based on humor, which we can immediately associate with a product.

Successful electronic media ad campaigns have also spun off well into the print media. This media mix combination has served the advertiser well by establishing both reach and frequency. When creativity is inspired and thus memorable, fewer impressions are needed to maintain frequency/awareness at a high level. Getting a commercial "sting line" to become a part of the popular culture vocabulary via word-of-mouth is an advertiser's dream and need not happen only on the national level. Good local advertising sculpted by hometown media professionals can also build reach and frequency and cause a consumer sensation.

The Optimum Effective Scheduling System

In the radio industry an exact schedule of commercials can be calculated to target any audience with the least amount of total waste. The information is contained in the National Association of Broadcaster's book, *Radio Advertising's Missing Ingredient: The Optimum Effective Scheduling System* by Steve Marx and Pierre Bouvard.[15]

Based on sound industry research, the calculation and usage of the resulting schedule, whose secret is schedule concentration over a period of weeks, will give advertisers the results they did not previously witness by the poor scheduling of a few spots here and a few spots there. The recommended OES schedule will show the advertiser exactly how many commercials to run each week to effectively reach the desired audience enough times to produce measurable results and build or maintain top-of-mind awareness within a given market.

The results of such OES schedules show that advertiser expectations are reached or exceeded eight times more often than with non-OES schedules. Reach and frequency are interesting to talk about, but they do not tell us if an actual schedule is going to work. An OES schedule is not a theory, but a proven, results-oriented system that is based on hard numbers.

The hard figures used, from Katz radio and Katz television that are a refinement of the twenty-year-old numbers of the Group W new math, are the results of hundreds of radio schedules actually run across the country for real-life advertisers. Such schedules enable the advertiser to rise above the media clutter and address the advertising research that finds that consumers must be confronted with a minimum of three commercials per week in order for that advertising schedule to be effective.

The OES system ensures that *effective reach,* or those hit three or more times each week, is at least 50 percent of the total reach of the station. Since "reach" in radio is defined as the number of different people who are exposed to a schedule of announcements, the OES effective reach system will guarantee to hit half of that total number at least three times each week, thus producing the results that advertisers want.

To calculate OES, an Arbitron rating book is needed along with two OES constants: the OES Spot Factor of 3.29 that tells how many commercials to buy, Monday through Sunday, 6 A.M. to 12 Midnight, to produce effective reach; and the OES Reach Factor that tells the advertiser the size of the audience effectively reached.

Three simple steps will then be used to calculate the exact numbers for each station, regardless of format or size of audience:

First, calculate the weekly turnover ratio. This is the crucial first step as stations with higher audience turnover will need more frequency than stations with a lower audience turnover. The example given to help understand this concept is of a radio station broadcasting inside a convenience store (a location with high traffic turnover) and from within a library (a location with low traffic turnover). Messages would need to be repeated more frequently from the convenience store than the library.

Stations with high turnover rates are those whose formats are geared to the younger audience, such as Top 40 and Contemporary Hit Radio (CHR) or adult All-News formats where information can be gotten quickly. Low turnover rate stations include classical or easy-listening stations catering to older, more mature audiences and country formats whose audiences are notoriously loyal.

This turnover ratio is calculated by dividing the average quarter-hour audience (AQH or the average number of people listening for at least five minutes in each quarter-hour over a specified period of time) into the station Cume figure, Cume/AQH. Second, the resulting number (turnover ratio) is then multiplied by the OES Spot Factor, 3.29, to determine the weekly schedule. Third, the station's Cume is then multiplied by the OES Reach Factor, .46, to determine how many people have been effectively reached.

A working example is presented in the following list, again from the NAB book from Marx and Bouvard, beginning with a range of typical weekly turnover ratios and the number of weekly spots required for the OES.

Turnover Ratio	OES Spot Factor	Spots Per Week
7	3.29	23
8	3.29	26
9	3.29	30
10	3.29	33
11	3.29	36
12	3.29	39
13	3.29	43
14	3.29	46
15	3.29	49
16	3.29	53
17	3.29	56
18	3.29	59
19	3.29	63
20	3.29	66
21	3.29	69
22	3.29	72

23	3.29	76
24	3.29	79
25	3.29	82

Now, following the example to its conclusion, assume we have a station with a Cume of 271,700 and an AQH of 18,100.

Step 1: Calculate the turnover ratio. Cume/AQH = 271,700/ 18,100 = 15.

Step 2: Multiply the turnover ratio by the OES Spot Factor 3.29. 15 × 3.29 = 49 units, Monday–Sunday, 6 A.M–12 Midnight.

Step 3: Multiple the Cume by the OES Reach Factor .46. 271,700 × .46 = 125,000 people effectively reached.

The commercial levels will seem high to advertisers used to spending similar amounts for newspaper space but not on a weekly basis with the electronic media. But as all businesses and media planners know, the schedule is always inexpensive when it works but expensive if it fails.

Television can produce similar results, but the cost will be due more to upfront production fees. Local television stations have computerized software that can match budgets with intended demographics to help advertisers target their message to the right group of consumers with frequency that can be afforded by the advertiser. There is no doubt about the powerful "double impact" of sight and sound in television, and retailers would do well to budget less newspaper and more television in markets served by a local television signal.

The following chapter, dealing with learning behavior, will assist the reader in understanding how truly powerful the electronic media are as educational tools. Both television and radio, however, need to be used correctly. The OES system, designed specifically for radio, is an example of how that medium can be used properly to produce long-term results that will surpass any one-time impression of even the largest series of ads in the daily newspaper of any market, regardless of size.

SUMMARY

Advertising of any type can only be expected to do one thing: bring a logical prospect or a potential customer into a place of business one time and one time only. From that point on, the product or service stands on its own. A variety of variables will either cause logical prospects to become loyal customers or take their business elsewhere where they perceive the service to be better or the price to be more competitive. Consumers become customers not because of advertising but in spite of it. Advertising does not make a store or a product successful; only well-run stores and good products make satisfied customers.

As an external variable, advertising must be viewed as a force whose effects are played out over the long run. Mistakes are made when advertisers view the ultimate goal of their advertising to be the generation of immediate sales. Such a view is misguided at best, as there exists minimal correlation between immediate sales and advertising expenditures.

If an advertiser desires immediate results from advertising, direct mail has been shown to be effective (although the response rate is under 5 percent at best). Short-term results can also be expected from businesses that have already established top-of-mind awareness from previous advertising efforts and wish to advertise legitimate sales or to remind the market of their continued presence. In this case, establishing store or brand awareness is not necessary and measuring immediate sales results would be appropriate.

Advertising that seeks to build market awareness through frequency and repetition (radio and television) is generally preferred over the one-time impression of the print media, whose ads are only viewed by a small percentage of readers who may be in the market and will be motivated by the price listed in the paper. Direct mail, billboards, or any type of printed advertising produces very little response in the media-conscious decade of the 1990s. The Yellow Pages, not even considered a form of advertising, competes heavily for the ad dollar via multiple Yellow Page directories in most markets.

What makes the electronic media so desirable is their intrusive nature. Commercials "intrude" into the programming and are consumed with no choice by the listener or the viewer. One cannot pass over an intrusive commercial and the impression is made, unlike print advertising where the reader chooses whether to note the ad or totally disregard it.

Intrusiveness builds reach and frequency, desired goals of advertisers who choose to position their businesses at the top of the consumer's mind. Reach and frequency, through radio, can be built by using the Optimum Effective Advertising Schedule (OES), which guarantees half of a radio station's reach will be hit three or more times on a weekly basis, the minimum number of times necessary to produce an advertiser response. Television produces similar results, with schedules figured for each client on local station software that matches a budget with the intended demographics of the advertiser.

NOTES

1. Karl Albrecht, *The Only Thing That Matters* (New York: HarperBusiness, 1992), pp. 15–16.

2. Ibid., p. 17.

3. David A. Aaker and John G. Myers, *Advertising Management* (Englewood Cliffs, N.J.: Prentice-Hall, 1987), p. 8.

4. Anthony I. Margan, "Point of View: Who's Killing the Great American Advertising Campaigns of America?" *Journal of Advertising Research* 24/6 (December 1984/January 1985): 34.

5. John Philip Jones, *How Much Is Enough . . . Getting the Most From Your Advertising Dollar* (New York: Lexington Books, 1992), p. 243.

6. Ibid., p. 294.

7. William G. Nickels, *Marketing Communication and Promotion* (New York: John Wiley and Sons, 1984), p. 71.

8. *Yellow Pages Update* 3/1 (Spring 1988): 4.

9. Ibid., p. 5.

10. David W. Finn, "The Integrated Information Response Model," *Journal of Advertising* 13/1 (1984): 28.

11. Ibid., pp. 28–29.

12. Laura M. Buchholz and Robert E. Smith, "The Role of Consumer Involvement in Determining Cognitive Response to Broadcast Advertising," *Journal of Advertising* 20/1 (1991): 16.

13. George B. Murray and John R. G. Jenkins, "The Concept of 'Effective Reach' in Advertising," *Journal of Advertising Research* (May/June 1992): 34–35.

14. Steve Marx and Pierre Bouvard, *Radio Advertising's Missing Ingredient: The Optimum Effective Scheduling System* (Washington, D.C.: National Association of Broadcasters, 1990), pp. 21–28.

15. Ibid., pp. 41–46.

OTHER WORKS CITED

Edell, Julie A. and Kevin L. Keller. "The Information Processing of Coordinated Media Campaigns." *Journal of Marketing Research* (March 1989): 149–163.

Greenwald, A. G. and C. Leavitt. "Audience Involvement in Advertising: Four Levels." *Journal of Consumer Research* (June 1984): 581–592.

Holbrook, Morris. "Situation-Specific Ideal Points and Usage of Multiple Dissimilar Brands." *Research in Marketing* 7 (1984): 93–131.

Krugman, Herbert E. "The Impact of Television Advertising: Learning Without Involvement." *Public Opinion Quarterly* (Fall 1965): 349–356.

Murdock, B. B., Jr. "Auditory and Visual Stores in Short Term Memory." *Acta Psychologica* 27 (1967): 316–324.

CHAPTER 4

The Psychology of Learning

> We are born to weakness, we have need of strength; we are born unprovided
> with anything, we need help; we are born stupid, we need judgment. All that
> we have not at birth and need when older is given us by education.
> — Jean-Jacques Rousseau

Of all the variables involved in the intricacies of advertising, the psychology of
learning behavior may be the most important. Corporate, business, and retail
media planners who understand how and why all of us as consumers learn and
can correlate this knowledge to the working intricacies of the advertising media
will be far ahead of those planners who see no correlation between learning behavior and the planning of business advertising.

EARLY CHILDHOOD EDUCATION

The study of early childhood tells us that education begins at birth, with the
most crucial years of learning occurring before age 5. The discussion of family
and culture in the previous chapter pointed out how greatly we are influenced by
our immediate family.

Early childhood educators Edith W. King and August Kerber have noted that
"The child's interaction with his family, beginning from birth, determines an essential aspect of his personality: his idea of himself. . . . Even before two years
of age . . . perhaps six months, the infant displays behavior reflecting his concept
of himself. . . . Self-concept, then, is not a biological phenomenon with which
the infant is born, but a phenomenon that evolves from the social and environmental aspects of living."[1]

Self-recognition is known as the looking-glass self: infants reflect the responses of those immediately around them and actually begin to take on the roles of those "significant others." Significant others or role-models are not confined to human characters. With television being on in the average household for more than seven hours per day, children also learn from the programs and the commercials they view on a daily basis.

Far from being a wholly negative influence in the educational or maturation process, television (and radio) assist with language development and enable children to understand and speak of difficult concepts such as space flight. Studies have shown that children whose parents read aloud to them and give them books at an early age show a preference for viewing television commercials, quiz shows, and weather reports as opposed to general programming such as cartoons.

Learning who we are, then, begins at birth. Cognitive learning, or the process of acquiring knowledge, also begins at a very early age. Learning, as educator Frank Smith writes, is social as well as developmental. It is a matter of identity and how we see ourselves. It is social because "we learn from the company we keep" and developmental because it is "continuous, spontaneous and effortless, requiring no particular attention, conscious motivation or specific reinforcement . . . and, it is not subject to forgetting."[2]

The manner in which we learn to do the things we all take for granted as mature adults is a key educational concept whose understanding directly correlates to the electronic media and the way in which they educate consumers through intrusive repetition.

We Are What We Are Because We Have Always Been

As products of our immediate environment, which includes family and significant others, we all learn what we know by being taught in essentially the same ways. We "mirror" those around us and become what they are. Our values, standards, and ways of behaving are programmed by our primary influences: parents, teachers, and cultural role-models. Indeed, there exists a correlation between a child's effective education and the family. If adults support learning at home, children do well on test scores. Second-tier influences of films, television, rented videos, radio, and the arts also play an educational role in the early developmental years.

Outside of the home, we matriculate for our formal education through a public or private school system that teaches us a certain body of knowledge and develops our self-concept by reinforcing the values we have received at home. How this reinforcement occurs is the heart of the psychology of learning, for everything we now know as adults is the result of one fundamental concept—repetition.

Repetition—How We Learn

Think about it. How is it that we know anything that we know? How do we know, instantaneously, that 7 times 3 equals 21 or that 8 times 7 equals 56? The simple answer is because of repeated exposure (repetition) to new information until it was memorized and, hence, became a part of our continuing knowledge base. All of us know that 9 times 6 equals 54 because we were exposed to the multiplication tables, probably via the flash card routine, in grade school. Continued exposure or repetition soon became knowledge that we carried with us for life, even though we never think about the educational process that caused us to learn this information initially.

Think of anything else you know how to do. How did you learn to tie your shoes, a necktie, or a bow? How did you learn to ride a bike, hit a baseball, or lift a golfball from a tee? By doing it over and over again until you mastered the concept.

How do you know what the state capitals are? Because of an exam you once had to prepare for. To learn the information, you went over it until you had memorized it and the information entered the long-term or permanent knowledge base. Granted, some of this information will be forgotten over time but most of us could name thirty-five to forty state capitals and probably more, even though that exam was decades ago!

We learn everything through repetition. That is precisely how we become good professionals in sales, law, medicine, teaching, or management. We become good over time. Wisdom through maturity is nothing more than doing what we do enough times to become proficient.

The Repetitive Nature of the Electronic Media

The electronic media educate consumers in the same way. Radio and television are affordable enough (have a low enough cost per thousand or CPM) for merchants to run their message over and over again until the mind of the consumer has been imprinted with the message of the ad, which becomes "old" knowledge or part of the consumer's own database. Where do most children want to eat when they go out? McDonald's. Teenagers pull up to the drive-in to order a hamburger and a _____. Can you finish it? A Coke. Name five automobiles you see every day on the streets.

Does such knowledge become a part of the brain's database due to the viewing of a newspaper advertisement or any form of print ad such as direct mail, billboards, or flyers? Clearly not. Any type of print advertisement represents one exposure to a product message; there is no repetition. The ad is read only if the reader chooses to read it. The electronic media expose consumers to ads without any action on their part.

Such intrusiveness is a plus. Most of the time, commercials are watched or listened to even if they interrupt the program. Since these ads cannot be selectively passed over, as with the newspaper, consumers are exposed to messages multiple times. In fact, if commercials are creative, people enjoy seeing and hearing them again. How many times is a newspaper ad read over and over again because it is so cute, creative, or attractive to the eye?

Do kids want to go to McDonald's because they have read a newspaper ad over and over again? McDonald's rarely uses newspaper for obvious reasons. Newspapers provide price-item, non-image building advertisements designed to appeal to the "now" buyer—the person in the market to whom the merchant wants to appeal with price alone at that immediate moment. No lasting images are built. No new knowledge is imparted via repetition.

For just one of these print images, newspapers charge an amount that would buy dozens if not hundreds of radio or television commercials (depending on rates and market size) that could work themselves into the database of the consumer's mind and become permanent knowledge.

Merchants do need price-item advertising to hit the "now" market, which is always a very small percent of the total market, but not to the extent that print outbills the electronic media by as much as ten times in some markets. Merchants and businesspeople must realize that radio and television can more cost-effectively deliver customers to them than can newspapers. The spot rate is low enough to enable merchants to afford continual repetition of their messages, which is the only way that particular message will ever become permanent in the minds of the majority of potential customers in their marketplace. Quick! Can you finish this! Two all-beef patties, special cheese . . .

THE FRANCHISING OF THE MIND

Every merchant or businessperson in every market in America would place the franchising process at the top of their list of goals, if only they would give more thought to the number one business challenge they ought to be facing: protecting the brand franchise, as David Martin would phrase it. This can be accomplished with little waste by selecting an intrusive media that can deliver multiple impressions to the defined target market.

Generic Products, Brand Names

Simply stated, consumers' minds are "franchised" when they refer to the generic product by the brand name. To make it more personal, when you have a cold with a runny nose, you do not reach for a facial tissue (generic product); you reach for a Kleenex (brand name). Even though you may be using a competing product to the Kimberly-Clark *Kleenex* brand (of which there are many) Kleenex is usually what you ask for and what gets written down on the grocery list. This franchising process is worth countless millions to the manufacturer over the lifetime of a product.

Other examples that come easily to mind include the generic products listed in the following chart and the franchised name brands we refer to them by. All of them have marketplace competitors, right next to them on the shelf, but which do you think has the greatest sales volume?

Generic Product	Brand Name
Adhesive Strips	Band-Aid
Petroleum Jelly	Vaseline
Cotton Swabs	Q-Tips
Gelatin Dessert	Jell-O
Soda/Pop/Soft Drink	Coke
Lip Balm	Chap Stick
Photocopy	Xerox
Adhesive Tape	Scotch Tape
Disinfectant Spray	Lysol

When consumers make grocery lists, they write down the brand name, not the generic one. Shoppers do not list petroleum jelly, adhesive strips, or cotton swabs. Such a phenomenon means millions of dollars in sales and can be achieved by local advertisers who understand how the media can be used to educate consumers through intrusiveness.

Top-of-Mind Awareness

When consumers can instantaneously recall the name of a product or business in recall surveys or just in answer to a direct question such as "Where is the best place to eat in this town?" a condition called "top-of-mind" awareness exists. Since most businesses have competition, being at the top of consumers' minds is the desired marketplace position for any business category. A direct correlation exists between market share and name recognition.

Although no one will ever substitute the name brand of "Bob's Cafe" for the generic category of "restaurant," true top-of-mind awareness for a business is just as good for bottom line sales figures as franchising the mind is for the types of products that lend themselves to the franchising concept. Name recognition in a given market means market share. It is that simple.

EDUCATIONAL LEARNING THEORIES

The behavioral response that causes a logical prospect to think of or buy a product automatically with little conscious thought is an example of the stimulus-response theories of Pavlov and Skinner. Although learning behavior may be slightly more complicated today than "see, hear, and do," the concept of learning through repetition still remains a sound educational practice.

Other theories include the Gestalt Theory, taken from the German word meaning "whole," which postulates that human behavior is dictated by a person's entire makeup—attitudes, perceptions, and culture. Consumers will therefore make buying decisions based on past experiences that make the present seem logical, a concept apart from the more elementary stimulus-response theories.

Advertising in this sense must be consistent with past experience that consumers expect. In other words, a nostalgia piece taking us back to the "good old days" would need to accurately recreate the proper atmosphere consistent with the memories of people who lived then in order to be effective in making an advertising impression.

Cultural and sociological motivations to buy have been previously discussed, although advertisers should be reminded that America is composed of many different cultures and subcultures, not the least of which is the growing Spanish or Latin American culture and the Asian or Eastern culture. Within these cultures exist racial, religious, and geographic subcultures, many of whom are aging; this elderly sector of our society may be one of the most important to advertisers as our population matures gracefully with improved health care and extended life expectancy.

Other Factors in Learning

Once certain behavioral patterns become evident through learning and personal skill or knowledge is acquired through actual practice (as in learning to play golf) or through formal education (nonexperiential learning where one learns and develops behavioral patterns based on the experiences of others), it is clear that a consumer will not act upon such behavior without the motivation to do so.

As consumers, we have choices. What motivates us to choose one particular restaurant over another when we are hungry or to choose one movie from a fourteen-screen cinema complex when we wish to be entertained is part of the motivational process that stems from learned behavior. Effective marketing can influence consumer choice, even though each individual is guided by different patterns of learned behavior, socialization, and acculturation. Essentially, though, the motivation that fuels consumer decision making is either internal and driven by the need to be comfortable or external and driven by the need to interact with and please others.

Applying this concept to buying behavior, consumers will either make purchases that conform to their own perceived needs, wants, and desires or to secure their social relationships and peer group status with others. Such motivating buying behavior can be described either as emotional or rational. John J. Burnette writes that "Emotional motives are characterized by innate feelings that may emerge without careful thought or without consideration of the social consequences. . . . A great many emotional motives exist . . . status, prestige, conformity, sex, loneliness, self-esteem and the desire to be different."[3]

Burnette argues that rational behavior, typified in marketing strategies by lower price campaigns and copy extolling endurance, quality, and convenience, "are supported by a systematic reasoning process that individuals perceive as being acceptable by their peers. . . . A homemaker . . . might insist on buying foods grown without chemicals and be willing to pay the higher price in order to enhance her family's health. . . . A man can rationalize purchasing an inexpensive pair of slacks because of the rough treatment they will receive at his place of employment."[4] Consumers are often motivated to do what is perceived as socially acceptable, even though buying behavior may be motivated by emotional motives.

The important concept here is not whether rational or emotional motives are valid, but that the consumer perceives them to be valid. Products and services in the marketplace only have value to the consumer if the consumer perceives such products or services as having value. Perceptions of value exist in all types of media campaigns in the marketplace and play an important role in the overall positioning process.

The perceived value of a product to a consumer, for example, can be enhanced by referring to the variables that motivate consumer decision making: overall store atmosphere can send the message of high quality and value; product features and quality packaging can position the product as being of exceptional value; competitive pricing related to overall benefits can enhance value, especially when products are legitimately marked down for clearance or originally tagged at $49.95 rather than $50.00 to instill the perception of great value for under $50.00; and, most certainly, value-driven consumer buying behavior is influenced by where a product might be manufactured. In a global economy, this is often difficult to discern, but since the 1970s the Japanese have succeeded in convincing the world that automotive value lies in the Land of the Rising Sun, not in American-made automotive products.

Positioning Strategies

Franchising and top-of-mind awareness are concepts that deal with the perception or impression that exists within a consumer's mind. Such positioning is the result of the total marketing and promotional efforts of a business that has succeeded in setting itself apart, in the consumer's mind, from its competitors. "To create a 'position' in the minds of consumers, marketers must show how their brands [store] are different from other brands in the same category and what makes them 'better.' The idea of 'better' may mean cheaper, longer lasting, better quality, more status and so on."[5]

As a concept, positioning strategies are nothing new. Beginning in 1972 advertising mavens Al Ries and Jack Trout wrote a series of articles entitled "The Positioning Era" for *Advertising Age* magazine. Arguing that unique products and images (such as the Marlboro Man) were no longer sufficient for market dominance due to the wide range of products delivered by advancing technology, Ries and Trout maintained that the real difference would lie in how products (or brands or stores) were positioned in the *minds* of consumers.

In other words, the advertising campaign rather than the product or the image that product conveyed to the consumer would be the positioning difference. Products could be positioned in consumers' minds via effective advertising touting a superior product or by showing how a product (or a store) was different from other brands in the same category by designing a superior ad campaign that contained a central selling idea the consumer could easily remember.

Product positioning meant centering manufacturing/marketing strategies on what the competition was *not* doing. Large, domestic gas-guzzling cars gave the VW bug the perfect market opening. VW positioned itself as the ugly "Lemon." Consumers were urged to "Think small" and not to worry if they could not afford a good-looking car as "Nobody's perfect." This appeal was perfectly suited to the values of the 1960s generation.

David Ogilvy looked at positioning, however, purely as image – and image is pure personality and should be consistent year in and year out. Products (and stores) have personalities, just like people, which will make or break them in the marketplace. He believed products were actually positioned before an advertising campaign began and that the image of the established product was what would sustain sales into the future.

Ogilvy's famous Hathaway shirt man with the eye patch is the prime advertising example of using imagery to create positive perceptions or warm feelings in the public's mind about a quality product. Advertising did not make the quality; it was already present and established. Advertising provided the warm feeling imagery. Feeling good about a product often can overcome potential objections about price by appealing to a buyer's sense of status and quality and thus expand the market.

Other memorable positioning campaigns over the years that have attended to either product or image/personality placement in the consumer's mind, creating tremendous growth and profits, include the following:

AVIS: "We're number two, so we try harder." Creates the perception as underdog. Everyone roots for the underdog, so why go with number one?

COCA-COLA: "Things go better with Coke." "It's the Real Thing." "Coke is it." All slogans position the brand franchise as the number one selling soft drink. So why buy number two (Pepsi) or even number three (7Up)?

COORS LIGHT: "It's the Right Beer Now." The positioning statement is the phrase itself.

CHEVROLET: "The Heartbeat of America . . . Today's Chevrolet." Creates the perception that the Chevrolet product is as vital to the American family as a heartbeat. You can't live without it.

ENERGIZER BATTERIES: "Still going. Nothing outlasts the Energizer. They keep going and going and going . . ." Energizer Bunny intrudes upon "regular" commercials, creating the perception that the battery never runs down. Why buy one that might not last as long?

MILLER LITE: "Everything you always wanted in a beer – and less." "Less Filling – Tastes Great." Creating the perception that low-calorie beer tastes as good as regular beer. So why buy regular beer?

MOTEL 6: "We'll keep the lights on for ya." Creates perception of an affordable, "down-home" alternative to overnight lodging in an expensive chain.

NIKE: "Air Jordan" and "Bo Knows." Creates the perception that the world's greatest athletes wear Nike. So why don't you?

7UP: The "Uncola." Positioning as the alternative to a cola drink.

SCOPE: "Medicine Breath." Creating the perception that mouthwash doesn't have to taste bad to be good.

DEAN WITTER: "We measure success one investor at a time." Gives the impression of individualized customer service from a caring, grass-roots company.

INFINITI: In a unique ad campaign, this luxury Nissan model was first introduced to the American public in 1989 via television commercials that broke through the clutter as the best recalled auto advertiser by never actually showing the car—only the sounds and scenes of nature. After the name "Infiniti" was established in 1990, the car began to appear.

Positioning will always be necessary with the number of companies, stores, and products available in a crowded and competitive marketplace. Positioning enables the store or product and its benefits to stand above the crowd and be recognized by potential consumers who make buying decisions based on their unique perception of store/product features or overall image compared to its competition.

Most of the time, the perceived differences exist within the mind of the consumer, but the strategy is effective as long as the consumer believes that 7Up is the uncola alternative or that Energizer batteries are the long-life alternative to any other brand of battery.

Effective positioning can be accomplished by appealing to a specifically defined demographic segment of the market or to the greater market and its many segments. The former is advisable when resources must be allocated sparingly or when the defined target market is well established. Copy can then be very specific with benefits tailored to the consumer.

The broader approach would contain more of a general, less specific appeal that would allow various consumer groups to interpret the benefits as they so desired. The caveat with this choice is that a broad brush appeal to the general market may end up appealing to no one. Much waste of the ad budget may also result from appealing to various market segments who will never be logical consumers.

Herein lies a specific problem with newspaper advertising. Advertisers pay for the entire circulation of the paper, not just for the desired target group; that target group can, however, be found listening to at least one particular radio station format.

Positioning strategies can best be played out using the electronic media to build awareness/reach and frequency, supplementing this approach with print media that can attract the "now" market who have entered the high-involvement stage. Impressions that have entered the long-term memory bank are placed there through repetition, not the one-time impression of a printed advertisement.

Today, with companies entering a new century in a questionable economic environment where downsizing is a reality, companies and stores will not only need to position brands, but themselves as industry leaders if consumers are to gain and retain confidence in the places they choose to do their business.

Remember Those Great Old Favorite Tunes?

Probably the best example of how learning occurs through intrusive repetition is the ability of most people to recall, word for word, their favorite songs they heard on the radio while they were growing up. Decades later, these tunes still retain a top-of-mind position; they are franchised in much the same way as are the familiar products like Band-Aids and Q-Tips that receive a disproportionate market share compared to their generic competitors. What retailer or business-person would not want the name of their store to be etched in the minds of marketplace consumers in the same way that the words to "Hound Dog" or "Satisfaction" are a part of the memory banks of millions of baby boomers?

Herein lies the key that will unlock unrealized profit potential for business-people who can apply the amazingly simple concept of sound and repetition to their own retail businesses. Baby boomers have been charmed and entertained into buying for decades while growing up as the first generation to be reared on the electronic media. Rock and roll found a huge and willing audience and positioned format radio (programming specific music to a defined target audience) as a viable way of successfully programming radio stations. Television found huge audiences, mainly in the evening hours, largely due to the fascination with a relatively new medium and fresh programming that was not familiar to audiences.

Radio found new life in the 1950s and the way in which it reaches smaller but well-defined market segments remains its strength today. Television's audience began its addiction to that medium in the same decade. Today television has become a megamedium for advertisers who can afford to reach its vast audiences. The baby boom generation, which has supported untold numbers of businesses with its collective spending power over the decades, is still sought out by advertisers who have targeted this spending group since they were teenagers.

The baby boomers have essentially been educated by sound. As the first generation to embrace radio and television as a part of a daily lifestyle, they have unconsciously been intruded upon and educated with no active involvement on their part. No one hears a song on the radio and says, "Hey, I like this song. I think I'll memorize the lyrics." Rather, over time the song becomes familiar and the lyrics become ingrained in the memory. Soon, consumers find themselves singing along with the song without much thought or effort. Years later, that song can be recalled word for word as it has become a part of the long-term memory bank, much as have the multiplication tables or the names of state capitals, or any other bits of knowledge that have taken the element of repetition to become habit.

Songs are easily memorized in a passive manner as their lyrics are usually simple rhymes. Children readily learn nursery rhymes and this ease of education carries over to songs and then to commercials, which are well written with uncomplicated lyrics or slogans and matching music that is memorable.

David Martin comments on the element of sound: "The sound track touches the heart by reaching the mind. Emotions stir to music. Basic instincts are titillated by sound effects synched to sight. What is channeled through the ear excites, saddens, delights, thrills. The mind absorbs, stores, then sends signals to the heart and glands; the pulse quickens and adrenalin begins to flow."[6]

This does not quite read like a description of a newspaper ad, does it? To help readers make their own connection with the concept of the intrusive nature of sound and how it franchises the mind with no effort on the part of the listener, look at the Cash Box number one songs from 1956, when rock format radio really began, through 1968. Older "boomers" will appreciate this listing.

If you grew to maturity in this era, how many lyrics come instantly to mind that you can sing to yourself right now? (A few are instrumentals, but chances are you can hum the tune.) You certainly could not do this if these songs had only been available to the public as printed sheet music.

Year	*Song & Artist*
1956	"Don't Be Cruel"—Elvis Presley
1957	"Tammy"—Debbie Reynolds
1958	"Nel Blu Di Pinto Di Blu"—Domenico Mudugno
1959	"Mack the Knife"—Bobby Darin
1960	"Theme From A Summer Place"—Percy Faith
1961	"Exodus"—Ferrante & Teicher
1962	"Twist"—Chubby Checker
1963	"Limbo Rock"—Chubby Checker
1964	"I Want to Hold Your Hand"—Beatles
1965	"Back In My Arms Again"—Supremes
1966	"The Ballad of the Green Berets"—S/Sgt. Barry Sadler
	"California Dreamin' "—Mamas & Papas
1967	"The Letter"—Boxtops
1968	"Hey Jude"—Beatles

For the "younger" readers, as well as those who never strayed from rock 'n roll, here are *Billboard* magazine's chart toppers from 1969 through 1986. Again, how many lyrics come instantly to mind? No memorization. No effort. That is how radio advertising works for businesses, too.

Year	Song & Artist
1969	"Aquarius"/"Let The Sun Shine In"—5th Dimension
1970	"Bridge Over Troubled Water"—Simon & Garfunkel
1971	"Joy To The World"—Three Dog Night
1972	"Alone Again (Naturally)"—Gilbert O'Sullivan
1973	"Killing Me Softly With His Song"—Roberta Flack
1974	"The Way We Were"—Barbra Streisand
1975	"Love Will Keep Us Together"—Captain & Tennille
1976	"Tonight's The Night (Gonna Be Alright)"—Rod Stewart
1977	"You Light Up My Life"—Debby Boone
1978	"Night Fever"—Bee Gees
1979	"My Sharona"—The Knack
1980	"Lady"—Kenny Rogers
1981	"Physical"—Olivia Newton-John
1982	"Ebony and Ivory"—Paul McCartney/Stevie Wonder
1983	"Billie Jean"—Michael Jackson
1984	"Like A Virgin"—Madonna
1985	"Say You, Say Me"—Lionel Richie
1986	"That's What Friends Are For"—Dionne & Friends

Not everyone in advertising agrees that music is an important ingredient in the creation of effective advertising. Ogilvy argues that musical vignettes are entertaining but impotent if you want to sell. Making the point that if you have nothing to say, sing it, Ogilvy writes: "If you went into a store and asked a salesman to show you a refrigerator, how would you react if he started singing at you? . . . Many people use music as background—emotional shorthand. Research shows that this is neither a positive or a negative factor. . . . Do great preachers allow organists to play background music under their sermons?"[7]

Ogilvy is not arguing that sound, music, and jingles cannot franchise the mind of a consumer. What he seems to be saying is that substituting catchy jingles or emotional music for good copy is not advisable. The message is the copy, not the music. He is, of course, correct. If the consumer remembers the tune and not the brand or the store, advertising has failed.

It is possible to make the message the copy even with music and jingles. It is just more difficult to make sure the message is not hidden behind the jingle or the music. Who can forget the award-winning California Raisin campaign, "I Heard It Through the Grapevine," the Ray Charles rendition of Pepsi's "You've Got the Right One, Baby" and "Uh-Huh," or Coke's "I'd Like to Teach the World to Sing"?

What would any feature film be like without a compelling music score? Good music builds drama, stirs emotion, and helps paint images in our minds, but it does not detract from the dialogue (the copy), which is the message or how we remember the plot. Music or jingles in advertising should not be emotional short-hand for poor copywriting. Good copywriting recognizes that the copy is the message but it can coexist with the elements of sound, sound effects, and a memorable musical scores.

The Case for McDonald's

Certainly another memorable musical line in advertising is McDonald's "We Do It All For You." Probably the best example in advertising of how to franchise the minds of an entire population by the time they are three years of age, McDonald's uses the electronic media almost exclusively in its efforts to maintain and build onto a market share that they have owned practically since Ray Kroc founded his corporation in 1955. Now a worldwide corporation, which first began selling shares to the public in 1965, McDonald's operates restaurants in Europe, Japan, China, and the former Soviet Union. This megaempire knows that in actuality, television does it all for them.

With thousands of different outlets, McDonald's does not worry about coordinating management or marketing techniques within each store in a given market. Everything that is done within the franchise is standardized through techniques learned at McDonald's Hamburger University; such uniformity of operation means that each store will be as clean and uniform in product and presentation as the next store. This coordination and integration of management and marketing efforts carry over to its advertising, which is handled by an advertising agency for all stores.

Demographically, McDonald's targets all market segments from children to adults to mature adults, but their most energetic and concentrated advertising is directed toward the 12 and under market, a segment usually reserved for toy manufacturers and cereal makers. This is no accident. McDonald's has discovered that they can enter the minds of children before they can even talk to begin the franchising process. They or their agency may not refer to their strategy by the term "franchising," but that is exactly what is happening with McDonald's television advertising.

Permit me to call upon personal situational examples for this section of the book, as some concepts are simply best explained by life's experiences. Many years ago, I was driving through a suburb of Milwaukee with a friend's child snugly strapped into her safety seat. She was not yet 2, could barely see out the window, and, to my knowledge could not yet speak anything intelligible. We drove by the Golden Arches, visible on one those hundred foot tall monster store signs that rise above the clutter. Her little hand lifted as she pointed to the sign and said, "Donald's, Donald's." Her mother later informed me that the only words she could say were "Mama" and "Donald's." This was the first time I became acutely aware of what McDonald's was on to and how powerful and intrusive television actually was.

The story does not end there, however. Several years later, I took this same person, now 8, to McDonald's along with her 10-year-old sister, They insisted on going to McDonald's in the mid-afternoon. So off we went. They both ordered "Happy Meals" and I was content with something more "adult." We sat down, they opened their meals to retrieve the toy that comes with each order, took exactly one bite out of their burgers, and poof(!), they were gone. Where? You guessed it. They were out in the McDonald's playground. Fifteen minutes later, I summoned them back in to finish their meals so we could go home. Almost in unison, they both exclaimed that they were not hungry! I tried to understand why they had wanted to come to McDonald's if they were not hungry, not accepting their attitudes as I ate two "Happy Meals" so the food I paid for would not be wasted.

Then it began to dawn on me. Kids do not want to come to McDonald's because they are hungry. They want to come to McDonald's for the *experience*. The colorful Saturday morning cartoons with Ronald McDonald and Hamburglar and all the other characters present a Disney-type atmosphere that all kids want to be a part of, even if they are not hungry! Now, there is some powerful marketing at work. How many restaurants that cater to adults can get us into their businesses to spend money even if we are not hungry? And a phenomenon like that can only happen with the electronic media. No newspaper or print media can franchise minds for life like McDonald's can by using television and, in some markets, radio. It is a powerful example of how an intrusive media plays a major role in the learning process and creates top-of-mind imagery that literally will last a lifetime.

I am also reminded of my college roommate's son. At five years old he sits at the dinner table singing, "You've got the right one, baby . . . uh-huh." It is his favorite song.

The Curve of Remembrance

The necessity of repetition in the franchising process is brought to light by the 1885 empirical experiments of Hermann Ebbinghaus, a German philosopher who found that diminishing returns set in within the first sixty minutes of learning. In other words, we forget quickly. Half of what we learn will be forgotten within sixty minutes, two-thirds within nine hours, and more than two-thirds within twenty-four hours, unless what we learn is reinforced through repetition, as in studying or being exposed to a continual, intrusive message.

Charting out his theory over a four-week period, a measurable decline in memory will occur without frequency and reinforcement of the message. By the second week, 75 percent of what was originally learned will be forgotten; by the end of the fourth week, a full 95 percent of the original information will be lost (see Figures 4.1 and 4.2). So much for the human memory.

Precisely because of this point, which has been reinforced by research (Ostheimer 1970; Ray, Sawyer, and Strong 1971; Calder and Sternthal 1980), advertisers should consider *consistency* in their approach to advertising. This point

Figure 4.1
The Curve of Remembrance

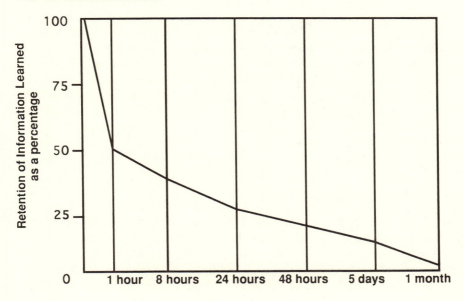

Figure 4.2
The Curve of Remembrance over a Four Week Period

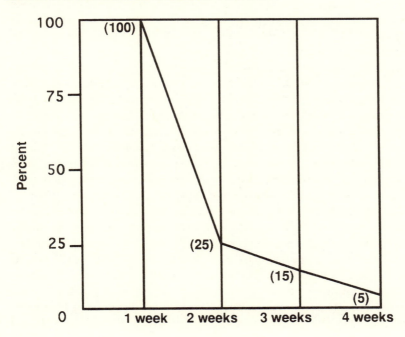

was well made in a 1984 study by R. A. Marquardt and G. W. Murdock, which analyzed data over an eight-year period for department store retailers and grocery store chains.

They found that the most consistent advertisers from this group were able to obtain 10 percent annual increases in gross sales from an 11 percent increase in advertising expenditures. Stores that were the most inconsistent advertisers were able to obtain the same 10 percent increase in gross sales, but only after a 17 percent increase in advertising expenditures. This same study also found a very significant correlation between retail advertising expenditures and retail sales, although, as has previously been demonstrated, much of that sales volume is generated over the long run from the carry-over effect of intrusive radio or television advertising.

The Key Role of Creativity

Since human beings tend to forget rather quickly, it is important for advertisers to understand that memory can be enhanced by learning, which results from repetition/frequency. But does there exist a point of diminishing return for advertisers where optimal frequency has occurred and consumer attention will ultimately decline? The answer seems to lie in the creative nature of the advertising copy itself. After a period of time, what is often referred to as the "wear-out" factor will emerge.

Audiences, having become accustomed to a particular message over a set period of time, simply stop paying attention. They are familiar with the presentation and are bored with seeing it presented yet another time. Such reaction seems normal and consistent with human nature, yet it can be minimized to offset the memory decay on the Ebbinghaus curve.

Simply stated, audiences react favorably over time to creative commercials that they perceive not to be boring or irritating. Entertaining and humorous commercials, like the Pesky Pink Percussionist (*USA Today*'s name for the Energizer Bunny), have a life of their own and command attention long after other commercials have withered into faded memory. The elements of music, like the Ray Charles "Uh-Huh" campaign for Pepsi or the soap opera drama of the middle-aged couple wooing and cooing each other from one tantalizing episode to another over cups of Taster's Choice, also stimulate audience attention over time.

Researchers have concluded that programming one commercial will produce a much quicker "wear-out" response than producing and rotating multiple commercials (usually three) on the same theme. The cliche that "variety is the spice of life" seems to be true in advertising as well.

Samuel C. Craig, Brian Sternthal, and Clark Leavitt (1976) studied the concept of "wear-out" and theme variation or multiple commercials. They found that there does exist some optimal level of repetition, with repetition enhancing attention through theme variation. "Although increasing repetition may facilitate learning, very substantial levels may cause cognitive responses that ultimately inhibit learning. Further, the nonbeneficial effects of high frequency campaigns can be mitigated by varying the execution of the same theme. This can be accomplished by stressing different benefits, using different spokespersons, or any other device that helps maintain audience attention."[8]

Bobby J. Calder and Brian Sternthal (1980) reported that higher levels of repetition were associated with inattention (boredom), leading to a negative assessment of the message. Hence, it is necessary to run multiple rather than single commercials when using the electronic media. Edell and Keller (1989) with support from Daniel R. Young and Frances S. Bellezza (1982) found that when consumers receive or encode information more than once, the chances of them storing such information for later retrieval is greater if the message is different each time. In other words, the theme of any advertising campaign must be consistent but multiple commercials should be produced. Edell and Keller also conclude that coordinated radio-television campaigns (same theme, different media) may be more efficient than using either radio or television alone.

It is also apparent that the more likeable or respected the source or spokesperson doing the commercial, the less boring a repeated message will become. A likeable, charismatic personality, however, is no substitute for adequate argumentation or the stressing of product benefits.

The Rest of the Story

It would be unfair, at this point, not to discuss what some researchers claim about the process of memorization in respect to repetition. The memorization or recall of arguments in commercials is no panacea. Repetition resulting in memorization can generate counterarguments, making copy more easily available for critical assessment. Even though a likeable source may lead to a more positive memory of the product or service, memorization itself may be counterproductive.

Should this be even remotely true, businesses that engage in advertising should attend to the other consumer variables outside of the realm of advertising previously noted on the Sales Wheel, such as customer service, friendly personnel, fair pricing in relation to benefits, parking, and store appearance.

If these and other consumer variables are positive, it will be difficult for consumers to construct counterarguments in response to a repeated advertising message. Weaker businesses in the marketplace, however, are sure to elicit mental responses like, "Sure thing. . . . I've been there before and nobody cared what I needed or if I was even there at all." If repetition generates negative counterarguments, it is the fault of the business and not the advertising.

How Much Reach and How Much Frequency?

It is obvious that each separate product or store within a given marketplace will be governed by different factors and circumstances that will cause it to need more or less frequency to accomplish its indigenous marketing goals within its area of shopper influence. Some retail outlets or businesses are well known, some are not; some have heavier competition than others; some, such as chain or franchise stores like Hardees, Ace Hardware, or Motel 6, rely on heavy national advertising to carry their message to the general public and will therefore spend fewer local dollars than some of their competitors.

Stores and businesses have different sales and profit goals, as well as different management philosophies and ways of looking at the communities of which they are a part. Determining how much of anything for each and every business is complicated enough, so the electronic media advertising industry uses a standard of measure for total exposure called gross rating points (GRPs), which help identify and answer the question of how much of the population is being reached at what cost.

How Rating Points Differ in Radio and Television

The concepts of GRPs and cost per point (CPP) are included in our overall discussion of reach and frequency, as many media planners, agencies, and stations use these figures in the selling and planning process. Such discussion, however, deals with the traditional way radio and television advertising has been measured and cost-factored.

The information on GRPs and CPP is essentially valid for television, as rating points are related to the total number of viewers at narrow time periods like the evening news or a college football game, so the total time spent is more concentrated and not as important as the total time spent listening to radio, which is bought by advertisers throughout the entire week in all dayparts.

As Steve Marx and Pierre Bouvard point out,[9] television surveys show household or metro area ratings (households tuned to a specific station as a percent of the metro DMA [Designated Market Area] television households) while radio surveys show cume and average quarter hour. The ratings are different, making television buying methods inefficient in radio.

Simply stated, GRPs do not tell the mixture of reach and frequency in radio; an advertiser could end up reaching 100 percent of the market at once or reaching 1 percent of the market 100 times, either of which spells disaster. This is precisely why the Optimum Effective Scheduling System (OES), discussed at the end of the previous chapter, was devised—so advertisers would know how many commercials to run to reach a defined number of people at least three times in one week. OES surpasses and may soon replace the concepts of GRPs and CPP.

Marx and Bouvard's answer to the time-worn cost per point (CPP) is trying to imagine a car being sold on the average cost per part, clothes being sold on the average cost per thread, or the cost of a college education being figured on the average cost per book. As silly as this sounds, radio is bought and sold like this every day. GRPs and CPP are fun academic exercises, but neither has much to do with getting results on radio. And results are what every advertiser in the world wants and deserves from a well-planned advertising budget. CPP also suffers from forcing advertisers to focus on the *cost* per point of building a mind share rather than on the overall *time* needed to accomplish results and the weekly (not per point) cost for that time.

Now that this caveat has been proclaimed, understanding the concept of GRPs can help television buyers and allow others to debate the differences between OES and calculating GRPs on a cost per point basis.

Gross Rating Points

Gross rating points are the gross impressions expressed as a percentage of the population being measured, with one rating point for radio being equal to one percent of the population. In television, one percent of the television households being surveyed is one rating point.

For radio, gross impressions divided by the population equals GRPs. GRPs are determined by multiplying reach (the percentage of a population exposed to the message; persons reached divided by the population equals reach rating) times frequency (the number of impressions that population receives). The higher the GRPs in a given campaign, the more thoroughly the market has been penetrated by that advertising effort.

For television, the important figures are for rating and share. As mentioned in the previous paragraph, a rating point is one percent of the television households; a program with a specific rating achieves that rating from the percentage of people watching a program from *all* television households in the survey area. Some households will have the television on, others will have it off. The rating figure is derived from the percentage of those watching compared to the universe of households which have television, whether turned on or off.

The share figure, on the other hand, represents the percentage of viewers watching a particular program from all of the televisions in the survey area that are *on.* In other words, a large share of a low-rated program may not be as good a buy as a lower share in a higher-rated program. Think about it!

Cost per Point

Tied in to GRPs is what is known as cost per rating point or CPP. CPP is the unit cost of one rating point or one percent of the population being measured. The schedule cost divided by GRPs equals CPP.

As an example, say a particular advertiser scheduled a commercial to run twenty times in a given week according to the following schedule, where frequency (impressions) times reach (the rating point or percent of population exposed) equals GRP:

5 impressions in a time period delivering a 10 rating: 50 GRPs

7 impressions in a time period delivering a 6 rating: 42 GRPs

4 impressions in a time period delivering a 4 rating: 12 GRPs

4 impressions in a time period delivering an 8 rating: 32 GRPs

Total GRPs for the week = 136

Figure 4.3
Cost per Gross Rating Point, Top Twenty Markets

Men 18 +		Women 18 +		Teens 12-17	
TV Prime Time	$6,728	TV Prime Time	$5,335	TV Prime Time	$5,061
TV Late News	4,959	TV Late News	4,191	Radio Daytime	2,764
TV Late Fringe	3,401	Radio Evening	2,962	TV Early Fringe	1,386
TV Early Fringe	3,052	TV Late Fringe	2,938	Radio AM Drive	1,371
Radio Evening	2,889	Radio PM Drive	2,615	Radio Evening	1,038
TV Early News	2,767	TV Early News	2,376	Radio PM Drive	995
Radio PM Drive	2,572	Radio AM Drive	2,341		
Radio AM Drive	2,391	Radio Daytime	2,274		
Radio Daytime	2,097	TV Early Fringe	1,988		
		TV Daytime	1,695		

Source: Radio Advertising Bureau.

CPP would be calculated by dividing the total cost of the schedule by the GRPs or 136. An example of cost per point (CPP) for the various media in the top twenty markets can be seen in Figure 4.3.

The periods with the highest rating, like the "10," will be the prime time periods or the local news segments that attract the largest number of total viewers. Different times of the day will attract more viewers or listeners than other periods.

With the sample schedule, there is the possibility that each member of the audience will be exposed up to twenty times since twenty commercials were scheduled, but the average consumer in the audience will obviously be exposed to fewer impressions. This exact number can be calculated by knowing more rating information, but what media planners and advertisers are mainly interested in are the GRPs generated. They can then measure overall GRP against the target GRP calculated from the reach and frequency ideal for the brand they are promoting or the type of store they are advertising in their market. So in our example, a GRP of 136 may be adequate or it may not be enough, depending on what is being advertised.

Advertising agencies, trade associations, and vendors can help advertisers determine the ideal GRPs for what they wish to advertise; but always remember to reduce total GRPs by 30 percent to 50 percent to account for remote control channel zappers (see Figure 4.4), button pushers, and those who do other things during commercial breaks. (It is interesting to note, however, that television "flippers" tend to flip into other commercials, thus still causing the intrusive consumption of advertising messages.)

When Heavy Repetition Is Required

One of the best works done in this area, which goes beyond the traditional cost-per-thousand (CPM) and reach and frequency discussions, was authored by

Figure 4.4
The Flipping Phenomenon

A new phenomenon: Flipping. A landmark study by J. Walter Thompson identified and measured a new kind of TV viewer, the flipper "... those who usually flip around to some degree rather than watching a show from beginning to end...One out of every three viewers describe their typical viewing pattern as mobile, not stationary, for most programs."

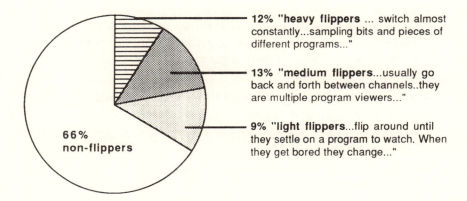

12% "heavy flippers ... switch almost constantly...sampling bits and pieces of different programs..."

13% "medium flippers...usually go back and forth between channels..they are multiple program viewers..."

9% "light flippers...flip around until they settle on a program to watch. When they get bored they change..."

66% non-flippers

Flipping is everywhere. Among JWT's other findings: flipping affects men more than women (43% vs. 29%) and young more than old (56% of 18-24s are flippers). Virtually all kinds of programs and all day parts are affected. The majority of flippers do so during commercial breaks. This tendency increases with the degree of flipping.

Source: Radio Advertising Bureau.

Joseph W. Ostrow, executive vice president of Young & Rubicam. Ostrow suggests that frequency be discussed in light of three factors: the marketing factor, the message or creative elements, and the media factor. This discussion should allow media planners and advertisers to focus on the question of "how much" may be needed to get the job done, a central question when buying a frequency medium such as radio or television. It should also be noted that Ostrow uses the word "brand" in his discussions; the words "store" or "business" could also be substituted, depending on whether the business or the brand is being advertised.

More or less frequency, according to Ostrow, would be required for each factor under the following conditions:[10]

Marketing Factors

- If the brand is new, it will need greater message repetition. Established brands generally need less frequency.
- If the brand has established a large market share (is dominant), or if

there exists high brand loyalty, it will need less frequency. Such brands have established customer acceptance and require less frequency.

- If the purchase or usage cycle is long, the brand will need less frequency. Products used in high volume and replaced often need high frequency to maintain top-of-mind awareness.
- Products or stores whose dominant marketing goal is to "beat" the competition will need higher frequency.
- Targeting "older" demographics will take higher frequency, as that age group absorbs material more slowly. On the other hand, children and teenagers learn faster, but they also forget quickly and may actually need more frequency than the former target group.

Message or Creative Factors

- A more complex message will need higher frequency than a more simple, easy to understand message.
- The more unique or different an ad or commercial is, the less frequency will be needed for remembrance.
- A new campaign to the market will need more frequency to register the message.
- A specific "price-item" campaign will need less frequency than one attempting to building an image.

Media Factors

- The more advertising clutter or the more a direct competitor is advertising, the higher the level of frequency needed.
- If advertising is consistent, less frequency is required.
- If advertising is sporadic, higher frequency will be needed due to campaign interruption.

Of course, final decisions on advertising schedules and overall frequency for each individual store or business is a budget determination made by the advertising manager or media planner. This information, however, should be helpful in the planning and implementing of an advertising schedule that will meet the overall short- and long-term objectives of the advertiser.

The Electronic Media as Teachers/Educators

Although a larger percentage of total media research has been devoted to the print media, it seems clear that a one-time exposure to any advertisement has little if any effect compared to multiple exposures through frequency. Newspaper can only provide a one-time exposure, at best, and then will not be available in the market for another twenty-four-hour period. Frequency can be built intrusively by using the electronic media throughout the day, vastly increasing the chances that the target consumer will be exposed to the advertising more than once.

Repeated exposure is the key to building the mind franchise, thus educating the consumer into brand or store awareness. This is vital to the total marketing efforts of any retailer due to the direct correlation between name recognition and market share.

DAGMAR

Repeated exposure can be charted in many different ways, but Figure 4.5 sums up the correlation between total number of commercial exposures and brand awareness with intent or probability of purchase within a four-week period. The vertical axis is based on the DAGMAR approach (Defining Advertising Goals for Measured Advertising Results), which attempts to describe the effectiveness of advertising or of each campaign or promotion run. A realistic goal of advertising would be to attract one-third of the available audience; the graph shows that such a goal can be accomplished with repeated exposures.

Figure 4.5
**The Correlation Between Commercial Exposures and Brand Awareness/Intent
to Purchase**

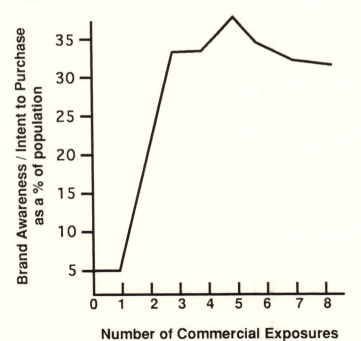

Weekly Consistency

Although the DAGMAR model demonstrates the advantages of repeated exposures scheduled with specific advertising goals in mind (for example, increasing
awareness of a new store among the 18–34 female demographic), and most advertising research indicates that at least three exposures within a buying cycle or
approximately a four-week period are necessary to maintain top-of-mind awareness and thus a competitive advantage within the market, the power of schedule
concentration cannot be ignored.

The DAGMAR concept would indicate that brand or store awareness is heightened beginning with the second exposure and is most effective within the three to
five exposure rate, although no responsible advertiser would schedule only three
to five commercials over such an extended period of time as four weeks. Why?
Simply due to the operational caveat at work here, which is the time period involved.

Schedule Concentration

Commercial impressions must be scheduled in a concentrated manner so that
subsequent impressions after the first exposure are not forgotten. Three to five
exposures are fine if the intended consumer is exposed within a one-week time
frame; if those exposures are spread out over a four-week period, the likely result
would be that when the second, third, or fourth commercial was consumed, the
first or earlier commercials would have been forgotten. Thus, subsequent exposures are merely repeated first exposures, as we know from the research of Ebbinghaus.

To ensure that specific advertising goals are met and that intended consumers
are impacted by at least three to five impressions within a given one-week time
frame, multiple commercials will need to be scheduled on a weekly basis, since
viewing and listening patterns vary with each consumer throughout the day and
week. This weekly schedule concentration over a period of weeks will produce
results since the targeted audience will be broad (commercials are scheduled over
a period of weeks, preferably from four to thirteen, depending on advertiser
goals) and can be considered preferable to a more narrowly focused concentration centered on days or dayparts and delivering fewer people.

When this is not done, such lack of weekly schedule concentration will result
in separate one or first-time exposures, which is the problem with print advertising. The ad budget will then have minimal market impact as pointed out in the
Optimal Effective Schedule (OES) discussion at the end of the previous chapter.

Remember, though, that the objective of awareness may be accomplished without a resulting increase in sales due to the long-term nature of advertising. Therefore, an advertising campaign must be consistent; businesspeople never know
"when" consumers are going to enter the market. Once they enter a high-involvement state and become logical prospects (a concept more fully developed in the
next chapter), being exposed to three or more messages will impact awareness
and intent to purchase.

A consistent campaign of this nature is most effectively and efficiently accomplished with minimal waste by using the intrusiveness of the electronic media, targeting the message to a specific demographic group who are the most logical prospects to consume the product or brands being advertised.

The Eye versus the Ear

It is quite possible that confusion over exactly which media can deliver effective, cost-efficient frequency still exists within the minds of may who have been successful with the print media over a period of time. This is not surprising since a direct correlation exists between advertising expenditures and the medium receiving those expenditures. Success always emanates from the medium that is given the budget.

However, it should be noted that many successful corporations are filing for bankruptcy in the 1990s after having used print exclusively for generations. Perhaps now is the time for successful retailers and those "on the margin" to consider reallocating advertising budgets to an intrusive medium that will educate potential consumers for a lifetime, which in turn may mean a lifetime of retail business for the advertiser.

A compelling reason to make such a switch lies in the very distinct educational differences between the eye and the ear. We have previously seen how we learn through our environment and our culture through the reinforcement of certain values or the repetition of certain tasks until learning has occurred. Since the electronic media itself works in this same manner by using the ear as the primary receptor (even television commercials are verbally driven), perhaps now is the time to discuss the role of the sensory organs in learning behavior—the ear, the primary receptor of radio and television advertising (remember, television is verbally driven), and the eye, the primary and only receptor of all print advertising.

Blindness and Deafness as Handicaps

To place the importance of the eye and the ear as educational "tools" in perspective, we begin by posing a very basic question: How many blind entertainers can you think of? Probably quite a few. Now, how many deaf entertainers can you think of? Probable one. Marlee Matlin.

Of course, one can always use the very remarkable and inspirational example of Helen Keller, the most famous of all exceptional human beings who overcame both blindness and deafness to become an author and teacher. The point is, however, that aside from exceptions, being born deaf appears to be a more serious handicap than being born blind. Many of these concepts were discussed in a videotape entitled *The Eye vs. the Ear,* featuring the advertising positioning experts Jack Trout and Al Ries. In the tape, experts like Dr. Elizabeth Loftus were interviewed and supported these general concepts about the handicapped and the "ear as teacher."

Blind students, as a general rule, graduate from high school at the same percentage rate as nonhandicapped students. About the same percentage of blind students go on to college as their nonhandicapped peers. As a percentage of their population, however, fewer deaf students go on to college and seem to have a far more difficult time obtaining a high school education. This has absolutely nothing to do with innate intelligence, which any student at Gallaudet University (the national university for the deaf in Washington, D.C.) would quickly inform you, but with the very real problems with learning that being deaf presents.

Deaf students, on average, graduate from high school reading at a fourth-grade level. Blind students graduate from high school, on average, reading by braille at a normal twelfth-grade level. These percentages may change over time with the very real advances taking place in deaf education, allowing many more students to enjoy higher education; however, the formal education of the deaf does seem to present some very real problems that lead many researchers to believe that it is sound, not sight, that plays the central role in the educational process.

This seems to be the case as there are many blind professionals representing all fields from entertainment to law and medicine, with limited membership from the deaf fraternity representing such professions. Again, this has nothing to do with innate intelligence, the deaf culture representing a highly sophisticated grouping of successful professionals, but rather with the difficulty of learning what cannot be heard.

Learning occurs primarily through sound. As infants, we hear words and begin associating those words with objects. Soon we begin to imitate the sounds or words our parents make and start forming our own syllables that describe those objects. In a word, we begin the process of language or of speaking.

We actually understand language before we can speak it or read it. Once we attribute certain sounds with certain meanings, cognition occurs and language is understood. Spoken words go directly into the brain for immediate understanding, allowing us to understand language and speak long before we can read.

Deaf children, however, cannot associate sounds with words; even though they may be able to see, they cannot know what an object is until a picture association is made. Even then, with no sound association, the learning process takes a longer time than with blind children who can associate sound with objects they can touch and feel; such touching and feeling take the place of seeing and education proceeds at the normal rate.

Relating the Concepts of Exceptional Education to Advertising

Blindness seems not to be a handicap in the learning process of young children, because the mind does learn by the ear rather than by the eye. Yet merchants attempt to "educate" and inform their marketplace by using the majority of their budgets in print, the eye-oriented medium. Since this is more often than not the case, the question of how adults respond to the stimulus of sound should be examined.

The learning of new information by sound does not stop as we mature. Just as with infants, the intrusive nature of sound directly enters the mind of adults; we, as adults, do not have to mentally process these sounds as we must necessarily process language when reading a print medium. The "fade-factor" that occurs immediately after we are presented with new information is not as acute when we read or review printed material.

Granted, consumers can read something over and over to increase retention, a concept supported by research. The ability to process information was studied by Walter Pauk (1984), who found that it was easier to remember what one read than what one heard, but this is likely due to the reality that when reading, one can slow down the pace if necessary (Buchholz and Smith 1991) or read the material over again for comprehension.

But who reads a printed ad over and over again? Also remember that a person is drawn to an ad only if he or she is a logical prospect in the market and will be attracted to the advertised price. Therefore, the research results pertaining to the processing of information via hearing or reading do not seem to pertain to retail advertising due to the way in which mass media is consumed. Printed ads are viewed only if desired and are not read over and over; the intrusiveness of the electronic media delivers the message without choice.

The difference between the verbal nature of the electronic media and the printed nature of newspapers is that spoken words go directly into the brain for instantaneous understanding. The written word takes longer for the brain to comprehend and has a more rapid "fade-factor" from the memory. This is because as we read we translate written symbols into phonetic or aural sounds in our mind; this mental detour takes longer than hearing and fades faster from the short-term memory than does hearing.

Hearing, being passive, takes less effort and the mind can be "franchised" intrusively over time, something that cannot occur with print. Therefore, using print media as major advertising vehicles does not appear to be in the best interests of businesspeople who wish to maintain top-of-mind awareness over time within their marketplace.

The Bottom Line — Where and How Print Fails

It has become clear throughout this chapter that print as an advertisement tool fails in the marketplace due to its inability to educate or franchise minds through frequency and because consumers learn more by sound than by sight. Newspaper is also handicapped by the fact that only one issue is available every twenty-four hours. The small percentage of highly involved "now" consumers who would read a printed ad will have to wait a full day before seeing that ad again, assuming it is even run two days in a row.

By that time, according to Ebbinghaus, a full 75 percent of the original information has been forgotten and the advertiser will, in essence, be starting over again with the educational process. The cost involved in this hit and miss approach far outweighs the benefits derived and may be a contributing factor to the failure of the many large retail chains going out of business after decades of using newspaper as the dominant method of advertising.

SUMMARY

As young children, our environment and immediate culture shape the way in which we think and act and establish a value base that we draw upon the remainder of our lives. We essentially know everything that we know from how to tie our shoes to knowledge that is a permanent part of our mind's information base because of repetition—doing something over and over again until we master the task.

Since we learn through repetition, the electronic media are able to educate consumers in the same way—by repeating a message over and over again until it becomes a permanent part of the knowledge base or what is known as "top-of-mind awareness." This franchising process is made possible by the intrusive nature of radio and television; the consumer cannot "pass over" a commercial as he or she can a newspaper ad and the commercial registers an impression. Advertising research shows that each time an impression is made, cognition is increased. Hence, over time, an indelible impression can be made by the intrusive nature of the electronic media at a far more affordable cost than the one-time impression of the print media. Repetition, in essence, causes familiarization, which elicits favorable or positive response. Hence, the act of repeated exposure itself enhances attitude (Zajonc 1968).

The research of Ebbinghaus and others points to the concept of memory decay and how quickly we forget. Constant reminding on the electronic media can offset such memory decay; newspaper, a one-time impression medium published only every twenty-four hours, essentially starts the educational process over again with each issue and is simply not a player in the long-term education of the consumer.

Media terms such as gross rating points (GRPs) and cost per point (CPP) are helpful with audience measurement and figuring the cost of reaching that audience, but are not valid measurements for determining end results of that schedule.

Since consumers are essentially educated by the ear and not the eye, the strength of radio and television is further underscored as the dominant educational media that cannot be ignored by advertisers and media planners who are concerned about positioning a business in the minds of marketplace consumers for perhaps generations to come.

NOTES

1. Edith W. King and August Kerber, *The Sociology of Early Childhood Education* (New York: American Book Company, 1968), pp. 45–46.

2. Frank Smith, "Learning to Read," *Phi Delta Kappan* 73/6 (February 1992): 432, 434.

3. John J. Burnette, *Promotion Management* (St. Paul: West, 1984), p. 99.

4. Ibid.

5. William G. Nickels, *Marketing Communication and Promotion* (New York: John Wiley and Sons, 1984), p. 342.

6. David Martin, *Romancing the Brand* (New York: AMACOM, 1989), p. 112.

7. David Ogilvy, *Ogilvy on Advertising* (New York: Vintage Books, 1985), p. 111.

8. Samuel C. Craig, Brian Sternthal, and Clark Leavitt, "Advertising Wearout: An Experimental Analysis," *Journal of Marketing Research* 13 (November 1976): 371.

9. Steve Marx and Pierre Bouvard, *Radio Advertising's Missing Ingredient: The Optimum Effective Scheduling System* (Washington, D.C.: National Association of Broadcasters, 1990), pp. 15–18.

10. Joseph W. Ostrow, "Setting Frequency Levels: An Art or a Science?" *Journal of Advertising Research* 24 (August/September 1984): 10–11.

OTHER WORKS CITED

Buchholz, Laura M. and Robert E. Smith. "The Role of Consumer Involvement in Determining Cognitive Response to Broadcast Advertising." *Journal of Advertising* 20 (1991): 4–17.

Calder, Bobby J. and Brian Sternthal. "Television Commercial Wearout: An Information Processing View." *Journal of Marketing Research* 17/2 (1980): 173–186.

Craig, Samuel C., Brian Sternthal, and Clark Leavitt. "Advertising Wearout: An Experimental Analysis." *Journal of Marketing Research* (November 1976): 371.

Edell, Julie A. and Kevin L. Keller. "The Information Processing of Coordinated Media Campaigns." *Journal of Marketing Research* (May 1989): 149–163.

Marquardt, R. A. and G. W. Murdock. "The Sales/Advertising Relationship: An Investigation of Correlations and Consistency in Supermarkets and Department Stores." *Journal of Advertising Research* (November 1984): 55–60.

Ostheimer, R. M. "Frequency Effects Over Time." *Journal of Advertising Research* (February 1970): 19–22.

Pauk, Walter. "Forgetting and Remembering." *How to Study in College* (Boston: Houghton Mifflin Co., 1984).

Ray, Michael, A. G. Sawyer, and E. C. Strong. "Frequency Effects Revisited." *Journal of Advertising Research* (February 1991): 14–20.

Young, Daniel R. and Francis S. Bellezza. "Encoding Variability, Memory Organization and the Repetition Effect." *Journal of Experimental Psychology: Learning, Memory and Cognition* 8/6 (1982): 545–559.

Zajonc, Robert B. "Attitudinal Effects of Mere Exposure." *Journal of Personality and Social Psychology Monographs* 9/2 (1968): 1–28.

CHAPTER 5

Target Marketing

Marketing in our lifetime has gone from the shotgun to the rifle to the laser.
. . . Today, you need surgical strikes for efficiency. Radio is the ultimate
strike weapon.

—Marvin Sloves, Chairman and CEO, Scali, McCabe & Sloves

—John B. Adams, President, The Martin Agency

TARGET MARKETING AND ADVERTISING

Some things in life just seem to go together. One cannot exist without the other.
Dagwood and Blondie. Baseball and hot dogs. Autumn and leaves of gold. Elvis
and rock 'n roll. Mutt and Jeff. And so it is with target marketing and advertising.
Advertising that is not designed to surgically strike at the heart of an identified
market segment carries with it an inordinate amount of waste. The concept of the
"surgical strike" itself is as important to corporate and business media planners as
any general knowledge of advertising, as therein lies the key to how advertising
must work if it is to be nonwasteful. A surgical strike is only possible when using
the electronic media, as only the narrowcasting nature of such a mass media can
pinpoint consumer markets efficiently.

Once this concept is understood, a business must then know what market segment or consumer demographic it needs to target its advertising to. Although
most businesses have a clear grasp of who they believe their customers to be,
consumer markets are constantly changing, with the graying of America and the
now mature baby boomers significantly influencing the buying behavior displayed in the consumer marketplace. Knowing and understanding these consumer markets will add to the advertising and media planners' prior knowledge of
advertising and consumer psychology, with the end result being more efficient

placement of advertising. Efficiency in advertising, of course, means minimal overall waste.

CONSUMER MARKETS – A DEMOGRAPHIC BREAKDOWN

The one certain factor about any market is that it will not last forever. As the population ages and society advances, consumer tastes, desires, and values undergo a transformation. What is accepted today may be anathema tomorrow. Today's fad is tomorrow's garage sale. This is precisely why businesses must know the demographic breakdown of the population and the unique characteristics of each market segment its products or services are attempting to attract.

Additional importance is given to this concept when advertisers turn their attention to what has sustained many of them over the years: the baby boom generation. As Robert Balon points out, the entire concept of today's niche marketing has been brought forward with the baby boomers in mind, with that generation alone being responsible for the decline of the mass market. He notes the writings of Paul Licht, who has studied the boomers and concluded that they "have not quite decided whether they are members of a distinct generation, bound together by history and demography, or merely a collection of small groups and individuals who just happen to share the same birthday."[1]

Indeed, there is an eighteen-year age span between the oldest and the youngest of the boomers, making 25–34 and 35–44 the two most desired demographics for today's advertisers. Role-models, as Balon notes, range from Robert Young to the Brady Bunch and the Waltons, meaning this generation is hardly homogeneous.

The one national neighborhood of the 1950s is now a mosaic of local neighborhoods that must be identified and presented to advertisers, along with information on how these niche groups can be effectively reached. Understanding the segmentation of micromarketing begins with understanding the demographics themselves and the characteristics that make each group unique.

Differentiating each indigenous consumer group and its current and projected characteristics into the next century essentially helps advertisers identify the factors they need to attend to over the coming years. The source of this demographic information is the *Almanac of Consumer Markets,* published by the American Demographics Press.[2]

Consumers Aged 18 to 24

Table 5.1 shows this shrinking age group and what its consumer impact will mean to merchants over the next ten years. This age group obviously will not have the market impact on the economy its baby boom parents did, although nonwhites and Hispanics will increase rapidly in this demographic as they will in all other groups.

The 18–24 group also spends more on alcoholic beverages than any other group, and of all groups, has the highest percentage of workers in the occupa-

Table 5.1
Consumers Aged 18 to 24

This market will be shrinking and changing during the 1990s. Here are some factors to watch.

There will be fewer young adults and fewer households headed by young adults.

■ Between 1990 and 2000 the number of 18-to-24-year-olds will drop 3 percent.

■ The number of households headed by under-25-year-olds will fall 5 percent during the 1990s.

■ In 1990 married couples head 33 percent of these youngest households; that share will be only 24 percent in 2000.

■ Eighty-three percent of men and 69 percent of women aged 18 to 24 have never married.

■ Seventy percent of these young women and 80 percent of the men are in the labor force. Most of the workers hold full-time jobs.

■ Twenty-seven percent of households headed by an under-25-year-old have household incomes between $20,000 and $35,000 and 13 percent have incomes of more than $35,000. But 60 percent of these households bring in less than $20,000.

■ Married couples have the highest median household income—$21,000—in this age group. The median income of dual-earner married couples is $4,100 higher than that.

■ These young households devote more of their spending dollar to food away from home, alcoholic beverages, shelter, apparel, and transportation than the average household.

■ Because of their dwindling numbers, households headed by under-25-year-olds will be spending an estimated three billion dollars less in 2000 than in 1990.

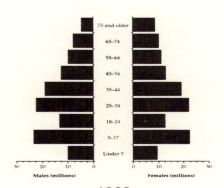

1990

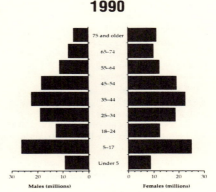

2000

tions of laborer, fabricator, service, sales, and administrative support. Due to declining households, this group will be spending $3 billion less in 2000 than in 1990.

Consumers Aged 25 to 34

This age group (Table 5.2) will be shrinking even more than the 18–24 group and will mean many changes for a market that once boomed for merchants (Table 5.3). There is a silver lining, though, as Table 5.4 depicts. Although households in this segment will be declining, more of them will have incomes between $50,000 and $60,000.

Table 5.2
Consumers Aged 25 to 34

Marketers beware. This age group will shrink the most and change a lot during the 1990s.

There will be fewer 25-to-34-year-olds in the next decade and they will head fewer households.

■ Between 1990 and 2000, the number of Americans aged 25 to 34 will fall 15 percent.

■ There will be 3 million fewer households headed by 25-to-34-year-olds in 2000 than in 1990.

■ During the 1990s, the number of family households will plunge 23 percent as the number of non-families will trend upward by 4 percent.

■ Men and women in this age group account for the largest share of all divorces and remarriages.

■ In 1987, 95 percent of men aged 25 to 34 were in the labor force; that share will decline slightly to 94 percent in 2000. In 1987, 72 percent of women in this age group were in the labor force; that share will climb to 82 percent in 2000.

■ Compared with other age groups, 25-to-34-year-olds head the largest proportion—31 percent—of households with incomes between $20,000 and $35,000. Of those remaining, an even 34 percent are above and below that range.

■ The median household income of these households is $26,900. Households headed by married couples have a median income of $32,800 and dual-earner married couples have the highest median income in the age group—$36,400.

■ This is the age group with the largest chunk of their spending dollar—33 percent—going to housing.

■ Between 1990 and 2000, the aggregate spending of these households will drop off by 72 billion dollars.

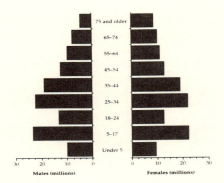

1990

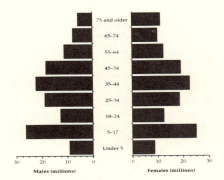

2000

This group also accounts for the largest proportion of all divorces and remarriages and will see 82 percent of its women in the workforce by the year 2000. Sixty-four percent of the 25–34 demographic are dual-income families that will spend approximately 40 percent of the food budget away from home. By 2000 these households will be spending $72 billion less than in 1990 due to a 15 percent decline in the number of households.

Consumers Aged 35 to 44

As Table 5.5 shows, this group is gaining economic clout and will be increasingly important to all businesses. Table 5.6 shows the booming numbers in this

Table 5.3
Number of Households, Consumers Aged 25 to 34

DOWNTURNING MARKET

As the small baby bust generation starts turning 25, this age group will see a sharp 15 percent decline, spelling big changes ahead for a formerly booming market.

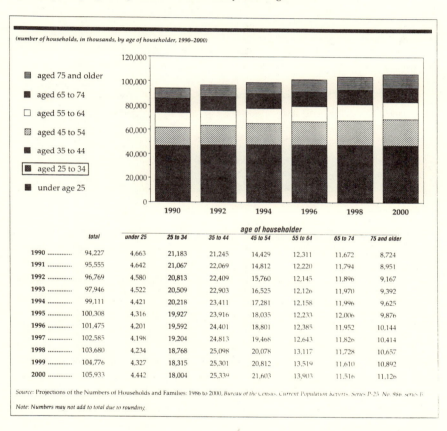

(number of households, in thousands, by age of householder, 1990–2000)

				age of householder				
	total	under 25	25 to 34	35 to 44	45 to 54	55 to 64	65 to 74	75 and older
1990	94,227	4,663	21,183	21,245	14,429	12,311	11,672	8,724
1991	95,555	4,642	21,067	22,069	14,812	12,220	11,794	8,951
1992	96,769	4,580	20,813	22,409	15,760	12,145	11,896	9,167
1993	97,946	4,522	20,509	22,903	16,525	12,126	11,970	9,392
1994	99,111	4,421	20,218	23,411	17,281	12,158	11,996	9,625
1995	100,308	4,316	19,927	23,916	18,035	12,233	12,006	9,876
1996	101,475	4,201	19,592	24,401	18,801	12,385	11,952	10,144
1997	102,585	4,198	19,204	24,813	19,468	12,643	11,826	10,414
1998	103,680	4,234	18,768	25,098	20,078	13,117	11,728	10,657
1999	104,776	4,327	18,315	25,301	20,812	13,519	11,610	10,892
2000	105,933	4,442	18,004	25,339	21,603	13,903	11,516	11,126

Source: Projections of the Numbers of Households and Families: 1986 to 2000, *Bureau of the Census, Current Population Reports, Series P-25, No. 986, series B*

Note: Numbers may not add to total due to rounding.

group composed of younger baby boomers and those starting over, while Table 5.7 shows that no other group has such a high proportion of workers in the managerial and professional category.

This is the most highly educated group of Americans, with men more likely to have high incomes in this segment than in any other. However, 71 percent of income-generating women aged 35 to 44 earn less than $20,000, although household spending will increase by $121 billion by the year 2000 due to a 19 percent rise in the number of households.

Table 5.4
Future Income, Consumers Aged 25 to 34

AFFLUENCE PREVAILS

Although the number of households headed by 25-to-34-year-olds will decline between 1990 and 1995, the good news is that more of them will have incomes between $50,000 and $60,000. The biggest drop will be in the number of households with household incomes under $20,000.

(projections of the number of households with householders aged 25 to 34, by household income, 1990 and 1995, numbers in thousands, income is in 1985 dollars)

	1990		1995		percent change
	number	percent	number	percent	1990-1995
All households	21,183	100.0%	19,927	100.0%	-5.9%
Less than $10,000	3,072	14.5	2,826	14.2	-8.0
$10,000 to $19,999	4,921	23.2	4,493	22.5	-8.7
$20,000 to $29,999	5,389	25.4	4,990	25.0	-7.4
$30,000 to $39,999	3,822	18.0	3,670	18.4	-4.0
$40,000 to $49,999	2,069	9.8	2,011	10.1	-2.8
$50,000 to $59,999	943	4.5	981	4.9	4.0
$60,000 to $74,999	530	2.5	524	2.6	-1.1
$75,000 and over	436	2.1	435	2.2	-0.2
Median household income	$24,823		$25,300		

Source: American Demographics, May to August, 1986, based on the national econometric model of Wharton Economic Forecasting Association and on household projections from the Bureau of the Census

Note: Numbers may not add to total due to rounding.

Consumers Aged 45 to 54

The growth group of the 1990s as Table 5.8 shows, this group will account for 21 percent of all household wealth and will be of prime interest to most businesses that have been tracking the boomer generation since they were teenagers. With children leaving home, much discretionary income will be available for luxury and leisure activities. Thirty percent of the workers in this demographic are managerial or professional, compared to 25 percent of all employees. By 2000, 75 percent of the 45–54 women will be in the workforce.

This market segment is at the top of the income chart and, as Table 5.9 shows, these households will spend $219 billion more in 2000 than in 1990.

Consumers Aged 55 to 64

An overall growth market as depicted in Table 5.10, this segment will spend an estimated $38 billion more in 2000 than in 1990 due to a 13 percent increase in households during this time. Within this group, however, comes a rise in widowhood and serious illness, although financial freedom allows each household to

Table 5.5
Consumers Aged 35 to 44

They will be 16 percent of all Americans in 2000, they are gaining economic clout, and their demographic profile is changing.

**More people and households
. . .and nontraditional households.**

■ Between 1990 and 2000, baby boomers will hike the number of 35-to-44-year-olds by 18 percent.

■ There will be a 19 percent increase in the number of households headed by members of this age group during the 1990s.

■ During those 10 years, family households will grow 12 percent; nonfamilies by 50 percent.

■ They are the most highly educated group of Americans—47 percent of them completed one to three years of college and 27 percent finished four or more years.

■ Women aged 35 to 44 are more likely to be in the work force than women in any other age group. Seventy-five percent of them were workers in 1987, a proportion that will increase to 84 percent by 2000.

■ They head 21 percent of all households but account for 26 percent of all household income.

■ Married couples in this age group have a median household income of $41,300. Median income is higher—$44,600—among the 68 percent of married couples that are dual-earners.

■ They devote a bigger share of their spending dollar to food, housing, apparel, entertainment, and insurance and pensions than the average American household.

■ Households headed by 35-to-44-year-olds will spend an estimated 121 billion dollars more in 2000 than in 1990.

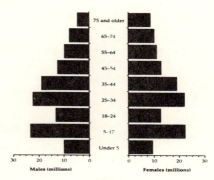

1990

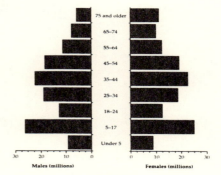

2000

spend $21,000 more than the average if the income is over $40,000. Home-ownership peaks in this age group, with 80 percent living in their own home. As with other age groups, though, white households (82 percent) are more likely to be homeowners than are black (61 percent) or Hispanic (58 percent) householders.

Consumers Aged 65 to 74

Table 5.11 shows this group to be shrinking, although fewer will be retiring and more money will be spent on food, health care, and personal care than in the average household. Households in this segment will decline one percent in the

Table 5.6
Number of Households, Consumers Aged 35 to 44

BOOMING NUMBERS

Younger baby boomers starting out and older boomers starting over will contribute to a 19 percent rise in the number of households headed by 35-44-year-olds during the 1990s. Family households will grow 12 percent, while nonfamilies will zoom up a full 50 percent.

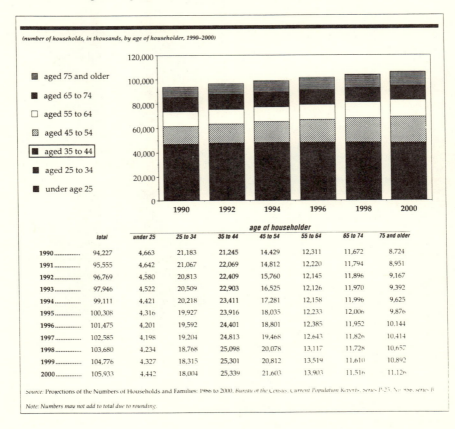

(number of households, in thousands, by age of householder, 1990–2000)

Legend:
- aged 75 and older
- aged 65 to 74
- aged 55 to 64
- aged 45 to 54
- aged 35 to 44
- aged 25 to 34
- under age 25

	total	under 25	25 to 34	35 to 44	45 to 54	55 to 64	65 to 74	75 and older
				age of householder				
1990	94,227	4,663	21,183	21,245	14,429	12,311	11,672	8,724
1991	95,555	4,642	21,067	22,069	14,812	12,220	11,794	8,951
1992	96,769	4,580	20,813	22,409	15,760	12,145	11,896	9,167
1993	97,946	4,522	20,509	22,903	16,525	12,126	11,970	9,392
1994	99,111	4,421	20,218	23,411	17,281	12,158	11,996	9,625
1995	100,308	4,316	19,927	23,916	18,035	12,233	12,006	9,876
1996	101,475	4,201	19,592	24,401	18,801	12,385	11,952	10,144
1997	102,585	4,198	19,204	24,813	19,468	12,643	11,826	10,414
1998	103,680	4,234	18,768	25,098	20,078	13,117	11,728	10,657
1999	104,776	4,327	18,315	25,301	20,812	13,519	11,610	10,892
2000	105,933	4,442	18,004	25,339	21,603	13,903	11,516	11,126

Source: Projections of the Numbers of Households and Families: 1986 to 2000, Bureau of the Census, Current Population Reports, Series P-25, No. 956, series B

Note: Numbers may not add to total due to rounding.

1990s and aggregate spending will drop by an estimated $3 billion. However, marketers and advertisers should realize that households headed by the 65–74 age group will increase by 7 percent by 1995, with 18 percent of these boasting incomes of $50,000 or more; high-income households will increase faster than low-income households.

Consumers Aged 75 and Older

Table 5.12 shows this group to be the second-fastest growing market, forecasted to be $28 billion larger in 2000 than in 1990. Half of this age group is widowed, but a major feature of the 1990s will be the 30 percent gain projected for the 75 and older householders. Obviously, a large share of the spending dollar in this category, 15 percent, goes to health care.

Future Expenditures in All Product Categories

Advertisers and businesses may wish to know what future consumer spending patterns may look like in major product and service categories. Table 5.13 shows projected aggregate expenditures in 1990 for all households with the same aggregate expenditures projected for the year 2000.

Use this information to determine how markets will change and how a particular business can adapt to this changing climate in order to prevent current market share erosion. Remember that no consumer market segment lasts forever and only by understanding the future can businesses today adapt for survival into the coming century.

WHAT IS WRONG WITH TODAY'S MARKETING?

Marketing plans today are often based on ignorance and compounded by mythology according to Kevin J. Clancy and Robert S. Schulman. They correctly see American businesses making advertising and marketing decisions based on concepts such as:

- Judgment or death-wish marketing—"This is the way we have always made decisions."
- Analyzing the competition to determine what should be done. How do you know the competition is not making a mistake?
- Top management demanding short-term results. Evidently, they have not read Tom Peters or Edward Deming or do not understand the long-term nature of advertising and marketing.
- Creative ad campaigns that please the business internally, usually put together by baby boomers who want to be different. Such campaigns do not address real customer needs with real solutions.
- Inefficient targeting with little emphasis on profitability.
- Inadequate research that concentrates on focus groups and "small, strange samples of atypical consumers (fewer than three hundred people) roaming through shopping malls in a semicomatose state with time on their hands."

Table 5.7
Kinds of Jobs, Consumers Aged 35 to 44

MANAGERS AND PROFESSIONALS

Thirty-two percent of working 35-to-44-year-old men and 31 percent of the women hold managerial and professional jobs. No other age group has such a high proportion of workers in that category—or such low representation among service and farming, forestry and fishing jobs.

(occupations of employed persons aged 16 and older and those aged 35 to 44, by sex, numbers in thousands)

	aged 16+	aged 35-44	males aged 35-44	females aged 35-44	percent aged 16+	percent aged 35-44
All employed persons	112,440	27,179	14,898	12,281	100.0%	100.0%
Managerial and professional	27,742	8,547	4,765	3,782	24.7	31.4
Executive, administrative and managerial ...	13,316	4,016	2,552	1,464	11.8	14.8
Officials & administrators, public admin.	549	195	119	76	0.5	0.7
Other executive, admin., & managerial	9,190	2,832	1,911	921	8.2	10.4
Management-related occupations	3,577	989	522	467	3.2	3.6
Professional specialty occupations	14,426	4,531	2,213	2,318	12.8	16.7
Engineers	1,731	455	434	21	1.5	1.7
Math & computer scientists	685	224	152	72	0.6	0.8
Natural scientists	388	111	84	27	0.3	0.4
Health diagnosing occupations	793	266	217	49	0.7	1.0
Health assessment & treating	2,148	624	95	529	1.9	2.3
Teachers, college & university	661	204	120	84	0.6	0.8
Teachers, except college & university	3,587	1,328	361	967	3.2	4.9
Lawyers & judges	707	241	197	44	0.6	0.9
Other professional specialty occupations .	3,727	1,078	554	524	3.3	4.0
Technical, sales, administrative support	35,082	8,078	2,914	5,164	31.2	29.7
Technicians & related support occupations .	3,346	862	424	438	3.0	3.2
Health technologists & technicians	1,142	308	39	269	1.0	1.1
Engineering & science technicians	1,100	272	213	59	1.0	1.0
Techs., except health, engineering, science	1,104	283	173	110	1.0	1.0
Sales occupations	13,480	2,949	1,690	1,259	12.0	10.9
Supervisors & proprietors	3,572	968	668	300	3.2	3.6
Sales reps., finance & business service	2,330	632	370	262	2.1	2.3

(continued next page)

- Inability to assess a marketing program's return on investment (ROI).
- Promoting managers before they have had to live with their brands or decisions and had to demonstrate a return on investment.

The concerns addressed in this chapter will be far from the complete answers needed for this comprehensive topic, but will note the key areas that corporate and business media planners must necessarily attend to if they do not wish to file Chapter 11 before the end of the century.

Table 5.7 (continued)

(continued from previous page)

(occupations of employed persons aged 16 and older, and those aged 35 to 44, by sex, numbers in thousands)

	aged 16+	aged 35–44	males aged 35–44	females aged 35–44	percent aged 16+	percent aged 35–44
Sales reps., commodities except retail	1,544	429	360	69	1.4%	1.6%
Sales, retail and personal	5,973	909	287	622	5.3	3.3
Sales-related occupations	60	11	5	6	0.1	0.0
Administrative support including clerical ...	18,256	4,266	799	3,467	16.2	15.7
Supervisors	723	227	107	120	0.6	0.8
Computer equipment operators.................	914	197	66	131	0.8	0.7
Secretaries, stenographers, & typists	5,004	1,204	15	1,189	4.5	4.4
Financial records processing	2,469	591	48	543	2.2	2.2
Mail & message distributing	961	253	171	82	0.9	0.9
Other admin. support including clerical...	8,185	1,795	394	1,401	7.3	6.6
Service occupations	15,054	2,885	1,041	1,844	13.4	10.6
Private household	934	141	3	138	0.8	0.5
Protective services	1,907	507	454	53	1.7	1.9
Service, except private hhld. & protective	12,213	2,237	584	1,653	10.9	8.2
Food service	5,204	699	177	522	4.6	2.6
Health service	1,873	416	35	381	1.7	1.5
Cleaning & building service	2,886	589	299	290	2.6	2.2
Personal service...	2,249	533	74	459	2.0	2.0
Precision production, craft, repair	13,568	3,339	3,019	320	12.1	12.3
Mechanics & repairers	4,445	1,125	1,078	47	0.4	4.1
Construction trades	5,011	1,144	1,119	25	4.5	4.2
Other production, craft, repair	4,112	1,070	822	248	3.7	3.9
Operators, fabricators, laborers	17,486	3,747	2,688	1,059	15.6	13.8
Machine operators, assemblers, inspectors	7,994	1,859	1,073	786	7.1	6.8
Transportation, material moving	4,712	1,171	1,062	109	4.2	4.3
Handlers, equip. cleaners, helpers, laborers ..	4,779	717	553	164	4.3	2.6
Farming, forestry, fishing	3,507	583	471	112	3.1	2.1
Farm operators & managers	1,317	252	210	42	1.2	0.9
Farm workers & related occupations	2,013	289	222	67	1.8	1.1
Forestry and fishing occupations	177	42	38	4	0.2	0.2

Source: Unpublished annual data for 1987, Bureau of Labor Statistics

Note: Numbers may not add to total due to rounding. Civilian, noninstitutionalized employees only.

Much has already been made of effective media choice and the need to partially abandon traditional print-oriented advertising in favor of an intrusive form of mind franchising. What now needs to be addressed is how an advertiser can determining exactly whom to target. Once a target group of consumers has been more efficiently defined, such a target group of people can be matched with specific radio stations and television programs that cater to their needs and tastes. Running commercials on these stations whose demographics match up with target customers means advertising with the least amount of waste and thus efficient use of a business's advertising budget.

Table 5.8
Consumers Aged 45 to 54

This is the growth group of the 1990s. Here are some reasons for watching them.

They have the highest incomes, they are the biggest spenders, and there will be many more of them.

■ The number of 45-to-54-year-olds will increase 47 percent between 1990 and 2000 when they will be 14 percent of the entire U.S. population.

■ They will head 20 percent of all households in 2000.

■ Households in this age group are most likely to include a married couple—66 percent of them do. However, only a third of those married-couple households contain children under the age of 18.

■ Nonfamily households with a householder aged 45 to 54 will increase 70 percent during the 1990s.

■ Ninety-one percent of men and 69 percent of women aged 45 to 54 are now in the labor force. By 2000, three-quarters of the women in this age group are expected to be labor force participants.

■ Compared with households headed by members of the other age groups, these have the highest median household income—over $37,000.

■ Married couples in this age group have a median household income of $45,200. Dual-earner married couples are at the top of the income chart with a median income of $50,300.

■ They account for 21 percent of all household wealth.

■ Households in this age group spend more on food, transportation, and insurance and pensions than households in any other age group.

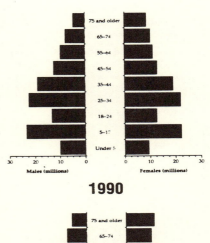

1990

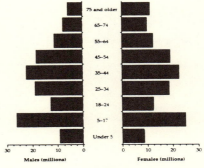

2000

Stated more precisely, the more clearly a business can define its target market, the more efficient advertising becomes. More time can then be spent advertising and marketing to genuine customers and prospects rather than to people who are not logical prospects and likely never will be.

Simply defining a target market is never enough. As Karl Albrecht notes in *The Only Thing That Matters,*

outstanding . . . organizations understand the very basic needs, instincts, life situations, problems, and buying motivations of their customers. They see their customers as unique people, not as market units. They know what critical elements of value will win and keep their business.

Table 5.9
Future Expenditures, Consumers Aged 45 to 54

MARKETERS, TAKE AIM

Households headed by 45-to-54-year-olds will spend a whopping 219 billion dollars more in 2000 than in 1990. Driving this spending boom is a 50 percent growth in the number of households in this age group during the 1990s.

(projected aggregate expenditures in 1990 and 2000 for all households and for households by age of householder, in billions of dollars)

	1990 aggregate annual expenditures in billions							
	all households	under 25	25-34	35-44	45-54	55-64	65-74	75+
Number of households (in thousands)	94,227	4,663	21,183	21,245	14,429	12,311	11,672	8,724
Total expenditures (in billions of dollars) ...	$2,203.1	$64.2	$476.6	$628.6	$441.2	$292.8	$197.2	$102.5
Food	330.8	9.4	70.3	93.7	64.1	43.9	32.3	17.2
Food at home	225.1	5.9	44.8	64.9	41.8	30.9	23.0	13.7
Food away from home	101.5	3.6	21.2	28.8	22.2	13.0	9.3	3.5
Alcoholic beverages	25.4	1.6	7.5	6.4	4.7	3.0	1.8	0.6
Housing...	667.6	19.2	158.3	193.5	121.9	80.8	58.3	35.6
Shelter	385.6	12.4	97.2	115.7	71.7	42.4	28.8	17.5
Owned dwellings............................	229.7	1.8	50.3	75.8	46.9	28.2	17.9	8.7
Rented dwellings	115.2	9.5	41.6	27.6	13.1	8.4	7.2	7.6
Other lodging	40.8	1.0	5.2	12.2	11.6	5.8	3.7	1.2
Fuels, utilities, and public services	160.0	3.7	32.0	41.2	29.6	23.2	18.6	11.8
Household operations..............................	34.2	0.7	9.6	10.2	3.8	3.7	2.9	3.3
Household furnishings, equipment..........	87.8	2.4	19.5	26.5	16.8	11.6	8.0	3.0
Apparel and services	111.0	4.1	24.6	33.7	22.8	13.8	8.3	3.6
Transportation	464.9	15.6	107.0	130.7	98.7	61.1	37.7	14.2
Health care	103.7	1.6	14.5	21.4	16.9	16.0	17.9	15.4
Entertainment	106.0	3.1	23.3	35.2	20.6	13.0	8.0	2.6
Personal care	20.1	0.6	3.7	5.2	3.8	3.1	2.3	1.3
Reading	13.6	0.3	2.6	3.8	2.6	1.9	1.6	0.8
Education	27.6	2.7	3.9	8.3	8.8	2.9	0.8	0.1
Tobacco and smoking supplies	22.0	0.8	4.9	5.8	4.5	3.3	2.0	0.7
Miscellaneous	31.5	0.6	6.5	8.1	5.9	4.5	3.6	2.3
Contributions and support payments	74.2	0.7	7.3	17.7	17.4	12.9	12.5	5.7
Personal insurance and pensions	208.9	3.9	46.4	65.2	48.5	32.6	10.0	2.3

It takes two kinds of research to understand your customers: research on the market and research on the customers themselves. Market research, in this connotation, is the investigation of the structure and dynamics of the marketplace you propose to serve. This includes identifying market segments, analyzing demographics, targeting critical market niches, and analyzing competitive forces.

Customer perception research goes at least one step further than conventional market research. It attempts to understand the expectations, thoughts, and feelings of the individual customer toward the service product and service provider. It hopes to discern one or more critical factors in the customer's perception of the total experience. This enables you to come up with a customer's value model, which is a set of criteria that drive the customer's choices between you and your competitors.[3]

Table 5.10
Consumers Aged 55 to 64

This is a growth market for the 1990s and the 21st century. Here are some key factors to watch.

During the 1990s, the number of these mature consumers and the number of households they head will be growing.

■ Between 1990 and 2000 the number of people aged 55 to 64 will increase by almost 14 percent.

■ Although three-quarters of the 13 million 55-to-64-year-old householders live in families, fewer than 10 percent of them still have children under 18 at home.

■ During the 1990s the number of households headed by 55-to-64-year-olds will climb 13 percent. The fastest growing types of households in this age group will be male-headed families (up 19 percent) and male-headed nonfamilies (up 31 percent).

■ Only 68 percent of the men in this age group and 43 percent of the women are in the work force.

■ Income per household member in this age group is $14,800 and median household income is $27,600.

■ Thirty-seven percent of married couples aged 55 to 64 are dual earners and their median household income is $45,200—$9,400 higher than the median for all married couples in this age group.

■ An above-average share of this age group's spending dollar goes to health care, contributions, and insurance and pensions.

■ Households in this age group will spend 38 billion dollars more in 2000 than in 1990.

■ Households headed by 55-to-64-year-olds account for 22 percent of all household wealth.

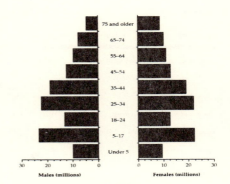

1990

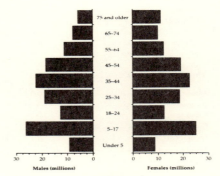

2000

Understanding customer value is what wins business for the future. Remember that advertising does not make a business or a product successful. Only quality products and outstanding customer service breed success. However, before a business can make a prospect a customer, that prospect must first be identified and informed about the business so he or she can then make the decision to come into the place of business for the first time.

Many smaller businesses will not wish to become overly involved in much of the information presented in this chapter. This approach is fine, as long as market and customer research is not ignored altogether. Much can be learned about the customers of a business, their current needs, and their buying preferences just by taking a cross-section of them out to lunch over a defined period of time, design-

Table 5.11
Consumers Aged 65 to 74

The number of these active retirees will drop slightly during the 1990s but they will be setting trends of the future.

The number of 65-to-74-year-olds will shrink during the 1990s along with the number of households they head.

■ Between 1990 and 2000, the number of people aged 65 to 74 will decline about 1 percent, dropping them from 7.2 percent of the American population to 6.5 percent.

■ The number of households headed by members of this age group will dwindle by about 1 percent during the 1990s.

■ Families are the rule among 65-to-74-year-olds—60 percent of the households they head are families and over half of them are married couples.

■ The three million women who live alone account for almost 75 percent of nonfamily households in this age group.

■ Although most of their peers are retired, 16 percent of men and 7 percent of women are still in the work force when they are aged 65 and older. Their labor force participation is expected to decline during the 1990s.

■ The median household income of households headed by 65-to-74-year-olds is $16,900. Married couples have a median income of $22,900 and dual-earner married couples come out on top with a median income of $37,200.

■ Households headed by a 65-to-74-year-old devote a larger chunk of their spending dollar to food, health care, personal care, and contributions than the average household.

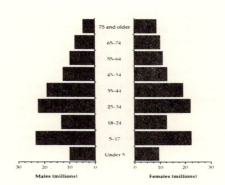

1990

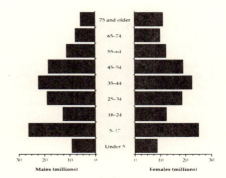

2000

ing a simple survey that can be filled out either in the store or sent out in the mail, or calling customers and asking them survey questions over the phone.

Speaking with customers one-on-one and asking them simple questions about why they shop your store, what you stock that they like, what they would like but cannot buy in your store, what they like about your competitors, what makes them feel uncomfortable about your store, and maybe a question or two about media preferences, can garner a wealth of information.

The importance of doing *at least* this much cannot be overstated. Besides helping identify exactly who the customer is in order to make better media buys, a businessperson conducting such informal research can keep abreast of subtle changes in market demographics that may be occurring but would not be noticed

Table 5.12
Consumers Aged 75 and Older

Although consumers aged 75 and older are beginning to slow down, they are the second-fastest growing market.

The number of elderly Americans will be on the rise during the 1990s along with the number of households they head.

■ Between 1990 and 2000 the number of Americans aged 75 and older will jump up 27 percent.

■ Between 1990 and 2000 the number of households headed by people aged 75 and older will increase by 240,200 each year, for an overall growth of 28 percent.

■ Of the nation's eight million households headed by someone aged 75 and older, only 33 percent are married couples and a full 57 percent are nonfamilies. Nearly all—97 percent—nonfamily elderly householders live alone, and 80 percent of those who live alone are women.

■ Only 9 percent of elderly Americans completed four or more years of college and most of them (58 percent) did not finish high school.

■ Fully three-quarters of households headed by someone aged 75 and older have household incomes of less than $20,000.

■ Elderly married couples have the lowest median household income of all married couples—$17,100—with only one in twelve bringing in $50,000 or more.

■ Food, housing, and personal care take a bigger chunk from the budgets of elderly households than from households in general. Compared with the other age groups, a large share of their spending dollar—15 percent—goes to health care.

■ The elderly market will be an estimated 28 billion dollars larger in 2000 than in 1990.

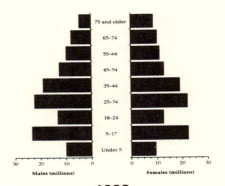

1990

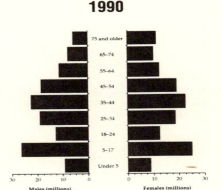

2000

without such research. By responding to these changes, businesses can hold on to customers that they already have and attract new ones that may have taken their business elsewhere.

A business, however, need not stop at this point. Understanding market segmentation and how to reach a more defined group of potential customers by advertising to them with the least amount of waste can be carried to further and even more interesting heights.

MARKET SEGMENTATION

Getting the right message to the right person in the most effective and cost-efficient manner possible, an operational goal of all advertising efforts, means developing marketing strategies that will appeal to the various segments within a defined marketplace. It has been established that consumers are motivated by behavior that is more or less consistent with their cultural heritage and personal value system, these behaviors having been learned and reinforced formally and informally through the repetitive nature of the learning process.

Manufacturers understand these differences and target their products, not to individuals, but to market segments. The way in which our society has developed, for example, has necessitated the use of automobiles by all except for those few who live in a densely populated urban area like New York City. Most of us need our own transportation, but we do not need or want the same vehicle. Each automobile— from the specialized and expensive Corvette to the inexpensive and practical Dodge Shadow—is designed, promoted, and advertised with a certain market segment in mind.

Think of all the products that you buy on a weekly or monthly basis—from over the counter medicines and hygienic products to soft drinks and cereals. Each of these products is positioned to appeal to either a youth, adult, or mature adult market with promotion and marketing efforts to match. Certainly, a middle-aged shopper does not buy a box of Fruit Loops for personal consumption (well, maybe just a handful!) no more than an adolescent would buy a high fiber cereal.

This difference in market segmentation becomes obvious after just one viewing of the commercials bringing your kids the Saturday morning cartoons and the sponsors of the network evening newscasts. The mature audience of news programs can be identified by the types of consumer sponsors, from laxatives and denture products to family vehicles and vans. In the same vein, the galaxy of games, dolls, and toys (not to mention the number of McDonald's commercials) identifies the youth market for the Saturday morning cartoons.

Benefit Segmentation

Since the late 1960s the concept of "benefit segmentation" has been employed for every conceivable product category, from beverages to computers. Russell Haley contended that the marketplace was driven by consumer needs, not necessarily by demographic profiles (factual characteristics) or even psychographic needs (consumer variables such as interests, activities, opinions, or lifestyles).

This consumer need or benefit segmentation seemed to make a great deal of sense as consumers with similar demographic makeups might purchase the same product for entirely different reasons. Studying buyers of toothpaste, Haley found that some consumers were motivated to buy the product in order to prevent tooth decay, others wanted sweeter breath or whiter teeth, and still others were only concerned about the price.

By utilizing these benefit segments as the principal driver, Haley could then incorporate demographic or psychographic data to more specifically define market segments. For example, he concluded that "decay prevention" was important to large families and that "whiter teeth" or "sweet breath" was important to to-

Table 5.13
Future Expenditures, 1990 and 2000

(projected aggregate expenditures in 1990 for all households and for households by age of householder, in billions of dollars)

	all households	**1990 aggregate annual expenditures in billions**						
		under 25	25-34	35-44	45-54	55-64	65-74	75+
Number of households (in thousands)	**94,227**	**4,663**	**21,183**	**21,245**	**14,429**	**12,311**	**11,672**	**8,724**
Total expenditures (in billions of dollars)	**2,203.1**	**64.2**	**476.6**	**628.6**	**441.2**	**292.8**	**197.2**	**102.5**
Food	**330.8**	**9.4**	**70.3**	**93.7**	**64.1**	**43.9**	**32.3**	**17.2**
Food at home	225.1	5.9	44.8	64.9	41.8	30.9	23.0	13.7
Food away from home	101.5	3.6	21.2	28.8	22.2	13.0	9.3	3.5
Alcoholic beverages	**25.4**	**1.6**	**7.5**	**6.4**	**4.7**	**3.0**	**1.8**	**0.6**
Housing	**667.6**	**19.2**	**158.3**	**193.5**	**121.9**	**80.8**	**58.3**	**35.6**
Shelter	385.6	12.4	97.2	115.7	71.7	42.4	28.8	17.5
Owned dwellings	229.7	1.8	50.3	75.8	46.9	28.2	17.9	8.7
Mortgage interest and charges	142.8	1.3	39.3	54.8	29.5	13.0	4.2	0.7
Property taxes	41.4	0.2	4.8	9.7	8.8	7.7	6.5	3.7
Maintenance, repairs, insurance, and other expenses	45.4	0.4	6.3	11.3	8.6	7.4	7.1	4.3
Rented dwellings	115.2	9.5	41.6	27.6	13.1	8.4	7.2	7.6
Other lodging	40.8	1.0	5.2	12.2	11.6	5.8	3.7	1.2

126

Fuels, utilities, and public services	160.0	3.7	32.0	41.2	29.6	23.2	18.6	11.8
Natural gas	24.3	0.4	4.6	5.9	4.4	3.8	3.1	2.1
Electricity	65.7	1.4	13.0	17.6	12.3	9.4	7.4	4.5
Fuel oil and other fuels	10.5	0.1	1.6	2.2	1.6	1.8	1.8	1.4
Telephone	45.2	1.6	10.3	11.6	8.4	5.9	4.7	2.8
Water and other public services	14.3	0.2	2.5	3.8	2.9	2.2	1.7	1.1
Household operations	34.2	0.7	9.6	10.2	3.8	3.7	2.9	3.3
Domestic services	27.9	0.6	8.5	8.4	2.6	2.7	2.1	2.9
Other household expenses	6.4	0.1	1.2	1.8	1.2	0.9	0.8	0.4
Household furnishings, equipment	87.8	2.4	19.5	26.5	16.8	11.6	8.0	3.0
Household textiles	8.2	0.2	1.4	2.6	1.5	1.2	0.9	0.4
Furniture	29.4	0.9	7.5	9.2	5.1	3.3	2.7	0.7
Floor coverings	5.1	0.1	0.7	1.9	0.9	0.7	0.6	0.2
Major appliances	14.9	0.5	3.2	3.5	3.0	2.4	1.6	0.7
Small appliances, misc. housewares	5.3	0.2	0.9	1.5	1.2	0.8	0.5	0.2
Miscellaneous household equipment	24.9	0.6	5.8	7.7	5.2	3.1	1.7	0.8
Apparel	**111.0**	**4.1**	**24.6**	**33.7**	**22.8**	**13.8**	**8.3**	**3.6**
Men and boys	27.5	1.0	6.0	8.9	6.0	3.3	1.7	0.7
Men, 16 and over	21.9	0.9	4.7	6.1	5.1	2.9	1.5	0.6
Boys, 2 to 15	5.6	0.1	1.3	2.7	0.9	0.4	0.2	0.1

Table 5.13 (continued)

(projected aggregate expenditures in 1990 for all households and for households by age of householder, in billions of dollars)

	1990 aggregate annual expenditures in billions							
	all households	under 25	25-34	35-44	45-54	55-64	65-74	75+
Women and girls	44.9	1.4	8.6	13.6	9.7	5.9	4.0	1.8
Women, 16 and over	38.2	1.3	7.0	10.1	8.7	5.5	3.8	1.8
Girls, 2 to 15	6.7	0.1	1.6	3.4	1.0	0.4	0.2	0.0
Children under 2	4.1	0.3	1.7	1.0	0.5	0.4	0.1	0.1
Footwear	11.9	0.4	2.5	3.8	2.4	1.5	1.0	0.4
Other apparel products and services	22.5	1.0	5.8	6.5	4.3	2.8	1.5	0.6
Transportation	464.9	15.6	107.0	130.7	98.7	61.1	37.7	14.2
Cars and trucks, new (net outlay)	137.8	3.5	31.7	39.9	29.7	18.0	11.1	3.9
Cars and trucks, used (net outlay)	85.4	4.0	22.3	23.5	18.9	9.8	5.2	1.7
Other vehicles	2.6	0.3	0.7	0.8	0.5	0.1	0.1	0.1
Vehicle finance charges	26.2	0.8	6.8	8.0	5.7	3.2	1.4	0.3
Gasoline and motor oil	88.2	3.1	19.5	24.3	17.6	12.5	8.0	3.2
Maintenance and repairs	44.2	1.5	9.4	11.8	9.1	6.3	4.4	1.7
Vehicle insurance	40.7	1.2	8.2	11.0	8.7	6.0	3.7	1.9
Public transportation	24.1	0.7	4.8	6.4	5.4	3.1	2.7	1.0
Vehicle rental, licenses, other charges	15.9	0.5	3.6	5.1	3.1	2.0	1.3	0.4

Health care	103.7	1.6	14.5	21.4	16.9	16.0	17.9	15.4
Health insurance	36.3	0.5	4.9	6.6	5.7	5.5	7.4	5.7
Medical services	49.0	0.8	7.8	11.6	7.9	7.4	6.9	6.7
Medicines and medical supplies	18.4	0.3	1.9	3.1	3.3	3.2	3.6	3.0
Entertainment	106.0	3.1	23.3	35.2	20.6	13.0	8.0	2.6
Fees and admissions	30.0	1.0	5.8	9.6	6.2	3.8	2.8	0.9
Television, radios, sound equipment	36.1	1.3	8.2	11.2	7.3	4.2	2.6	1.3
Other equipment and services	39.9	0.9	9.3	14.4	7.1	5.1	2.6	0.5
Personal care	20.1	0.6	3.7	5.2	3.8	3.1	2.3	1.3
Reading	13.6	0.3	2.6	3.8	2.6	1.9	1.6	0.8
Education	27.6	2.7	3.9	8.3	8.8	2.9	0.8	0.1
Tobacco and smoking supplies	22.0	0.8	4.9	5.8	4.5	3.3	2.0	0.7
Miscellaneous	31.5	0.6	6.5	8.1	5.9	4.5	3.6	2.3
Contributions and support payments	74.2	0.7	7.3	17.7	17.4	12.9	12.5	5.7
Personal insurance and pensions	208.9	3.9	46.4	65.2	48.5	32.6	10.0	2.3
Life insurance and other personal insurance	28.9	0.3	4.7	7.8	6.4	5.0	3.7	1.0
Retirement, pensions, Social Security	179.9	3.6	41.7	57.3	42.1	27.7	6.3	1.3

Source: The 1986 Consumer Expenditure Survey. Bureau of Labor Statistics and Projections of the Number of Households and Families:1986 to 2000. Bureau of the Census, Series P-25, No. 986

Note: Aggregate expenditures are the sum of the total expenditures of all households in the nation or of all households in an age group. Projections are based on the average annual expenditures in 1986 and have not been adjusted for inflation. Projections show how total annual expenditures would change as the number of households in the age group changes during the 1990s. All other factors such as price and expenditure pattern are held constant and are not accounted for in these projections.

Table 5.13 (continued)

(projected aggregate expenditures in 2000 for all households and for households by age of householder, in billions of dollars)

	all households	under 25	25-34	35-44	45-54	55-64	65-74	75+
2000 aggregate annual expenditures in billions								
Number of households (in thousands)	105,933	4,442	18,004	25,339	21,603	13,903	11,516	11,126
Total expenditures (in billions of dollars)	2,532.4	61.1	405.1	749.7	660.6	330.6	194.6	130.7
Food	379.7	9.0	59.7	111.7	95.9	49.5	31.9	22.0
Food at home	258.9	5.6	38.1	77.4	62.6	34.9	22.7	17.5
Food away from home	117.2	3.4	18.0	34.3	33.2	14.7	9.1	4.5
Alcoholic Beverages	28.3	1.5	6.4	7.6	7.0	3.4	1.7	0.7
Housing	760.3	18.3	134.5	230.8	182.5	91.3	57.5	45.3
Shelter	438.2	11.8	82.6	137.9	107.3	47.9	28.4	22.3
Owned dwellings	265.8	1.7	42.8	90.4	70.3	31.9	17.6	11.1
Mortgage interest and charges	163.9	1.2	33.4	65.4	44.2	14.7	4.1	0.9
Property taxes	48.9	0.2	4.1	11.6	13.2	8.7	6.4	4.7
Maintenance, repairs, insurance, and other expenses	53.0	0.4	5.3	13.5	12.9	8.4	7.0	5.5
Rented dwellings	123.4	9.1	35.4	32.9	19.7	9.5	7.2	9.7
Other lodging	49.1	0.9	4.4	14.6	17.4	6.5	3.7	1.5

Fuels, utilities, and public services	183.6	3.5	27.2	49.1	44.3	26.2	18.3	15.0
Natural gas	27.9	0.4	3.9	7.0	6.6	4.3	3.1	2.7
Electricity	75.6	1.3	11.1	21.0	18.4	10.6	7.3	5.8
Fuel oil and other fuels	12.0	0.1	1.4	2.6	2.4	2.0	1.8	1.7
Telephone	51.4	1.5	8.7	13.8	12.6	6.7	4.6	3.5
Water and other public services	16.7	0.2	2.1	4.6	4.3	2.5	1.7	1.3
Household operations	38.0	0.7	8.2	12.2	5.7	4.1	2.9	4.2
Domestic services	30.6	0.5	7.2	10.1	3.9	3.1	2.1	3.7
Other household expenses	7.3	0.1	1.0	2.1	1.8	1.0	0.8	0.5
Household furnishings, equipment	100.5	2.3	16.6	31.6	25.2	13.1	7.9	3.8
Household textiles	9.5	0.2	1.2	3.1	2.3	1.4	0.9	0.5
Furniture	33.1	0.9	6.4	10.9	7.6	3.8	2.7	0.9
Floor coverings	6.0	0.1	0.6	2.3	1.3	0.8	0.6	0.3
Major appliances	17.0	0.4	2.7	4.2	4.4	2.7	1.6	0.9
Small appliances, misc. housewares	6.2	0.2	0.8	1.8	1.7	1.0	0.5	0.3
Miscellaneous household equipment	28.7	0.6	4.9	9.2	7.8	3.5	1.7	1.0
Apparel	**127.6**	**3.9**	**20.9**	**40.2**	**34.2**	**15.6**	**8.2**	**4.6**
Men and boys	31.8	0.9	5.1	10.6	8.9	3.7	1.6	0.9
Men, 16 and over	25.3	0.9	4.0	7.3	7.6	3.3	1.5	0.8
Boys, 2 to 15	6.5	0.1	1.1	3.3	1.4	0.4	0.2	0.1

Table 5.13 (continued)

(projected aggregate expenditures in 2000 for all households and for households by age of householder, in billions of dollars)

	2000 aggregate annual expenditures in billions							
	all households	under 25	25-34	35-44	45-54	55-64	65-74	75+
Women and girls	52.2	1.3	7.3	16.2	14.5	6.6	3.9	2.4
Women, 16 and over	44.6	1.3	6.0	12.1	13.0	6.2	3.7	2.3
Girls, 2 to 15	7.6	0.1	1.3	4.1	1.5	0.4	0.2	0.0
Children under 2	4.4	0.3	1.5	1.2	0.7	0.5	0.1	0.1
Footwear	13.7	0.4	2.1	4.5	3.6	1.6	0.9	0.5
Other apparel products and services	25.5	1.0	4.9	7.8	6.4	3.1	1.5	0.8
Transportation	**533.7**	**14.8**	**90.9**	**155.9**	**147.7**	**69.0**	**37.2**	**18.1**
Cars and trucks, new (net outlay)	158.6	3.3	27.0	47.5	44.5	20.4	10.9	5.0
Cars and trucks, used (net outlay)	97.5	3.8	19.0	28.1	28.3	11.1	5.1	2.1
Other vehicles	2.9	0.3	0.6	0.9	0.8	0.1	0.1	0.1
Vehicle finance charges	29.9	0.8	5.8	9.6	8.5	3.6	1.3	0.4
Gasoline and motor oil	101.0	2.9	16.5	29.0	26.3	14.2	7.9	4.1
Maintenance and repairs	50.7	1.4	8.0	14.1	13.7	7.1	4.4	2.2
Vehicle insurance	47.0	1.2	7.0	13.1	13.0	6.8	3.6	2.4
Public transportation	27.9	0.7	4.1	7.7	8.1	3.5	2.7	1.3
Vehicle rental, licenses, other charges	18.2	0.4	3.0	6.0	4.6	2.2	1.3	0.6

Health care	120.0	1.5	12.4	25.5	25.3	18.1	17.7	19.6
Health insurance	41.8	0.5	4.2	7.9	8.5	6.2	7.3	7.3
Medical services	56.7	0.8	6.6	13.8	11.8	8.3	6.8	8.5
Medicines and medical supplies	21.6	0.2	1.6	3.7	5.0	3.6	3.6	3.8
Entertainment	121.7	3.0	19.8	42.0	30.9	14.7	7.9	3.3
Fees and admissions	34.7	0.9	5.0	11.4	9.3	4.2	2.7	1.1
Television, radios, sound equipment	41.5	1.2	6.9	13.4	11.0	4.7	2.6	1.6
Other equipment and services	45.5	0.9	7.9	17.2	10.6	5.8	2.6	0.6
Personal care	23.1	0.5	3.2	6.2	5.7	3.5	2.3	1.7
Reading	15.7	0.3	2.2	4.5	3.9	2.2	1.6	1.0
Education	33.2	2.6	3.3	10.0	13.1	3.3	0.8	0.2
Tobacco and smoking supplies	25.2	0.8	4.2	6.9	6.8	3.7	2.0	0.9
Miscellaneous	36.2	0.6	5.5	9.7	8.9	5.0	3.5	2.9
Contributions and support payments	88.2	0.6	6.2	21.1	26.0	14.5	12.3	7.3
Personal insurance and pensions	243.2	3.7	39.4	77.7	72.7	36.8	9.9	2.9
Life insurance and other personal insurance	33.8	0.3	4.0	9.4	9.6	5.6	3.7	1.3
Retirement, pensions, Social Security	209.3	3.5	35.4	68.3	63.0	31.2	6.2	1.6

Source: The 1986 Consumer Expenditure Survey, Bureau of Labor Statistics and Projections of the Number of Households and Families:1986 to 2000, Bureau of the Census, Series P-25, No. 986.

Note: Aggregate expenditures are the sum of the total expenditures of all households in the nation or of all households in an age group. Projections are based on the average annual expenditures in 1986 and have not been adjusted for inflation. Projections show how total annual expenditures would change as the number of households in the age group changes during the 1990s. All other factors such as price and expenditure pattern are held constant and are not accounted for in these projections.

bacco users or single people. From this point, these market segments of larger families or single people can be broken down into even smaller segments based on purchase volume; the combination of all of the segmentation data can then present the marketer with information about how consumers are likely to act depending upon the following variables:[4]

age	lifestyles	product images
sex	values	corporate images
income	needs	brand images
social class	wants	education
attitudes	personality	race
interests	self-image	religion
opinions	media habits	decision variables
desired benefits	users versus nonusers	user social activities

From analyzing this data, it becomes clear that the most common factor among similar market segments is that they are not alike at all. People with similar characteristics buy the same product for entirely different reasons. Traditionally the most popular demographic, women aged 18 to 49, is far from a homogeneous segment as are other so-called market segments like the baby boomers or the elderly.

As Clancy and Schulman argue in *The Marketing Revolution,* "when a company looks at such a target, it is asking in effect, 'Are these groups—whether heavy users or light, taste-conscious people or price-conscious, or any other defining variable—different in terms of anything other than the variable that defined the group in the first place?' And the answer is often, no. Heavy users, for example, are rarely very similar in terms of anything other than their usage patterns and, perhaps, family size."[5]

Companies and advertisers need to understand that there are limits to market segmentation. Heavy users of any product may have only that one commonality, making them extremely difficult to define and reach. Women aged 18 to 34 or 18 to 49 have widely different cultural, environmental, educational, social, and economic backgrounds and will purchase similar products for diverse reasons difficult if not impossible to define. There will, of course, be some common consumer demographic characteristics but these similarities will account for only a small percentage of total purchases.

Advertisers interested in precisely defining a target market need to ask further questions concerning the most appropriate way to segment and define their market and, even more important, which target will likely produce the best return or be the most profitable. More people in a demographic grouping or heavier users in one market segment does not necessarily mean that is the segment or demographic that ought to be targeted in an advertising campaign using any media.

Targeting the Heavy User

A business, of course, should target the heavy user and many do — to the exclusion of all other potential prospects. Such strategy begs the question of whether there are other groups that would be more profitable for a business to target other than the heaviest user.

Assume that there are "x" number of annual potential dollars in a given market for any type of business. There are "hot" prospects or those in a high-involvement stage for any product or service. Likewise, there are "warm" prospects who are in a low-involvement stage, and those totally out of the market in a no-involvement stage.

First, no business is going to get 100 percent of the market. And since the percentage of those in the "now" market who are hot prospects is so low (2 percent), perhaps those who are in the warm or replacement stage ought to be looked at.

Since that figure is 8 percent, the warm market offers greater potential to the advertiser than does the "now" market or those consumers in the market who will definitely buy today. The hot prospect group has already made up their minds anyway, so advertising to them at this point is too late.

The group that needs to be targeted is the warm prospect group who will be in the market, depending on the product or service needed, within one to three months. Therefore, targeting the "now" buyers, who are probably the heaviest users, offers less profit potential than getting to those who will eminently need a product or service but have not fully decided on where to purchase that product or service.

Values and Lifestyles (VALS)

Probably since the initial person bartered the first crude stone ax for winter foodstores or an animal skin for ornamental beads, the question was likely asked, "Who else would be interested in what I have to offer or can provide?" So began the thought process of identifying consumer groups, broken down into their patterns of living and shopping according to attitudes, interests, and opinions. Each identified group or segment could then be considered logical prospects for the multitude of goods and services offered in the local, regional, or national marketplace.

This same question has since been posed by every merchant who has gone into business and by each media outlet that has attempted to identify and quantify its unique audience for those merchants searching for an advertising vehicle to carry their message to the right public.

Simply stated, when this first hypothetical question was posed, times were easier: fewer products, less competition, a seeming unlimited market spawned by pent-up post-World War II demand. Go into business, place an ad in the newspaper, and open the store to sell brands advertised coast to coast on network television shows like "I Love Lucy," "The Dinah Shore Show," or "The Jack Benny Show."

But something happened along the way as the Rolling Stones were informing the baby boomers that they could not get "no satisfaction" from a man coming on television to inform them "how white my shirt can be" and that you could not be a man unless you smoked "the same cigarette as me." The largest generation in history was resisting a national label. Not everyone in this demographic would go to Woodstock or San Francisco or buy a Janis Joplin record.

The boomers were maturing. They had disposable income, probably from their parents who wanted them to have more than they had grown up with during the Depression, and they were spending it on blue jeans, rock concerts, and stereo equipment to be sure, but also on education that would lead to affluence and the suburban homes, automobiles, and lifestyle they had rejected—until they could afford it.

The boomers were one generation, but they were not about to be labeled as homogeneous and they entered the workforce and began rearing families of their own. The workforce was not to be what their fathers saw, either. It was no mirror image of the 1950s or 1960s. It was kaleidoscopic in nature, revealing ethnic diversity and working women with each turn of the economic base.

More radio stations than ever before were catering to musical tastes that ranged from heavy metal to easy listening. Cable television had begun its coaxial march from coast to coast. In short, audiences were being pulled apart and fragmented, becoming harder to define than the "Leave It To Beaver" viewers of more homogeneous times. A standard tool was needed that would define, quantify, and delineate the psychographic characteristics of a diverse group of consumers so that better advertising decisions could be made at the local, regional, and national levels.

In 1978 SRI International introduced the VALS market research concept, based on original research from Arnold Mitchell. Since that time VALS has been the only generally accepted means for psychographic segmentation, making it important to advertisers who want a tool to better understand their market and for advertising agencies that provide segmentation data to their clients.

In 1990 VALS 2 was developed in response to the valid concerns of agencies that America had changed from a more single-dimension population to a multidimensional people, responding to a multiplicity of consumer choices in the marketplace and needing a more specific tool to predict consumer behavior. In a word, something new was needed to discover why Americans act as they do.

Essentially, SRI dropped values and lifestyles as the basis for its consumer segmentation and modernized its approach, feeling lifestyles as a predictor of purchasing choices had lost its effect with the aging of the baby boomers and the diverse nature of a population living in a global economy.

"The new VALS typology utilizes a broader psychographic profile, and initial reports are that it is easier to link to actual consumer buying behavior because the vast pool of attitudes that are measured by it are more constant over time and less subject to change than the lifestyles that dominated the earlier VALS typology."[6]

Figure 5.1
The *VALS™2* Consumer Segments

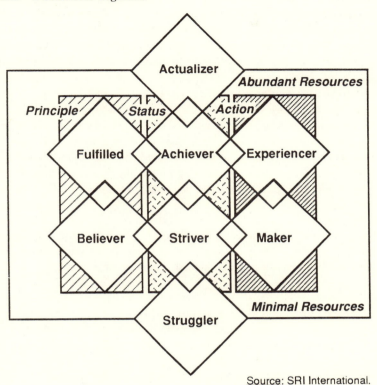

Source: SRI International.

Using broader psychographic profiles means more smaller segments in VALS 2, with the American population divided into eight consumer segments (see Figure 5.1). The driving concept behind this new approach is finding a correlation between opinions and behavior. Respondent opinions are given in answer to forty-three questions and these are correlated with actual consumer purchase and media behavior.

VALS 2 Psychographic Groupings

The VALS 2 eight psychographic groupings are stacked vertically according to resources (strugglers to actualizers) and horizontally according to self-orientation—consumers are either principle-oriented, status-oriented, or action-oriented. Each of these orientations has two segments: high resources and low resources.

Principle-oriented consumers are guided in their buying decisions by the way they feel the world could or should be. The well-educated and professional fulfilleds have high incomes, support social change, and are value-oriented when buying. The believers have more modest incomes, are more conservative, and (predictably) favor established American brands. Their lives are centered around the family, church, and community – traditional American values.

The status-oriented consumers care a great deal about what others think. Achievers are successful and very work-oriented, respecting authority (their bosses/any authority figure) and are politically conservative (status quo). They love to buy products that show off their financial success to families and neighbors.

The strivers have similar values but fewer resources and continually attempt to "keep up with the Joneses."

The action-oriented experiencers and makers are younger demographically and prefer more variety in their lives. Experiencers, usually single and with few responsibilities, are heavy consumers of fast food, new cars, music, sports bars, and nightclubs. The makers are more laid back and personally focused, unimpressed with material possessions and not as anxious to be "Joe Cool" as are the experiencers.

The strugglers obviously have the lowest incomes and are not of great interest to advertisers, who do not target to the lowest resource segment. Actualizers are of enormous interest as they basically can buy and do anything they want; they represent a wide range of upscale interests and activities.

Importance of VALS to Advertisers

This information is important to advertisers, as utilization of this approach will not only allow a business to better understand its own customers but to properly identify the appropriate radio station or television program listened to or viewed by audiences with similar profiles.

The transition has been from that broadbrush approach to one of micromanaging – identifying the differences in consumer segments and clusters region by region across the country. All populations today are indeed more heterogeneous than homogeneous.

What Advertisers Will Demand in the 1990s

Advertisers in the 1990s will be demanding more research from the radio and television stations that wish to serve them on a continuing basis. The new VALS 2 system is now on-line with the databases of several companies offering local and regional profiles of consumers based on what they term "neighborhood clusters." Stations with local databases can draw neighborhood audience profiles complete with psychographic and demographic characteristics. This information presented to an advertiser or potential advertiser would go a long way in molding the image of the electronic media as a professional, customer-oriented industry.

Advertisers who wish to profile their intended customers or radio or television stations that wish to profile their audiences to identify the various segments using the VALS 2 system can either enlist the services of an advertising agency for assistance or purchase an annual subscription to VALS and do the research themselves. SRI will analyze the data and assist with the tabulation of other marketing factors.

The agency route would be advantageous if their databases included the VALS 2 system on-line with the companies that offer the local or regional profiles: Donnelly Marketing Information Services, National Decisions Systems, Claritas, or CACI.

EFFECTIVE TARGET MARKETING

As Clancy and Schulman discuss, advertisers must first understand the distinction between prospects and customers. Prospects are consumers who have never bought a company's product or who have never done business in a particular store. They are either the warm prospects or the consumers out of the market completely who will be in the market at some undetermined point in the future.

Customers are those who have bought a particular product or have done business with a particular store—the logical prospects who have come into the business or tried the product at least once and will likely return again providing they were satisfied after the first or subsequent visits.

Customer Loyalty

Understanding these two groups is critical in the fight for brand loyalty, as even satisfied users must be continually reminded about their chosen brands or stores to offset competitor attempts to get them to switch allegiance. Loyalty is paramount to businesses such as car dealers, banks, insurance companies, restaurants, auto service centers, and upscale retailers where consumers will likely choose only one or two with which to do the majority of their business. Businesses must keep this segment loyal simply because it is easier to keep a satisfied customer than it is to find a new customer who is doing business elsewhere.

Encouraging to advertisers is the fact that in recent years brand loyalty has been steady, despite an 8 percent decline over seventeen years (see Figure 5.2). In commenting on this figure, Tod Johnson, president of the NPD Group, noted that where "manufacturers have not maintained share of advertising voice, brand equity has declined." Adding further insight into this figure from the NPD Group, loyalty fell to 95 from 100 for brands that did increase ad spending. This may be due to increased competition within brand category, however.

Brands that decreased ad expenditures witnessed a loyalty drop to 84, while brands that fluctuated their advertising spending or received little ad support dropped to 82.

That name recognition and market share are correlated was borne out by this study, which also found brands with the highest level of consumer-recognized promotion indexing at 91.

How Much Are Current Customers Worth?

Since most businesses spend a majority of their resources attempting to attract new customers rather than on satisfying and keeping current ones, managers ought to understand what a blunder this is. Tomorrow's profits will come from

Figure 5.2
Brand Loyalty

NPD Group, which has been charting consumer loyalty to 45 major brands since 1975, found that while loyalty has declined 8% in 17 years, it has remained steady for four years. For the 6 months ending June 19,1991, brand loyalty indexed at 92.

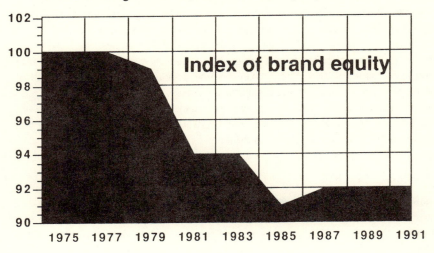

Source: NPD Group.

today's satisfied customers. New customers, of course, will be important but cannot sustain a business as can a base of loyal followers.

In the spring 1991 edition of *Marketing Science Institute Review,* Philip Kotler noted that current customers are worth five times the value of new customers. "Many markets have settled into maturity. There are not many new customers entering the product category and the costs of attracting new customers are rising and competition is increasing. In these markets it costs about five times as much to attract a new customer as to maintain the goodwill of an existing customer."

A business does not have to be perfect to retain its customers or to implement strategies designed to reduce customer defection. Products and service certainly need to be excellent, but as Clancy and Shulman point out, high levels of cost directed toward this effort may be overkill; beyond a certain point, profits will decline. "If bank customers, for example, will tolerate waiting in line for as long as five minutes, why add enough tellers to reduce the wait to 30 seconds? The cost will not bring another dollar into the bank. . . . Corporations should seek to find a financially optimal balance between customer needs and expectations and the firm's resources, capabilities and the associated costs of implementation."[7]

What's In A Name? Billions

This was a *USA Today* headline from the August 12, 1992 edition. The article, taken from information published in *Financial World* magazine, claimed that the most valuable asset many companies owned was their name. Marlboro, the most well-known brand of cigarette on earth, is worth $31 billion or about twice its annual revenues. The most valuable brands on the heels of Marlboro are: Coca-Cola, $24.4 billion; Budweiser, $10.1 billion; Pepsi-Cola, $9.6 billion; Nescafe instant coffee, $8.5 billion; Kellogg cereals, $8.4 billion; Winston cigarettes, $6.1 billion; Pampers disposable diapers, $6.1 billion; Camel cigarettes, $4.4 billion; and Campbell Soups, $3.9 billion.

It all ties together. Name recognition. Franchising of the mind. The better known the store or product, the higher the market share. Stores and products become known intrusively via the electronic media—through a message that is repeated over and over again to the point that it becomes a part of the subconscious memory base like the songs remembered from our earlier years.

Of the most valuable brands, perhaps Winston is the best example of a product whose brand and slogan were built by the intrusive nature of radio and television. Virtually everyone born prior to the mid-1950s can finish this singing jingle without hesitation: "Winston tastes good . . ."

Of course. "Like a cigarette should." However, virtually none of these people can tell you what Winston's current slogan is, even though untold billions have been spent on newspaper, magazine, and billboard advertising ever since cigarette advertising was taken off radio and television on January 1, 1970, by mandate of the federal government.

Their current slogan, in place for years, is short, easy to remember, and plastered coast to coast via the nonintrusive print media. But few people know, "Winston . . . America's Best."

Some Product Categories and Businesses
Will Not Have Loyal Customers

In the overall discussion of brand, store, and customer loyalty, such feelings seem to be less important to some store or product categories than others. Convenience stores, many fast food outlets, and multiple brand grocery items like paper towels, crackers, cookies, and snack items have less customer loyalty than other product or store categories.

Reasons for these types of categories never gaining a high percentage of loyal customers deal with consumers buying and accepting different brands and changing brands or stores with each purchase. These businesses or product categories will have to attract a higher volume of prospects since loyal customers are scarce.

Since these types of stores or product brands will be advertising to attract more prospects than loyal customers, it does not mean that each different product purchase cannot be made at the same store. This is a factor all-purpose merchants should keep in mind. Large-scale merchandisers and outlets like convenience stores or weakly positioned fast food outlets can position their store above the product and attract new prospects through outstanding service, friendly personnel, or other consumer buying variables.

The Role of Research in Market Segmentation/ Target Marketing

Once an advertiser or media planner has determined whether prospects, customers, or both are the critical marketing factor of the business and that the name of their product or store should be advertised within a given market to increase the value of said brand, consideration should be given to the hiring of a research firm that can conduct appropriate marketing research including consumer interviews, survey questionnaires, and the sampling of national trends. The end result of this endeavor is to isolate which target groups, from the thousands of possible consumer variable combinations, ought to be targeted via marketing and advertising efforts.

In other words, the question of how a business can identify and effectively reach that large consumer group in the warm market as well as those in a high-involvement state will be answered.

Such a comprehensive research approach will, of course, consume a time frame of several months and will be coupled with a corresponding budget that will be beyond the reach of all but the largest of businesses. But there are things moderate- and lower-budgeted businesses can do to identify the appropriate target market for their advertising and marketing efforts.

An Alternate Approach to Targeting the Right Market

In order to plan marketing and advertising efforts without committing the sins discussed at the beginning of the chapter, one must begin anew with an open and determined mind to approach advertising and marketing in a different light: to be creative and different, but not overly cute just to entertain the office staff; to meet the goals set for today but not fall into the trap of myopic thinking that abandons long-term planning; to identify multiple target groups and how best to reach them, not merely making the misguided assumption that "everybody" wants what the business offers or wants to come into the business ("everyone" could be a potential customer for stores like large discount chains where there exists no particular characteristics for such a large target market, but not everybody chooses to shop at any particular store); and, finally, to target the groups with the most profit potential by using advertising that can be identified as being successful.

Narrowing markets from available data to properly identify the consumer or retail group that a business ought to target is the focus of target marketing or advertising. A store or business is successful insofar as it is able to be accepted in the consumer marketplace, which means communicating the message of that business to the proper group of logical prospects. None of the results, of course, will guarantee or predict consumer behavior in an ever-changing market of available products and services, but all businesses can do more to quantify and verify their marketing and promotional efforts. The end result? More effective and results-oriented advertising.

How to Optimally Define Your Market Segment

Refining and targeting the specific market that exists for a particular business can be done either by the advertiser, a media planner at an advertising agency, or the advertiser with the help of computerized programs and possibly a market researcher from a local college or university.

Remember what needs to be accomplished here: the definition of exactly *who* the customer is. Many businesses think they know, but in reality it may be someone else; in that case, their target market is being missed. The following steps can serve as guidelines in helping to define the exact target market while answering the question, "Is my customer who I think he/she is?"

The suggested steps for helping define a customer or target market begin with the elementary and move toward the more complex. The first two steps deal with consumer research or the identification of exactly who shops and buys in the store, where they live, what and when they buy, how often they shop, how much they spend, and how they use the product purchased.

The third step deals with product or actual in-store opinion tabulations via focus groups or informal meetings with customers. The fourth step involves market analysis, while the fifth procedure involves a breakdown of the competitive situation within the marketplace.

First, a business must determine from how wide a geographic area shoppers come. This will assist in the proper media planning, that is, buying stations that cover the proper geographical area. This can be done by either tracking checks written to the store over the previous three years (or starting now!) and pinpointing hometowns on a wall map or, less precisely, by regularly surveying license plates in the parking lots. Home address and zip code information can also be gathered from personal checks. Again, identifying the actual customer is the goal, even when this information may be generally known.

Second, customer profiles can be drawn by asking each buyer to fill out a customer survey card, responding to questions like place of employment, family income range, types of purchases, frequency of visits, hours and days shopped, or other questions deemed appropriate by the business in this consumer research effort to identify the correct target market.

Third, research must be done on the specific product or products offered by the store or on the store itself if it offers a variety of products. This information will tell the retailer if the products or services offered are appealing to and in demand by who he/she thinks the target market is.

In other words, is there a match between the perceived or real target market and what the store or business offers? Adjustments to an ever-changing marketplace of consumer opinion are continually needed; what shoppers want today may be rejected tomorrow.

The research done on the product(s) or service(s) the business offers would review them in terms of price, quality, packaging, image, uses, and lifecycle.

The research done on the overall store itself in which the products or services are offered would survey perceived image, consumer likes and dislikes about any and all products and services offered, customer service, and virtually anything that would be of concern to the public from their point of view—not management's.

Focus groups of approximately eight to ten paid or volunteer recruits who are collectively interviewed by researchers to gather data for a particular business should be considered at this point to provide more concrete or empirical evidence about both the business and the product or services it offers. Such groups oftentimes yield very useful, spontaneous comments that researchers could never get with a more formal, written survey.

Such focus groups, however, have developed a reputation of being unreliable by offering nothing to management other than what management already decided they wanted to hear.

If groups are not moderated by a professional, answers to questions in these groups can be easily slanted, depending on how questions are asked. Moreover, a few people in each group tend to dominate and sway the opinions of others, thus sometimes making them unreliable as indicators of actual circumstances.

Clancy and Schulman recognize the problems presented with this research approach. "Focus groups are among the most preposterous approaches to message development. Yet companies love a good group, particularly if it's done in an interesting place. They take this approach all the time. While focus groups may be a place to start, unfortunately it's where many companies end as well. The unquantifiable, unstable opinions of paid informants become the basis for message strategy."[8]

However, call them what you will, but Stew Leonard's Dairy in Norwalk, Connecticut, has these questions and more answered for them each Saturday morning when management meets with customer groups who tell them what they like and dislike about the grocery operation. Management listens—and then responds. It is that simple.

And management knows exactly who these people are as they volunteer for this "duty" in droves simply because they know management will listen and respond immediately, not tomorrow. Stew has a large suggestion box in his business that is filled to capacity daily; each suggestion is typed into a master list and circulated to every employee by 11:00 the next morning. When a business knows its customers personally like this, it is much easier to identify the market that ought to be targeted.

It may be best not to totally disregard focus groups, however, as many researchers have good success with them. If a business does elect to go this route, care should be taken to make sure the group is moderated by a professional; this provides a needed, objective leader who will hear what needs to be heard. If such a group is moderated by the general manager or the advertising planner, that person is sure to hear only what he or she wants to hear and the group will be a waste of time.

Fourth, the market analysis phase involves analyzing the data collected from the first three steps. Who is the customer? Is that person who the business thought he or she was? Where are these customers? What are the demographics of this customer group? How do they use our store, our products, or our services? How profitable is this group to our business? Are they the really "hot" prospects for our business or the "warm" prospects? Are there other groups in which potential profit lies? What do these respondents tell us from our informal (focus groups) meetings? How best can we continually change and respond to meeting the needs of this group so we can attract more of them?

Market analysis would be incomplete if this identified customer profile were not then matched to a specific radio station format or formats or to particular television programs in the market that cater to this identified group, provided television is a significant player. Print, of course, can be used to achieve marketing objectives but as a nonintrusive medium, should be used to supplement an aggressive electronic media campaign that is working to franchise the minds of the identified group in an attempt to make them loyal customers for life.

The final step involves an analysis of the competitive situation within the market. What is their market share compared to yours? How similar is their customer profile? How do they advertise? What media do they use? What are their advantages or disadvantages compared to yours? Is their location preferable? Go into the business and find out first-hand about their customer service, pricing, and other variables that can tell you how you stack up competitively.

The competition may be doing a lot of things wrong, but what they are doing right should be acknowledged. In fact, hope that they are spending thousands in the newspaper as their main source of advertising so you can then use the electronic media to overwhelm them in the marketplace!

A Final Word on Research

It was earlier mentioned that a local market researcher from a nearby college or university might help in providing more statistical correlations in the marketing effort. If no one is available for personal assistance, ask the university librarian for a short psychographic test that could be given over the telephone or to selected customers in the store. In this way, any business can begin to develop a customer profile that would certainly be of local use.

As Clancy and Schulman recommend, if a local resource person such as a professor or librarian is available, begin with the individual respondent and the potential profitability of that person in relation to the forecasted dollar revenue of the business. The goal of an outside resource is having someone who can use a computer to provide a description of the "optimal" target by searching through the billions of possible choices available from the combination of the many consumer variables previously noted.

Have the researcher feed the profit potential estimates into a nonlinear math model that is programmed to simultaneously determine volume potential, media exposure, cost, positioning, and other variables. The computer must be linked to a larger database such as the Simmons Market Research Bureau (SMRB) or Mediamark Research (MRI) that can draw upon data already available for the entire industry.

Both companies collect massive amounts of data from ongoing consumer surveys about brand usage and media consumption. These syndicated data are then sold to subscribers and provide solid consumer-based information about various market segments. The information, however, is available only to those who subscribe or pay for the desired information.

If such resources are available, information will then need to be provided to the researcher on the maximum dollars feasible for an advertising budget, the potential size of a particular product category in units and dollars, the minimum size of the target or media group desired, and some information on the costs of the local media and any available ratings figures.

A target group can then be identified that will represent a large percentage of all prospects. This will be the target group or the "optimal" group that will produce a better return on advertising investment than any other group.

The program can also show the GRPs possible from using various media, but remember not to buy using gross ratings points as a base criterion, as they represent a one-dimensional measure that may be good for buying television but not radio. In radio, GRPs give no information on the most important criteria of all—cume or unduplicated audience and the total time each listener spends listening. The important factor here is effective reach.

DEMOGRAPHIC AND GEOGRAPHIC VARIABLES

To be consistent with what most marketing and advertising planners are most familiar with, demographic and geographic variables as well as market segmentation strategies need to be discussed in more detail to assist businesses in the overall positioning process.

Market segments are traditionally broken down into categories reflective of identifiable demographic and geographic characteristics such as sex, age, income, and region of the country. Such distinctions are important to advertisers as motivations to buy are different depending on these demographic or geographic variables. "Demographic variables have long been the most popular basis for distinguishing significant groupings in the marketplace. One reason is that consumer wants or usage rates are often highly associated with demographic variables; another is that demographic variables are easier to measure than most other types of variables."[9] Table 5.14 lists the major demographic variables used in segmenting consumer markets.

Table 5.14

Major Segmentation Variables and Their Typical Breakdowns

Variables	Typical Breakdowns
Geographic	
Region	Pacific, Mountain, West North Central, West South Central, East North Central, East South Central, South Atlantic, Middle Atlantic, New England
County size	A, B, C, D
City or Standard Metropoliton Service Area (SMSA) Population	Under 5,000; 5,000-19,999; 20,000-499,999; 50,000-99,999; 100,000-249,999; 250,000-49,999; 500,000-999,999; 1,000,000-3,999,999; 4,000,000 or over
Density	Urban, suburban, rural
Climate	Northern, southern
Demographic	
Age	Under 6, 6-11, 12-17,18-34, 35-49, 50-64, 65+
Sex	Male, female
Family size	1-2, 3-4, 5+
Family life cycle	Young, single; young, married, no children; young, married, youngest child under six; young, married, youngest child six or over; older married, with children; older, married, with no children under 18; older, single; other
Income	Under $10,000; $10,000-$25,000; $25,000-$50,000; over $50,000
Occupation	Professional and technical; managers, officials and proprietors; clerical, sales; craftsmen, foremen; operatives; farmers; retired; students; housewives; unemployed
Education	Grade school or less; some high school; graduated high school; some college; graduated college; advanced degree
Religion	Catholic, Protestant, Jewish, other
Race	White, Black, Oriental, Hispanic
Nationality	American, British, French, German, Eastern European, Scandinavian, Italian, Latin American, Middle Eastern, Japanese, African
Social class	Lower-class, upper-lower, lower-middle, middle-middle, upper-middle, lower-upper, upper-upper
Psychographic	
Life-style	Swinger, status seeker, family oriented, plain Joe
Personality	Compulsive, gregarious, authoritarian, ambitious
Benefits sought	Economy, convenience, prestige
User status	Nonuser, ex-user, potential user, first-time user, regular user
Usage rate	Light user, medium user, heavy user
Loyalty status	None; medium; strong; absolute
Readiness stage	Unaware, aware, informed, interested, desirous, intending to buy
Marketing-factor sensitivity	Quality, price, service, advertising, sales promotion

Source: From information in Philip Kotler's Marketing Management
(Englewood Cliffs, N.J.: Prentice-Hall, 1976), p. 146.

These variables, however, are not etched in stone as the desires and needs of consumers change as they mature from the more carefree teenage years, to the responsibilities of adulthood, to the desired security offered during the retirement years. However, not everyone matriculates through life in the same way. For example, America currently has 41 million never-marrieds. And those who marry do it later; the median age of women who marry is now 24.2 years, men 26.3 years.

Knowing demographically and geographically exactly who your target market is and how they can be most effectively reached can help advertisers and marketers maximize ad dollars with a minimal amount of waste. Most businesses need only concern themselves with the region in which they do business and they will know the characteristics of shoppers within that region. Consumers in New Mexico, for example, will have somewhat different tastes in food and clothing due to the influence of native American and Hispanic culture than consumers in Boston, who are influenced by traditional European values and a centuries-old fishing industry.

Geographic Variables—The South versus the West

Many demographers would certainly agree that there exist important geographic differences in values and lifestyles among the populace of the four regions of the United States. For example, generalized differences exist between the West and the South, while each region has its own idiosyncrasies.

Westerners seem to regard self-respect as less important and being a "maverick" as highly important. In the West, the individual is king. Drinking imported beer is important to Easterners who tend to be somewhat "elite." Southerners value family relationships, stress religious values, and are defiantly independent in buying habits and the stressing of personal accomplishment. Retailers understanding such general conclusions could offer wider selections in the Dixie states and tie advertising copy to the value of personal accomplishment ("You've worked hard, you deserve this.").

Such geographic information can assist advertisers and planners in tying product benefits to consumers' personal values and what is meaningful to them. To illustrate, since Westerners place less weight on core values than do Southerners, advertising in the Southern states might do better in emphasizing value fulfillment, whereas a media schedule in the West might be more successful if the emphasis is placed on the benefits derived from owning or consuming a product.

Many behaviors, however, are homogeneous. It seems that all of us view security, fun, and enjoyment no differently; therefore, advertising that ties into these values need not be given any special attention other than that of creativity to catch the attention of the intended target audience.

As an aside, many researchers believe that no other region of the country studies itself as much as does the South. Witness the many books still published each year on the Civil War, most of them by Southern writers.

Southerners are described as having a "dual identity." They are Southerners first and Americans second. Rebel flags abound from backyards to state capitols; country music and Richard Petty are as traditional as Jack Daniels or Kentucky Bourbon; hot, humid nights will forever be a part of Southern summers. This though, is the traditional South. Atlanta, arguably the capital of the New South, is as metropolitan as any American city and has developed a homogeneity thrust upon it by Northern migration. Still, it is uniquely Southern by tradition if not by modern-day appearance.

Businesses that operate in the Southern states are no doubt quick to understand this very distinct regionalism that is different from the more wandering and independent ways of "Western folk" and can adapt advertising copy accordingly.

This is not to say there is not "Texas loyalty," or a sense of identity and attachment to Vermont for native New Englanders, or even a sense that Floridians have about not being a part of the "South" as much as they are a paradise retreat apart from the concerns of other regions of the country, but only that the South seems more introspective.

Age, Sex, Education, and Income

Perhaps the most useful discussion, however, would center around the more readily identifiable demographic characteristics of age, sex, education, and income. Most retailers have these characteristics in mind when they promote and advertise their businesses, although such data that can be used to construct consumer profiles are not always accurate in a constantly changing economic climate that has recently witnessed the emergence of the working woman and the influx of minorities into a workplace once dominated by the white American male. Figure 5.3 shows the labor force growth by race or ethnic origin up to the year 2000.[10]

The United States is currently the fourth largest Spanish-speaking country in the world, making ethnic, cultural, and racial realities a part of today's advertising in many markets.

Market Segmentation by Age

The importance of the under 12 market, as well as the increasingly important teenage market, is not lost on advertisers. Young children can certainly influence the decision-making process of parents as exemplified by the advertising of McDonald's, the various toy manufacturers, and the major breakfast cereal companies like Kellogg's and General Mills. The most effective and least expensive way to target this influential market is by using the electronic media, as young adults usually do not rely on the newspaper for news, information, or entertainment.

Young people also have access to a great deal of spendable income. Table 5.15 shows that the 32 million American children aged 4 to 12 have a combined annual income of $8.6 billion. The chart from Texas A & M University shows where they obtain this money. By the year 2000, there will be more than 15 mil-

Figure 5.3
Labor Force Growth by Race or Ethnic Origin

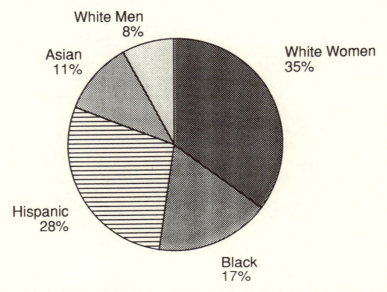

Percent of growth each group will account for 1986 - 2000.

Source: Bureau of Labor Statistics, in Small Business in the Year 2000,
cited in Future Vision, ed. Eric Miller (Naperville, Ill.: Sourcebooks Trade, 1991), p. 227.

Table 5.15
Annual Income of Children Aged 4 to 12

Source	earnings (in millions)
Allowances	$4,580
Household tasks	1,296
Parental gifts	1,296
Work outside of home	1,037
Gifts from others	432
Total	**8,641**

Source: James McNeal, Texas A&M University, as cited in *Future Vision*,
ed. Eric Miller (Naperville, Ill.: Sourcebooks Trade, 1991), p. 98.

lion 14- to 17-year-olds. Teenagers currently receive a mean allowance of $64.20 per week, which will undoubtedly increase by the end of the century (Table 5.16).[11]

As the baby boomers continue to gray (the lead pack is now approaching age 50), marketing to senior citizens becomes more important to many companies

Table 5.16
Mean Amount of Money Received per Week by Age Group

age group	amount of money
12 - 15	$ 24.00
16 - 17	61.70
18 - 19	134.80
Average	**$ 64.20**

How teens get their money

	male	female
Full-time job	13.2 %	11.9 %
Part-time job	33.3 %	30.0 %
Odd jobs	37.9 %	38.6 %
Regular allowance	27.8 %	27.3 %
Obtain money from parents when needed	37.5 %	48.4 %

Source: Teenage Research Unlimited, cited in *Future Vision*, ed. Eric Miller (Naperville, Ill.: Sourcebooks Trade, 1991), p. 98.

and businesses. The median household income for 55- to 64-year-olds will be $27,020 by 1995, with the number of households exceeding $50,000 increasing by 7 percent.[12]

Market Segmentation by Sex

Many consumer products and services are obviously intended for either the male or female buyer, but with the emergence of the working woman (65 percent of women with children under 18 are now in the workforce), many businesses that traditionally targeted only the male shopper will need to change their focus and then decide how best to reach a mobile, working female consumer. Examples of these types of businesses would be car dealers, automobile service centers, tire stores, professional services, and electronics stores.

This change in America's workforce also means that more men will be doing the shopping, going to the dry cleaners, dealing with diaper services and cleaning services, and more or less engaging in what was once considered "women's work." Advertisers, take note!

Market Segmentation by Education and Income

Education, closely aligned with occupation and income, is of interest to advertisers who wish to target the high-end or upscale market. This seems to be important, as highly educated consumers such as college professors may be in the market for entirely different products and services than nondegree union workers or laborers who may earn as much if not more than educators.

With college enrollment increasing nearly 4 percent, a lower high school dropout rate, and an increasing emphasis on continuing education and job training in the workforce, workers are becoming more discriminating in their tastes and attitudes. Targeting these people with the right message becomes even more important as we enter the twenty-first century with more consumer choices than ever before.

Household income is important in the demographic picture quite simply because it dictates what products and services a family can afford. Naturally, the higher the price the more selective the demographic becomes.

Advertisers who become frustrated at slow days should understand that if people have money, they will likely spend it. Annual household expenditures are on the rise, partly due to dual-income families, which may also be a reason why the largest increase has been in vehicle purchases (Table 5.17).

Other Demographic Variables

Although the concept of target demographics and market segmentation implies that an advertiser or marketer direct the advertising message to the heavy user of a product or service, John J. Burnett warns us that this is not always the proper strategy, as was earlier discussed. "Many companies have allocated most of their resources to attract the heavy user; ultimately, the competing campaigns cancel one another out."[13] He suggests finding alternate characteristics that correlate with usage rates: purchase occasion, user status, consumer loyalty, and stage of readiness.

Purchase occasion refers to the advertiser or media planner determining the reason for the purchase. This would make a difference in how the copy was prepared for the demographic and how receptive they may be to such copy.

User status refers to the differing communication strategies that would be used if the copy were directed to product or service nonusers, ex-users, one-time users, or regular users. Exactly whom the message is attempting to reach should be defined before the copy is written to appeal to nobody in particular.

The third subcriterion of *loyalty* references the brand-loyal customer, the exact number being very difficult to determine and "loyalty" being a challenging word to quantify. Many stores and products certainly have their share of loyal customers, but copy should not assume that "everybody" has the same feelings toward a store, product, or service as would a loyal customer.

Burnette's final characteristic, *stage of readiness,* is patterned after the consumer behavior model that suggests potential consumers advance through several stages before becoming customers: unaware, aware, informed, interested, desirous, and intending to buy. Marketing and advertising strategies can be designed to move consumers through the various and appropriate stages, although the

Table 5.17
Annual Expenditures of All Consumer Units and Percent Changes, Consumer Expenditure (CE) Survey, 1987 to 1988

	1987	1988	% change in CE
Number of consumer units (households)	94,150	94,862	.8%
Item			
income before taxes	$27,326	$28,540	4.4%
income after taxes	$24,871	$26,149	5.1%
average number of persons in consumer unit	2.6	2.6	
average age of reference person	47	47	
Average number in consumer unit:			
earners	1.4	1.4	
vehicles	2	2	
children under 18	.7	.7	
persons 65+	.3	.3	

Long-term constant dollar growth rates for selected consumer expenditure categories 1988-1993

	1989	1990	1991	1992	1993
Total personal consumption expenditures	3.1%	2.2%	3.7%	3.8%	2.8%
Total durable goods	4.4%	2.8%	7.1%	6.2%	3.7%
motor vehicles/parts	4.7%	2.2%	8.1%	6.3%	3.3%
furniture/mattresses	2.2%	2.3%	4.7%	5.3%	3.2%
kitchen/household appliances	2.5%	1.9%	4.4%	5.0%	3.4%
china/glass/tableware	2.5%	2.0%	3.6%	4.8%	2.6%
radio/TV/records/music inst.	7.4%	6.2%	11.2%	8.1%	5.4%
jewelry	4.1%	1.8%	4.9%	5.4%	2.8%
wheel goods/toys/sports equip.	3.8%	2.8%	5.1%	6.2%	4.4%
Total nondurable goods	2.3%	1.7%	2.8%	2.8%	1.8%
food/beverages at home	1.2%	1.6%	1.8%	2.0%	1.3%
food/beverages in restaurants	3.3%	1.9%	3.5%	3.8%	2.9%
shoes/footwear	4.4%	2.6%	3.7%	4.3%	2.8%
women's clothing	4.9%	2.9%	4.8%	4.3%	3.1%
drugs/sundries	2.3%	2.0%	1.8%	1.6%	0.7%
non. dur. toys/sports sundries	3.9%	3.1%	5.2%	5.7%	3.5%
Total service expenditures	3.3%	2.4%	3.3%	3.8%	3.1%
medical care services	3.8%	3.4%	4.0%	4.6%	3.9%
personal business services	5.2%	3.3%	5.0%	5.8%	4.7%
recreational services	4.5%	3.7%	4.6%	5.3%	4.7%

Source: Economic Perspectives, cited in Future Vision, ed. Eric Miller
(Naperville, Ill.: Sourcebooks Trade, 1991), p. 78 and 80.

stages of readiness are vague and difficult to measure and can only provide general guidelines for copy preparation.

The obvious challenge for the advertiser is to properly identify the correct market segment and the corresponding strategy that will appeal to that segment. Consideration must be given to proper allocation of resources (advertising budget), overall marketing objectives, the current position of the store or product within the marketplace, and the potential return (profit) for the investment required.

Advertisers and planners should also remember that most businesses are divided into two or more "profit centers" or areas that generate revenues independently of one another. These centers may often appeal to different demographic segments. The profit centers that generate the highest revenue or offer the greatest revenue potential should be the areas advertised, not the least profitable that have the lowest customer count.

Determining how best to achieve success in advertising to various market segments may be easier to understand once more information is given on the numbers of potential consumers who are actually in the market at any given time for any product or service being advertised to any market segment and the number of daily advertisements and ad dollars chasing those potential customers.

SUMMARY

Consumers come in many sizes, shapes, colors, and age groups. Segmenting consumers into various blocks according to age, sex, income, geographic location, or other related variables is the science of demographics. The more a business know about customer demographics, the better it will be in minimizing advertising waste and maximizing sales and profits.

Marketing to these various population sectors in an efficient manner can be anything but exact, with many marketing and advertising decisions being made by businesses by knee-jerk instinct. Rather than using consumer-based research of any type, what guides the decision-making process is tradition—"that is the way we have always done it."

Showing businesses how to become efficient in target marketing was a main concern of this chapter. There are, however, drawbacks to segmentation, and advertising to the heavy user is not always the wise course of action as more profit potential may exist within the larger "warm" market. Defining optimum markets so the right segment can be targeted efficiently can be done, even within the smaller, local community of most advertisers.

Of prime importance to any advertiser is the loyal customer. This person can be worth up to five times more to a business than a new customer, who is both somewhat difficult as well as expensive to find. When loyal customers are found, even if some are alienated due to risky marketing decisions, as happened with Coca-Cola (discussed in the following chapter), they can be brought back into the fold with further repositioning and effective product advertising.

Efficient target marketing means understanding the difference between prospects and customers, a critical distinction in the fight for brand loyalty. Quite simply, it is far easier to keep a satisfied customer than it is to find a new customer who is currently doing business elsewhere and may be satisfied.

Name recognition and market share are strongly correlated: the more the business is known, the higher the market share. Name recognition is enhanced through effective target marketing and the franchising process, which occurs through intrusive repetition. Defining the proper market segment to "intrude" upon is a major step toward reducing advertising waste in the overall corporate planning effort.

NOTES

1. Robert E. Balon, *Radio in the 90's* (Washington, D.C.: National Association of Broadcasters, 1990), pp. 2, 4, 60.

2. Margaret K. Ambry, *1990–1991 Almanac of Consumer Markets* (Ithaca, N.Y.: American Demographics Press, 1989), pp. 39–355.

3. Karl Albrecht, *The Only Thing That Matters* (New York: HarperBusiness, 1992), pp. 66–67.

4. William G. Nickels, *Marketing Communication and Promotion* (New York: John Wiley and Sons, 1984), p. 341.

5. Kevin J. Clancy and Robert S. Shulman, *The Marketing Revolution* (New York: HarperBusiness, 1991), p. 64.

6. Balon, *Radio in the 90's,* p. 80.

7. Clancy and Shulman, *Marketing Revolution,* p. 240.

8. Ibid., p. 171.

9. Philip Kotler, *Marketing Management* (Englewood Cliffs, N.J.: Prentice-Hall, 1976), p. 145.

10. Eric Miller, ed., *Future Vision* (Naperville, Ill.: Sourcebooks Trade, 1991), p. 227.

11. Ibid., p. 98.

12. Ibid., p. 96.

13. John J. Burnette, *Promotion Management* (St. Paul: West, 1984), p. 163.

CHAPTER 6

The Surgical Strike
How to Target
with Creative Copy

> There have never been more media—new television networks and channels,
> video and film, record numbers of new magazines, newsletters, journals and
> newspapers—dedicated to delivering you the changing news of the day. . . .
> But . . . how much information are you absorbing? . . . The vast amount of
> data that comes your way each day will probably whiz right by you.
> —John Naisbitt and Patricia Aburdene,
> *Megatrends 2000*

"Surgical strike," as defined in the previous chapter, is an apt metaphor since, as
this chapter will show, the number of consumers in the market for any given
product or service on any given day is minute. Knowing how to effectively target
and attend to this small group within any defined market, along with the majority
of consumers who are not in the market and will therefore not be receptive to
advertising efforts, is crucial to reducing advertising waste. Targeting the right
group on the right station, however, is inefficient without the right copy. Creativity in this business is mandatory, not merely suggested procedure.

It is not enough to understand advertising, consumer behavior, the psychology
behind learning, and the market segments a business may wish to target. To effectively impress a message upon a defined group, a company must first have a
product or a brand that is or can be in demand once it is made known through
advertising. That advertising must then surgically strike at the heart of that defined group if the budget supporting it is not to be wasted.

Second, that business or product must have a name that is trusted by the public.
Remember, products or businesses make customers; advertising can only deliver
a logical prospect to the door of the business. However, once a business has a
product or a name that has been generally accepted by the public, advertising

reinforces the overall feeling of trust and confidence in that product or business. Such reinforcement helps keep customers loyal for years.

Trust and confidence are important ingredients in the marketing mix as consumers will enter a business such as a department or discount store, which they believe to be credible, to buy any number of retail goods. And consumers who have trust and loyalty in a product or a business will remain loyal, regardless of the turmoil that may surround that product or business.

Turmoil within the marketplace is indeed a reality. Products and entire businesses may need to change or reposition themselves to adapt to changing market conditions. This can be difficult. The temptation to refuse change is powerful. Changing from a predominantly print form of advertising to one based in the electronic media, for example, will not be done without a willingness to experience some risk.

MARKETING AND ADVERTISING AS RISK TAKING

The decision to reposition a business or a product—to change the way in which something has been done for decades or even generations—takes a fair amount of confidence in the future, coupled with the willingness to take that calculated risk today that will reap the expected rewards and profits in the future.

Managers today must plan for tomorrow's business by understanding that lifestyle changes in an era of the working woman and an increasingly mobile population mean that reaching these new consumers via the traditional print media will no longer be as effective as in past decades. Tomorrow's consumers can only be reached by changing marketing directions and advertising campaigns today from mostly print to mostly electronic media.

Risk, however, is not something traditionally conservative businesspeople like to entertain. As Daniel Kehrer points out, "rather than encourage the type of cautious experimentation that defines good management, many American companies have so far spent their greatest resources trying to *avoid* risk."[1]

He explains that even when businesses say they welcome change or innovation, they often still resist it: "There is a potent natural tendency toward caution in the face of uncertainty. This is the dividing point. It is the difference between *accepting* change when it happens to come along, and beating change to the punch by *creating* it, and thus maintaining greater control over it, yourself."[2]

The most often cited case study in recent marketing and business literature, including the writings of Kehrer, was the decision of one of the oldest and most conservative of America's corporations, Coca-Cola, to change the formula of the world's most successful soft drink to something called "New Coke." Some call it the worst marketing blunder of all time, others say Coke panicked in face of the highly successful "Pepsi Generation" advertising campaign that surpassed Coke in both consumer recall of its advertising and in the marketplace.

Actually, it was neither a marketing blunder nor a panicked reaction. But it did have a lot to do with the competition. Coke was willing to change, to take a risk.

And it paid off. If Coke is willing to change after one hundred years, any business in America can change its direction to take advantage of the new advertising realities.

Coca-Cola's advertising and product had dominated the American scene since the Depression era. Consumers' minds were franchised with the theme "The Pause That Refreshes" that began on radio in 1929 and with the idea that Coke was "The Real Thing," introduced in 1942 and again in 1969.

The boyish blond with the white fountain cap serving Coke and the Coke bottle itself were familiar American popular culture images. It was almost un-American to drink anything else. But, like any other successful product or business, Coke had its competition. Consumers were not drinking Coke to the exclusion of all other brands.

Many locally successful brands, like Duffy's of Denver, had their niches, but on the national scene Pepsi-Cola had begun an almost unnoticed marketing and advertising invasion targeted to the most influential and spendfree generation of all—the baby boomers. By the end of the 1980s Pepsi was indeed the drink of choice for this huge consumer group. After enjoying years of 10 percent to 15 percent growth, by 1980 Coke's growth was stymied at 2 percent. Coke drinkers dropped an amazing 39 percent while Pepsi tripled its consumer group. Oddly enough, Coke was still number one in terms of total volume, so these statistics, which should have made management quiver, were shrugged off by Coke management.

Not until Roberto C. Goizueta took the helm in the early 1980s did Coke decide to squarely face the fact that its market share was eroding due to direct competition from Pepsi. In 1984 Pepsi surpassed Coke in grocery store sales volume, despite the fact that Coke was spending more on advertising and had a superior worldwide distribution network firmly in place.

Goizueta could face these new, disturbing figures or turn his back on the reality to rely on Coke's past reputation to take the company to its 100th anniversary birthday party in 1986. Surely, Coke could hang on to its number one position until then.

The prospect of reaching that 100-year milestone as number two must have given Goizueta sleepless nights. It was clearly time to do something, to take a risk, to step out from tradition and change the way of business as usual. Business as usual was no longer good enough.

"On April 23, 1985, the chairman and chief executive officer of the Coca-Cola Company stunned everyone from Wall Street to Main Street with a blockbuster announcement: The company was scrapping its ninety-nine year old formula for the world's most financially successful soft drink. A new Coke would take its place."[3]

The result? A consumer outcry that caused many critics to dub the decision as a marketing blunder unparalleled in corporate history. Consumers, by and large, rejected the new taste and demanded a return to the "old" Coke.

With overall sales in jeopardy, such a consumer revolt could have torpedoed most other companies. But this was Coke under new leadership. What did Goizueta do? He reintroduced the old Coke under a new name, "Coke Classic," to recapture traditional business, kept the new Coke that had the sweeter taste of the competing Pepsi product that many younger consumers preferred, and took another risk by introducing Diet Coke to the marketplace.

In 1985, the year of the great marketing blunder, Coke's soft drink brands grew two and a half times higher than the industry average. Worldwide volume increased 25 percent in the first five years of Goizueta's leadership—and Wall Street loved it. From a dip to $66 after the announced formula change, in 1986 the stock rose to $125 and split three for one.

So much for the willingness to take risks to preserve market share and reposition for the future. Of course, we are talking about Cola-Cola here, but no product is invincible from market share erosion if poor marketing decisions are made and the product is not generally accepted by the public. Witness General Motors.

During this whole scenario, not only did Coke have to advance a new product to a partially skeptical public, but they also had to protect the brand franchise of the classic "old" Coke and introduce the new Diet Coke as well. Publicity in the news media during this time certainly did help, but the vast number of consumers were informed of these product decisions via advertising on radio and television.

If today's corporations and businesses do not begin to reposition themselves competitively and reach their markets or market segments by making surgical strikes with the intrusive media of radio and television, they may not be able to hold back the competitive advances of businesses that know how to identify and effectively reach this new consumer group of the 1990s.

Reaching this group is far more of a science that one may think, since the number of people interested in buying any given product on any given day or going into any particular store at all, is so small. Even those who will buy Coke today, still the number one sales leader by volume in its product category, are a very small percentage of those who will actually shop for groceries.

This is why advertisers must understand the numbers. Knowing the numbers will help businesses understand why they must choose the electronic media to get their message out to an identified target demographic or a particular market segment within their sphere of business influence.

THE ADVERTISER'S MOST IMPORTANT FIGURES: 2/8/90/20/5,200

A general misconception of many businesses that utilize any form of advertising, from the electronic media and newspapers to direct mail and flyers on car windshields, is that large numbers of consumers in the surrounding marketplace are actually interested in what that business sells or offers on any given day. It is probably quite natural for a business owner or manager to assume or to believe that "everybody" is a potential customer for what they offer or that large numbers of people are logical prospects and are in the market for their services.

Probably nothing is further from the truth. Understanding this concept can help the advertiser or media planner better choose which media will best serve the advertising needs and goals of the business (Figure 6.1). Keep in mind that the figures discussed are only averages, with some product and brand categories either above or below the indicated figures.

2 Percent

This first number is a percentage figure that represents the actual number of potential customers any business has on any given day, or the percentage of consumers in the marketplace who can be considered in the high-involvement stage and who are actively seeking the products or services offered by a particular category of business. This is a very small bulls-eye that businesses are attempting to target on a daily basis and runs counter to the general thinking that "everybody" wants what is being sold or offered. It does, however, clearly point out the need to utilize the laser approach in advertising by surgically striking this small percentage group with the appropriate electronic media.

A few examples will underscore this 2 percent retail phenomenon. One of the items most frequently found on grocery lists is soft drinks, specifically Coca-Cola. Often, it is the top item, listed more often than even milk or bread. But even though it may be the number one item listed, only about 6 percent of daily shoppers will actually purchase Coca-Cola. Grocery items are purchased far more frequently than other consumer goods, so the percentage of consumers in the market for such items will be higher than the 2 percent average, but the point remains that on any given day, a very small percentage of consumers will actually purchase an item as in demand as the leading soft drink brand.

Figure 6.1
Consumer Marketplace Behavior (Percentage of Total Population)

2%	**Hot Prospects.** In the "now" market for any particular product or service. Will likely buy today. *Highly Involved.*
8%	**Warm Market Prospects.** In the "replacement" market. Will likely buy within two to three months. *Low to Moderate Involvement.*
90%	*No Involvement.* Could care less about any advertising.
5200	Average number of advertising impressions confronting the typical consumer in one day.
20%	Average annual market population turnover rate.

Most retailers are generally aware of this phenomenon. Shoe retailers, to use another example, know that only about 1 percent of women in their market area are in the high-involvement stage, ready to buy shoes on any given day. And how many places are there in any city or town in which women can buy these shoes? Because a woman is going to buy a pair of shoes today does not mean that she will buy them in *your* or any given store. There may be dozens of retail outlets competing for this 1 percent of market share.

It now becomes apparent how crucial advertising choices actually become and how important the understanding of advertising and market segmentation are to overall marketing and promotional strategies.

8 Percent

Beneath the small percentage of those who are the hot prospects for any given product or service lies the 8 percent of the market who can be considered "warm" and in the low-involvement stage of consumerism. This percentage of the market can be considered the "replacement" market or those whose appliances, cars, furniture, or whatever are making those funny little pings, creaks, and groans that indicate a new unit will have to be purchased at some point in the future.

Likely to be in the 2 percent high-involvement market within one to three months, these potential customers are attentive to advertising messages but not yet ready to seriously shop for purchase. The only thing that could move them up into the 2 percent bracket, aside from complete product failure at the moment, would be a legitimate sale on what they will likely need in the future but could not buy at the price offered today.

Consumers in the low- or high-involvement state certainly harbor individual moods or frames of mind that predetermine a capacity to absorb information (audience involvement). The higher the level of involvement (hearing a commercial for tires when new tires are needed), the more attentive the consumer, who easily comprehends the given information and integrates it with prior or existing knowledge. This sets the stage for a purchasing decision that can be spurred by creative copy or a legitimate sale.

90 Percent

This leaves 90 percent of the market that could care less about anything being advertised. These are the consumers in the no-involvement stage who simply will not be motivated to read or even note a newspaper ad and will passively attend to the electronic media for entertainment value, only because they cannot help but attend to the intrusiveness of the medium. These people will only enter the low-involvement stage or become hot prospects when complete product failure befalls them unexpectedly and they need to buy within a short, defined period of time.

When that time for imminent purchase does occur, however, as it will sooner or later for all consumers using any manufactured product, where will that consumer in need go to shop for whatever product needs replacement? The answer is apparent. To the store or the business that has established top-of-mind awareness or share of mind with that particular consumer.

Attempting to build brand or store awareness at this point in the consumer buying cycle is too late. Such awareness was built over the past weeks, months, or even years of advertising and promotion. The store that gets the business will be the one that, due to this awareness, consumers think of in time of need—providing, of course, that such store has the brand selection desired, a competitive price, and well-trained sales personnel and attends to the remaining variables discussed earlier in the Sales Wheel.

Being able to attract this business in time of need is exactly why merchants need to be consistent in their advertising and marketing efforts. Consumers enter the market at all times with the intent to purchase. Since no one can predict exactly when this time will occur, the Ebbinghaus research points to consistency as the one defense against consumers forgetting about a particular product or business at exactly the time when they need it.

20 Percent

This figure, explains in part, why many people in a given market have never heard of a particular business, even if it is advertising. This is the average annual market population turnover rate. Twenty percent of the population moves every year, meaning, on average, a full one-fifth of the potential customers of any business are so new to an area they have not yet developed consumer behavior patterns. They are probably unfamiliar with the city streets, much less all of the businesses that cater to their needs, and will rely heavily on what the people they do know tell them.

If a business has established itself with this secondary group of new acquaintances and office or work associates, word-of-mouth customer traffic will result. If not, needed stores will be chosen on a random basis using available print media and possibly, the Yellow Pages.

5,200

This number gets to the heart of the difficult task advertisers have in effectively reaching potential consumers within their area of marketing influence. This figure, drawn from the *New York Times,* represents the average number of advertising impressions that the typical consumer will be confronted with each day from radio and television commercials and newspaper ads to large eye-catching billboards and store signs. Also included in this number would be T-shirts and specialty advertising items like pens, caps, jackets, or buttons.

Although this figure varies from source to source, it is reflective of the media clutter that exists in all markets and underscores the importance of properly selecting the right media to target the desired audience with the least waste.

Moving Consumers from No Involvement to High Involvement

At this point, one central theme seems to become apparent. Since consumers will only note a newspaper ad if they are in the market and looking for the right price, the retail practice of spending the majority of allocated budgets on a medium that will only be noted by the smallest percentage of potential consumers does not seem to be consistent with sound media planning. The prudent choice would be to effectively target the market via the radio format or television program that targets the correct demographic in an attempt to have the advertising message "intrusively" heard, even by those who are not in the "now" market, which is the vast percentage. This is advertising with the least waste that can effectively move consumers from the no-involvement, to the low-involvement, to the high-involvement stages of buying behavior.

This can be accomplished even though those in the 90 percent no-involvement stage will only passively attend to an intrusive electronic media message, since there is no active interest if the receiver of the message is not a logical prospect. Media research tells that even when the message is passively attended to on the subconscious level, it registers an impression. Over time, many impressions have educated the consumer to the point of being able to recall the store or the product in time of need.

Newspaper Weakness

Herein lies the major weakness of newspaper. Since newspaper ads are selectively passed over by those out of the market, they are never noted by the 90 percent or so in a circulation area who do not need or want what is being advertised. Newspapers are the antithesis of the laser psychology of advertising that mandates the need for surgically striking the target market. The entire circulation of the paper must be bought in order to hit the desired demographic. Worse waste does not exist in advertising.

Those same consumers whom advertisers inefficiently attempt to reach via newspaper advertising can be targeted by a radio or television advertisement that will intrusively register with them whether they want it to or not.

As inefficient as newspaper can be, the message here is not to eradicate it from the advertising budget altogether. Newspaper ads most certainly will be noted by those in the market who are logical prospects, and advertisers should use the print media to reach that "now" market or the 2 percent who need that is being advertised. What they should be cautioned against is using the majority of their budget to target this small 2 percent bulls-eye.

Recommended would be the usage of 20 percent to 30 percent of the total advertising budget to target this 2 percent, with the remaining 70 percent to 80 percent of the ad budget being set aside for an educational and intrusive medium that will surgically strike virtually every person in the listening or viewing audience of the desired target demographic, not just a small percentage of that available audience.

Preference Levels

It would indeed be a fanciful world for merchants if that 2 percent of a market area who wanted to buy shoes or tires or new clothing had only one store to go to in each product category, thus ensuring that store of all the available business. In this scenario, that small 2 percent bulls-eye would provide enough business to overwhelm any retail operation. That, however, is not the situation in an often-times crowded retail marketplace where consumers can literally choose from dozens if not hundreds of outlets in which to buy the same or similar items.

Consumers will shop in the store or business that comes to mind in time of need. This consumer behavior, for the merchant whose store is being shopped, is representative of the preferred shopper response. It is, however, only one of five possible consumer behaviors and is the level indicative of the top preference level that the 2 percent of consumers in the "hot prospect" mode can make.

Of that target bulls-eye who will buy today, which could number in the hundreds or thousands depending on market size, the total number of shoppers will be divided among five different preference levels. Understanding this concept will underscore the need to advertise efficiently with the least budgetary waste.

With the number one or top preference level already defined, we will now work our way from the number five or least preferred level to the top position that all advertisers ideally want. For ease of understanding, we will use a hypothetical store that could be representative of any store in the country open for business today.

Five: Of the total number of people in a given marketplace who will purchase shoes today (1 percent to 2 percent), a certain percentage of that total have never heard of Smart's Shoe Store even though they may be advertising. Although they will buy, Smart's has no chance of getting the business as these consumers have no awareness of the store. Instead, the percentage of consumers in this category will purchase shoes from another retail outlet that has succeeded in establishing top-of-mind awareness.

Four: The percentage of today's buyer at this level may be aware of Smart's Shoe Store, but since the store cannot be immediately recalled and no top-of-mind awareness has been established, Smart's will likely not be thought about when the consumer leaves the home or office to buy shoes.

Three: Consumers in this category know about Smart's and will consider going into the store to shop, but only if they have the time and happen to remember them when driving into the area to buy their shoes. In this case, store awareness does exist but it is not top-of-mind awareness. Smart's may or may not get the business.

Two: Consumers involved at this level will shop Smart's for shoes, but they will also visit competitor stores. Smart's may or may not get the business depending on the sales variables involved, but consumers will at least enter the store to see if they can find what they want or need. Chances for making a sale are good but certainly not guaranteed.

One: At this level, the consumer will buy shoes from no other retailer but

Smart's. Smart's has total top-of-mind awareness with these buyers, who will willingly drive by competitor shoe stores to get to the store they know will have what they want or need. Obviously, past positive experience has brought these customers back, but at some point in the past, even these loyal customers were not aware of Smart's. Through advertising and other variables, Smart's was able to get them to enter the store and they became loyal customers for life.

The point is clear. Even though dozens, hundreds, or thousands of potential consumers, depending on market size, will buy shoes today, not all will buy from Smart's Shoe Store. Smart's is engaged in a competitive struggle with all other stores that sell shoes to bring as many potential buyers as possible into their store. This can only be done over time by establishing top-of-mind awareness within the minds of as many citizens in the marketplace as possible.

Advertising is designed to assist Smart's and all other retail stores by moving potential customers up the hierarchy scale from unawareness to awareness, to top-of-mind awareness. Stores that exist at this level enjoy a disproportionate share of business within their area of service and need not be concerned about building brand or store awareness, but rather with maintaining a positive attitude and avoiding attitude decay.

This can be done by engaging in "reminder advertising" that merely reminds consumers to shop as opposed to a schedule designed to build frequency and reach and is more suited to businesses that do not enjoy large market shares. Most businesses, however, do *not* exist at the level where they can enjoy a lion's share of the business and must design their advertising on a weekly basis to position themselves as competitively as possible within their area of business.

How a particular business chooses to establish itself in the minds of the marketplace is, of course, up to that business, but becoming top-of-mind through the regular use of the electronic media, supplemented by the newspaper for today's market, would seem to serve the majority of the business community quite well.

The Switching Idea

This brings us back to the very real fact of media clutter and the 5,200 ad impressions that confront each of us on a daily basis. A schedule of commercials in and of itself running on a particular station, even if it is the right station serving the audience of the advertiser's customers, will not produce short- or long-term results if the copy is not creative enough to stand above the media clutter of these 5,200 advertising impressions that confront the average consumer in one day.

To stand out from such clutter, effectively written radio and television commercials must contain either a central selling idea or a switching idea that gives consumers a reason to become one-time triers or shoppers. A switching idea is basically a highlighting of the attributes of a particular product or service.

Newspapers, by definition of their price-item orientation, use price listings as their approach to the switching idea, although few businesses wish to position themselves as the low-price leader within their particular product or business category.

The positioning campaigns discussed in the previous chapter are good examples of well-written, memorable efforts that certainly give consumers a reason to try a new experience or a different product. These commercial examples, which included the Pepsi "Uh-Huh" theme and the Energizer Bunny, were able to successfully present product ideas or attributes using new, fresh themes.

The basis for arriving at such new ways of thinking is a brainstorming process used at many major advertising agencies and developed by Alex Osborne of Batten, Barton, Durstine and Osborn (BBDO). Designed to stimulate ideas for changing product attributes, it involves a group of creative people posing questions to one another in a free-flowing, criticism-free environment. Such questions stimulate critical and creative thinking about how the product or the store to be advertised can be positioned or repositioned in the marketplace against competing products or stores. Results from this exercise often produce commercials that are more important to the success of the product than the actual product attributes themselves.

Brand Loyalty

Brand loyalty has been one central concern of this chapter. Giving consumers reasons to switch to different brands or different stores or to change their shopping patterns in general is a crucial ingredient in a marketplace mix as consumers are not generally brand loyal in a marketplace of competing products and retail outlets in which to buy these products. Media clutter is one thing, but such clutter is merely symptomatic of the competitive clutter that exists throughout our society.

As reported by The Public Pulse and the Roper Organization in *Future Vision,* "The clutter-confronted consumer is becoming more perceptive in distinguishing between and among brands, and he/she likes having many high-quality brands to choose from. However, marketers are not succeeding in presenting the salient attributes of their products amid the clutter and consumers are not seeing new products as new. . . . [They] have become numb to newness for the sake of newness."[4]

Also noted in this same work published by the editors of *Research Alert* are the ways in which the shopping habits of Americans have changed, giving credence to the absolute necessity of efficiently targeting the right message to the right consumer group.[5]

- Old-fashioned brand loyalty has been replaced by nutritional and environmental concerns.
- Of twenty-five products used, more than half the users of seventeen of the products say they are brand switchers.

- Brand loyalty is stronger among older consumers; consumers aged 18 to 29 are less likely to have strong brand allegiance.

- Higher-income consumers are also more brand loyal. The bottom end of the market buys whatever is less expensive, regardless of brand. The baby boomers are the wild card, showing less allegiance so far than their parents.

- Older, more educated consumers rely on their own abilities to evaluate products, rather than brand cues. Well-known alone is not enough.

- International consumers in diverse product categories find no relevant differences, as technological advances allow competitors to immediately clone new products from brand leaders.

- Brand names, however, can still carve a niche. In dual-income families, they function as trusted time-savers. Newly arrived minorities (e.g., Hispanics and new Asian arrivals) often use them as a means of reducing risk.

Advertising Expenditures as a Percentage of Sales

Many advertisers often feel that they do not have an advertising budget large enough to accomplish the goals of mind franchising needed to build the share of awareness within a defined target demographic. A common advertiser response to the expenditure of large sums of money for a frequency-building ad campaign is that they do not have the required amount of money in their budgets. The money is there and it always has been; it is just that available monies are often disguised as being unavailable.

The key point to attend to at this point is the actual advertising budget itself and how that budget is determined for the fiscal or budgetary year. Most businesses work with an overall ad budget that is a certain percentage (usually 3 percent to 6 percent) of gross sales, working from figures indicating the past year's gross sales and figures projecting sales into the coming year.

If this is the situation, then there is no "budget problem." If there is a problem at all, it is an inventory/sales problem. The more inventory that is moved, the higher the advertising budget will become since that budget is figured from a percentage of gross revenues.

The second factor that often disguises available revenues within the total advertising budget is the amount of money slated for newspaper advertising. Since it has been previously shown that only a small percentage of newspaper readers will attend to a printed ad, that ad can be reduced in size and still attract the same number of readers since those readers are in the now market and will be looking for an ad of that nature, regardless of size. The savings from this simple act of ad reduction can then be put toward a frequency-building campaign on either the radio or television without actually increasing the number of dollars in the advertising budget.

If an advertiser reduces the size of a newspaper ad from a full page to a half-page, the "noting" will only drop around 8 percent but the cost will drop a full 50 percent! This frees up many "disguised" ad dollars that can be put to use in the electronic media, thus creating many more impressions than if those dollars remained in newspaper alone. In addition, the advertising budget is being more efficiently used with less waste as targeting a specific demographic is much easier on the electronic media than through the dozens and dozens of newsprint pages that are viewed only on a one-time basis and if the consumer is in the market as a logical prospect.

That Fickle, Fickle Consumer

All of this, of course, can be viewed cynically by those whose understanding of human nature leads them to believe that consumers are about as loyal in the marketplace today as a wolf would be loyal while guarding a flock of sheep and that consumers are motivated to purchase by price alone. This could logically seem to be the case with all of the low-price-oriented print advertising that screams "sale, sale, sale!" in each edition, while noting few product or store attributes or the number of coupon-clippers who buy whatever product on which they can receive a discount.

Advertisers, however, need to understand that consumers are not as fickle as they appear. Certainly, a degree of so-called fickleness does occur in the marketplace and some products are shopped solely for price, but despite the rush to become the "low-price" leader by many merchants, consumers are savvy enough overall not to buy into the "low-price" spiel in large numbers.

This may be partly due to the overuse of the term, to the point that consumers simply do not believe that "low-price" means low price anymore, but rather *low-price leaders* designed to get one into the store. Shoppers have then figured that once they are in the store, the retailer attitude is that they will pay the "regular" price for whatever they need when they discover the low-price product may not have the desired or needed features.

It is generally true that consumers no longer believe "low-price" any more than they believe in the terms "quality" or "service" even when it is true that a particular store does indeed have these variables. Consumer skepticism is directly born from the overuse of these terms in most advertising.

It is not true, however, that low-price advertising or the preaching of better service and overall quality will extinguish brand loyalty for those products or stores that are well positioned in the minds of consumers. With the vast selection of products available today, consumers will trust what they consider to be the established brand or store. Why?

Consumers do not have the time to stop and study the label or the product attributes of a new or unfamiliar brand. They will buy what they trust and get on with it. Brands or retail outlets that are weak or not distinctively different will have a difficult time carving out their share of the market, especially if the mainstay of their advertising is to push "low-price" and "sale" in the newspaper several times per week.

If these weaker businesses that are not established are serious about competing and carving out a niche in the consumer's mind, they will need to explain their differences on an intrusive medium that will allow an element of explanation directly to the intended target demographic. Once a brand or store is established, they will enjoy what is known as consumer clout and can hold back the tide of brand or store erosion caused by the advertising claims of competitors.

Consumers, then, are probably more loyal than fickle. They just need to be encouraged to remain loyal through good product attributes and advertising that explains or shows these attributes.

ADVERTISING VERSUS PROMOTION

Two terms that are often interchanged in the business community during the strategic planning effort are the terms "advertising" and "promotion." Advertising can certainly be promotion as well as promotion can be advertising, but they are not the same thing.

Promotion is anything that a business does to advance marketplace acceptance or sales or its product(s) or service(s), preferably without needing to lower price or even after raising the price. It is essentially any form of communication, printed or verbal, within the entire channel of distribution, which advances a product or service to logical prospects/prospective customers. This includes everything from promotional literature and wholesaler incentives to retailers for preferable shelf space to nonpaid news publicity and paid retail advertising.

Advertising, then, is a part of the overall promotional effort. In fact, it is exactly 25 percent of the promotional effort according to John J. Burnette, who defines the remaining quarters as personal selling, publicity, and sales promotion.[6]

> *Advertising* — Any paid form of presentation by an identified sponsor. Ranges from efforts to reach specific individuals, as in direct mail, to the more popular form of reaching large groups via the mass media, in both electronic as well as print forms.

> *Personal Selling* — Oral presentation with one or more prospective purchasers for the purpose of making sales. It includes sales calls to retailers from manufacturers' representatives (field selling), assistance of a sales clerk (retail selling), or door-to-door/in-home selling from companies like Avon or Fuller Brush.

> *Publicity* — Stimulating demand by planting commercially significant news in a published medium or obtaining radio or television news coverage. Although this represents "free" coverage, it is not a cost-free form of promotion if a business pays salaries and other expenses for a publicity department.

*Sales Promotion—*The remaining marketing activities that stimulate consumer purchasing and dealer effectiveness, such as in-store displays, shows and exhibitions, or demonstrations aimed at either consumers, the trade, or the manufacturer's own sales force.

THE CREATIVE FACTOR

Much has been mentioned in this book about the value of ideas in effective advertising, creativity, positioning, and franchising the minds of consumer groups through musical or slogan repetition in order to properly reach the identified market segment or target demographic. The creative element, then, may seem to be the central factor if a business is to meet a defined advertising goal of increasing market share or of introducing a new product or store to the general public.

Creativity is the key ingredient in advertising and marketing efforts, however, only if the product or the service of which that advertising or marketing speaks is first worthy of creativity.

Stewart Washburn accurately notes that

advertising for most consumer products which most people are exposed to is pure hype. The reason given for buying most consumer products has very little to do with the quality or efficacy of the product being offered. . . . [These] advertisements to which we are exposed in the print media and which catch our attention on television, for the most part, have very little to do with the intrinsic qualities of the products being touted. To get fancy about it, "The benefits are associative, not attributive."*

Washburn takes on blue jeans being sold by suggestive, seminaked maids, the cry babies and idiots who sniffle through television shows hawking cold remedies, and a whole host of other products designed to prevent our bodies from otherwise deteriorating; television commercials that do not identify the sponsor until it is almost over, and the exploitation of patriotism or wrapping products of inferior quality in the American flag to convince us to "Buy American!" when a less expensive, quality import can be had.

What reasonable observer can argue that "Art directors produce to astonish other art directors and copywriters write to terrorize other copywriters . . . [with] the reader or viewer . . . never given a legitimate reason to buy. Flash and trash replace actual benefits. Production values replace product performance [while] clients pay the bills because they don't know any better."[7]

This, of course, is what happens when the client or business gets sidetracked from what it is actually supposed to do, mainly provide quality service and a quality product to its market, and becomes more involved and interested in the hype at the expense of the product or business.

*Stewart Washburn, *Managing the Marketing Functions* (New York: McGraw-Hill, 1988). Used with permission of McGraw-Hill.

Advertising can only work if the benefits it proclaims can truly be associated with a superior product or service. Remember what advertising can and cannot do? Advertising cannot make a satisfied customer. Only superior products and services can make satisfied customers.

Where to Begin

The creation of effective advertising is the result of a mutual effort between the businessperson and the advertising representative handling his or her account. This representative can be either from an advertising agency, the local radio or television station, or other media outlet.

The business advertising manager handling the details from the business end, however, cannot afford to simply relinquish creative control over the entire project as many are inclined to do. Nor can he or she refuse to allow for the guidance of the assigned sales representative and backup creative resources. A symbiotic relationship must be established with equal concern at both ends. Otherwise, the end result may very well mean ineffective advertising promoting the wrong items and using the wrong approach with bland copy written for the wrong reasons.

To adequately prepare for the discussion of advertising with the appropriate account representative, the advertising manager for a business should prepare in advance by following a few suggested guidelines.

Know the goals of any advertising the business will do in any media for the next twelve months. What is it that the company wants to accomplish? What is the exact dollar amount of sales the business wants to generate? Does the business want to advertise image or price-item as would a low-price leader? How does the business wish to be perceived in the marketplace compared to its competition?

From knowing the desired sales volume for the next twelve months, *decide on an appropriate advertising budget for that period of time.* The advertising figure is usually a percentage of the gross sales volume falling somewhere between 3 percent and 6 percent, the amount depending on market size and overall marketing goals.

Obviously, 3 percent of gross sales in the large metro market of Chicago will be a larger figure than 3 percent of gross sales in downstate Jacksonville, Illinois. Merchants in the smaller city may need a higher percentage to have an adequate budget.

Keep in mind that budgets are not to be carved in stone, but rather should serve as flexible indicators of available monies to be used for image investment. This investment, like any investment, will produce a long-term result provided it is managed and used correctly.

Having a general idea of what the competition spends is fine, but remember that they may not be "doing it right." Also be careful not to use this budget for an excess of "donation" advertising or "below the line" trade show promotions that cannot possibly produce a return on investment.

Examples of these types of unhelpful "advertising investments" that are not designed to produce direct retail results as are the major mass media, aside from previously discussed trade shows and Yellow Pages courtesy displays, include the buying of space in the high school annual, buying space on the local sheriff's calendar, or appearing on one side of the waste receptacle on the downtown square.

Understand everything possible about what the business offers to the public—from the product line to the various consumer variables. Know how the product or store differs from the competition. Many products and businesses are different only because of their advertising.

What is the real difference between beers other than one is "Less Filling and Tastes Great" and the other "Is the Right Beer Now"? What is the real difference in coffee products other than the advertising that sets them apart? What is the difference in bran cereals or margarines with no cholesterol that are supposed to taste like butter other than their advertising campaigns? What is the real difference between fast food hamburgers and the standard chocolate, strawberry, and vanilla drinks that they all mislabel as "shakes" and make from some sort of mix?

Will your business be different because of its product or perceived reputation or because of its marketplace advertising? In other words, "Where's the Beef?" to coin Clara Peller, who successfully positioned Wendy's against its fast food hamburger rivals in the early 1980s by use of that memorable phrase.

Know exactly what products or services need to be promoted or moved via any advertising effort. Vendor shipments, floor space, and season of the year can help determine what needs to be promoted when. Avoid a knee-jerk reaction when advertisement is placed and copy is needed; just instructing the sales representative to prepare copy on whatever comes to mind when you are speaking is no way to meet the overall marketing goals of the business.

Know exactly who the intended target market for the store and its products is. If this remains a quantity unknown, ask for assistance in determining the exact market. Watch for this variable to change over time as today's customers may leave, for whatever reason, and be replaced by yet another consumer group.

What type of advertising will this identified group respond to? Humor or seriousness of purpose? Do you use the rubbery face of Jim Varney ("Know what I mean, Vern?") or the more serious approach of a Karl Malden ("Don't leave home without it")?

Demand good copy. Do not accept dull, boring, or pedestrian copy that will not touch the intended target market in some way.

Understand the strengths and weaknesses of the mass media both in general and in your market. Although this book recommends buying the electronic media over and above the print media, refuse to buy from unprofessional sales representatives who use pressure tactics or who cannot answer concerns or prepare good copy. Also, do not buy a radio station whose target audience is not your target customer or place your commercial on a television program that is not viewed by your intended market.

Do not buy something because your buddies at the club are buying it. Their goals may not be your goals; if there are similarities in goals and budgets, fine, then buy. But do not go out of business trying to "keep up with the Joneses."

Always monitor what you are doing in the marketplace and communicate what is happening to all store employees. Do not advertise a sale that floor salespeople know nothing about.

Be patient. Understand the long-term nature of proper advertising and promotion. If your organization is sound, the results will come. "Management by Impulse" is a title yet to hit the bookstore shelves.

WHAT GOOD COPY REALLY IS

Good copy is essentially the preparation of a message that promotes the strongest attributes and consumer benefits of a business to the intended target demographic. Even more basic, good copy is good advertising that is remembered.

The Top Down/Bottom up Advertising Approach

Good copy is copy that is local in nature, regardless of the national scope of the store or product being advertised. A trend beginning to emerge has been set by progressive advertising agencies like Scali, McCabe & Sloves, and The Martin Agency. Together these agencies began handling the Mercedes-Benz account in 1992. Scali is the national New York-based agency that is providing input from the "top down" and Martin the Richmond-based regional/local sister agency that is working on the account from the "bottom up." They are building a national voice for Mercedes with four local accents, realizing that the Southeast is different from the Northeast and that diesels sell better in the Southeast than in California. Here is their creative Western region thirty-second radio commercial, with all the appeal an affluent and educated Southern Californian could ask for:

There are only five signed van Gogh portraits in the world, just a few hundred bottles of 1983 Le Monterarchet, and a mere six Faberge Eggs held in private hands. If you don't own any of these rare treasures, take heart. Your authorized Southern California Mercedes-Benz dealers remind you that there are fewer than 100 Mercedes 600 SLs available. Not many. But then, would you want there to be?

These agencies realize that establishing an appeal for Mercedes-Benz can also be done nationally in the large markets or from the top down by writing copy with strong verbal consistency for all regions of the country, still leaving room for the local accents like the "Faberge Eggs" commercial just described.

Multitiered Positioning

What these agencies and other progressive advertisers are beginning to realize is the necessity for multitiered positioning. Many products and services seek to appeal to a broad, national market while simultaneously appealing to the indigenous needs of identified target segments.

Local and regional businesses, a microcosm of the national scene, should also understand that they have a broad customer base with common needs that can be appealed to in a more general way through local or regional advertising media. However, not to be forgotten are the marketing tiers that fall below this broader base: the various ethnic groups within the community or the different demographic groups that would need a similar product or service, such as insurance, but for different reasons need special appeals on different radio stations or television programs.

Insurance companies or telephone companies that offer the same basic product or service to an entire population certainly sell to different target markets in different ways. Even though the service (having insurance or a telephone in the home) may be basic, there are certainly many different options and packages with different price structures available to choose from, depending on customer needs. One general product or service may be offered by the company, but that product or service becomes many when it is offered in different ways to different marketing segments.

Reaching These Marketing Segments Creatively

The need for creativity to catch the imagination and attention of these identified target groups has been discussed throughout the preceding chapters and although it is unnecessary to parrot the many advertising books written on this subject alone, some specific guidelines ought to be mentioned at this point.

It is not the purpose of this book to discuss creativity in the newspaper industry: creative print is an oxymoron at best. Although price-item print advertising will attract those 2 percent of prospects in the "now" market, those so motivated will be inclined to read anything simply because they are in the market. That is why creativity is not essential in newspaper advertising.

The real challenge advertisers face is how to attract the masses of potential customers who are *not* interested in what they are selling to the public, while franchising their minds in the process. This can only be done on the intrusive medium of radio or television.

The Competition for Attention

Earlier in this chapter, we saw that the average consumer is confronted with 5,200 advertising impressions per day. Over a year's period of time that would equal 1,898,000 impressions from a company's name on a ball point pen to the larger forms of the mass media. Of this total, approximately 50,000 per year or 137 per day will be television commercials. A lesser number will be from radio as television dominates total attention, although mostly in the evening hours.

Even though radio and television have the advantage of being intrusive, an intrusive ad that does not register to a nonattending audience will not be remembered. Since we know that most people are not interested in what is being advertised anyway, because they are not in the market, they need to become involved—much like a viewer of a movie who did not want to watch the film but decided to anyway and ended up totally involved and interested. To accomplish this takes creative clout.

Creative clout is what sustains memory over time. It is that edge that certain advertisers have that makes an ad jump out in the minds of consumers as they enter their cars to begin the drive to the main shopping areas of their local markets. These creative market impressions must be consistent, ever-present in the marketplace since advertisers never know when potential customers in their markets are at the end of the buying cycle for whatever they sell and are ready to buy again. Memory needs to be sustained until it is time to get that consumer to park in *their* parking area.

In this case, your friend and ally should be the sales representative from the radio or television station who is professionally trained to help businesses identify and solve existing problems and concerns. Part of this effort means working with businesses to identify proper segments of the market to advertise to and developing creative copy to reach those segments.

Do not make the mistake, however, of assuming that a local radio or television station will devise good creative copy. Many will, of course, but responsibility for effective copy rests with both the advertiser as well as with the media outlet represented by your sales representative. And do not accept just one commercial. To avoid wear-out, you will need more than one commercial in rotation.

David W. Schumann, Richard E. Petty, and O. Scott Clemons (1990) found that for products with little consumer relevance, or those purchased on impulse without much thought (like snack items, candy, or produce), less variance over multiple exposures was effective (one commercial would suffice), as the mere recall of a store or product was sufficient to stimulate buying. However, for products that commanded higher levels of involvement (higher-priced items with brand distinction), copy needed substantive variation over multiple exposures to avoid loss of interest.

GUIDELINES FOR CREATIVE COPY

To help guide businesses in that elusive search for creative copy, here are several general suggestions to follow. The specifics can be devised by the advertiser and the radio or television station through the assistance of the advertising sales representative whose job it is to place the right message on the right station at the right time.

Remember that the electronic media are first and foremost an entertainment media. Even hard news is presented with the flair of entertainment. When consumers want news, but find it presented in a dull, boring, and pedestrian manner, they will quickly change the channel.

Commercials need to draw listeners and viewers to their message in an entertaining and trustful way. There is no need to club audiences over the head with messages of "buy, buy, buy!" That is what the newspaper does and always has done with its price-item approach. The message is clearly "this is the price today, so buy today." Since most consumers do not want to buy today, it is best to have entertainment value for memorability.

Examples of these commercials have been previously discussed in earlier chapters: The Energizer Bunny, the California Raisins and the classic "Mean Joe Greene" Coke commercial come to mind when thinking of television. The genesis of these memorable television commercials can be traced to good ideas coupled with good writing. The superior production values apparent in these large budget examples may not be able to be duplicated on the local level, but no large market monopoly exists on original ideas or quality writing. Smaller market television advertisers should consider concentrating more on creativity and less on overall production costs. The idea is to avoid the "electronic billboard" or the use of voiced-over slides. This may be good for the budget, but such a non-creative approach will not easily franchise minds or enhance top-of-mind awareness.

In radio, Motel 6 ("We'll leave the light on for you") has top-of-mind awareness on the national scene and Nynex Yellow Pages, a regional player, was recognized by *Advertising Age* as having the best radio ad for 1991.

Radio, though, is primarily a local medium, hence different business categories dominate the mind in each different market (although, as we have seen, "local" is becoming the buzzword for national products and stores). Wrangler, for example, is beginning to dominate minds through creative radio as well as television commercials geared to different regions of the country. Handled by Scali, McCabe & Sloves, and The Martin Agency, the philosophy is similar to Mercedes-Benz. Make the product local. Here are two radio commercial examples, with the main characters Jake and Clint in two different situations that would play in different regions of the country. These commercial examples are also uncomplicated and easy to understand. Simple is better.

Wrangler :60 Radio, "New Dog"

SFX: Dog panting throughout
JAKE: Clint, sit up.
JAKE: Clint, roll over.
JAKE: Clint, play dead.
JAKE: Clint, go over and get my hat off that chair.
JAKE: Clint, fetch the . . .
CLINT: Jake?
JAKE: Oh, hi, Clint.
CLINT: New dog?
JAKE: Uh, yeah.

CLINT: Kind of homely, isn't he?

JAKE: Not good looking at all.

CLINT: Is he smart?

JAKE: Dumb as dirt.

CLINT: Ooo. Doesn't smell too good either. Why'd you get him?

JAKE: Well, I heard having a dog is a great way to meet girls.

CLINT: Hmm. What's his name?

JAKE: Rover.

VO: Getting a dog is one way to get a woman to notice you. Another way is getting a pair of Riata jeans from Wrangler.

Wrangler :60 Radio, "Wild Ride"

SFX: Sounds of the rodeo at an indoor arena.

CLINT: Jake?

JAKE: Yeah, Clint.

CLINT: How long we been coming to this rodeo?

JAKE: Five years, I guess.

CLINT: Jake?

JAKE: Yeah, Clint.

CLINT: I don't know about you, but that was the worst ride I ever had.

JAKE: I can't remember when I've been that scared.

CLINT: Me too.

JAKE: I just held on and prayed for it to be over.

CLINT: My whole life flashed before my eyes.

JAKE: Did you see those people's faces when we almost jumped that barrier?

CLINT: I thought they were goners for sure.

JAKE: Well, one thing's certain. The next time we come to New York, no more taxi cabs.

CLINT: Yep. From now on, we're walking.

VO: No matter where cowboys roam, they always take a piece of the true West with them. Brushpopper shirts from Wrangler.

Another example of excellent creative advertising that is simple and easy to understand is the Clio Award winning script for Motel 6, brought to life by a down-home delivery created by The Richards Group for airing on network newscasts carried locally by thousands of stations.

Hi, Tom Bodett for Motel 6 and I'm here to wax a little philosophic. You know, at Motel 6 we have a philosophy: People sleep, therefore we are. And the way we figure it, since you don't appreciate artwork when you're sleepin', why hang it in the rooms. I guess if you wanted to be technical though, our walls can be considered art. Abstract art. You know, nothing to get in the way of individual interpretation. Sort of like an empty canvas to be painted on with the mind. Holy smokes. That's deep. I'd just better do the commercial. At Motel 6, you get just what you need. A clean, comfortable room and a good night's sleep for around 22 bucks in most places. A little more in some, and a lot less in others, but always the lowest prices of any national chain and always a heck of a deal. It's a simple philosophy, but it makes good sense. Sort of like a rolling stone not gatherin' any moss. Or that bird in the hand stuff. Ah, I think you get the drift. I'm Tom Bodett, art critic, for Motel 6 and we'll leave the walls bare for you.

In Chapter 3, one of the buying variables discussed on the Sales Wheel was price related to benefit. The key word here is "benefit." Every commercial obviously wants their target demographic to buy and every audience is certainly smart enough to know this. Few people will buy if there is no apparent benefit, either real (the newest model with all the latest features not on last year's model) or psychological ("All my men wear English Leather . . . or nothing at all.").

Much has been made so far about store or product uniqueness, but many stores and brands are so similar that the only differentiating factor is the advertising itself. Why go to K-Mart if Wal-Mart is closer? Why go to Arby's if the Dairy Queen is closer? And so it goes. In a homogenized world where convenience stores rent videos while they sell gas and one store tries to be like every other, does it matter where anybody shops. What makes *you* so unique?

If the answer is nothing, it will be hard to develop a believable ad that will franchise the minds of a public already skeptical when they hear the words "service," "quality," and "low-price."

Go back to the Sales Wheel and determine where your strengths are that the creative people in your marketplace can turn into a huge marketing advantage for you. They are there. You just have not discovered them. And, when you think you have, look again. If all the competition has the same advantage, it is not an advantage – unless they are not advertising it.

Understand human nature and the fact that it has not changed and will be constant into the next century. David Martin says it best:

We will always have a desire for food and drink, for rest, comfort and security, for a sense of self-worth or social acclaim, for independence, power and success. Parental feelings will always run strong: the desire to nurture, protect and provide. Human nature is a constant. It's dependable. We were born with our four instincts: fear (self-preservation), hunger (for food and drink), sex (love), rage (anger). People have five senses: sight, touch, smell, hearing and taste. The instinct and senses are often a starting point for advertising appeals.[8]

To tap into these instincts and senses, copy needs to be written that appeals to the instincts and to the senses since that is what humans will most readily respond to. The impulse to buy is often emotionally driven, disguised as logic. Instincts (fear, hunger, sex, and rage) are varying degrees of emotion. The senses are more logically based. Copy can appeal to one or both, depending on the business and the inventory tabbed for advertising.

Most of us buy what we want, not what we need, motivated by how we see ourselves and how we want others to see us. Our cultural and social values never leave us and human behavior will be consistent with learned behavior and the desire to advance ourselves beyond our current circumstances. This means we will buy products and services that are newer, improved, or better.

Satellite emotions and feelings that have been identified by researchers like Poffenberger and Plutchik that can help produce strong copy include:

- Family affection — Nurturing instinct.
- Anticipation — Expectation or impatience for something good or better.
- Health — A major concern of older baby boomers.
- Surprise — Reaction to something unanticipated — lower price than expected, better quality or service than expected, more product uses than expected.
- Activity — Sports activity to maintain health and vitality.
- Conformity — Desire to be up to date, not out of date. Fear of scorn if more old-fashioned than modern.
- Joy — Exuberation and satisfaction.
- Superiority — Ambition to improve, to be better, to stand out as unique.
- Disgust — Disdain or rejection, being miserable. Maybe from a competitor's product.
- Sadness — Disappointment — again, possibly from doing business with a competitor.
- Group spirit — The "I'd like to teach the world to sing" Coke commercial.
- Economy — Doing the right thing as a consumer.
- Recommendation — From a likable or respected role-model like a celebrity or athlete, either local or national. The more likable the spokesperson, the less boring and more effective the copy. The spokesperson, however, does not have to be recognizable, only believable.

Do not be afraid to try different approaches. Look how often the large, national advertisers change themes. When something seems to work or catch on, keep it. It will eventually wear out, but not as quickly as you may think. When something successful has run its course, have a follow-up campaign or idea waiting in the wings so there is no void or "dead-air" between campaigns.

Finally, *demand good copy.* Do not accept the everyday, ordinary stuff that you yourself could ad lib into a microphone. If you ask for it, you will get it eventually. If not, take your business elsewhere. In this case, you are the customer.

SUMMARY

Most businesses are probably not aware of the small (2 percent) number of people within their marketing area who are actually "hot" prospects or interested in what they are selling on any given day. With a bulls-eye this small, it becomes amazingly clear how efficient any advertising effort has to be to be done without waste. The surgical strike advantages of the electronic media over those of print in reaching the 90 percent to 98 percent of the market who will *not* note an advertiser's message if it runs in the newspaper, simply because they are not in the "hot" or the "warm" market, become apparent.

The revelation of preference levels within that small group of "hot," "now," or "today's" buyers revealed how competitive the overall business environment actually is and, again, how vital reaching them in nonwasteful ways becomes. One way that advertisers can reduce waste is by more efficiently identifying their correct market segment through the incorporation of the VALS 2 system that looks for specific relationships between expressed opinions (attitudes) and buying behavior.

Advertisers who have succeeded in identifying their correct target group cannot confuse advertising with promotion. Advertising is a form of promotion and should not be attempted (although this is done every day) without consideration for the creative factor and for the elements of good copy.

Appealing to human emotions, needs, and desires can be done as suggested by many researchers and can be counted on to be effective simply because human nature is a constant. What we all fear, love, and dream will be as alive tomorrow as it has been throughout the ages.

NOTES

1. Daniel Kehrer, *Doing Business Boldly* (New York: Times Books, 1989), p. 6.
2. Ibid., p. 7.
3. Ibid., p. 8.
4. Eric Miller, ed., *Future Vision* (Naperville, Ill.: Sourcebooks Trade, 1991), p. 101.
5. Ibid., p. 102.
6. John J. Burnette, *Promotion Management* (St. Paul: West, 1984), p. 18.
7. Stewart Washburn, *Managing the Marketing Functions* (New York: McGraw-Hill, 1988), p. 16.
8. David Martin, *Romancing the Brand* (New York: AMACOM, 1989), p. 136.

OTHER WORKS CITED

Schumann, David W., Richard E. Petty, and D. Scott Clemons. "Predicting the Effectiveness of Different Strategies of Advertising Variation: A Test of the Repetition–Variation Hypotheses." *Journal of Consumer Research* (September 1990): 192–202.

CHAPTER 7

The Advertising
Managers Speak

The advertiser . . . is the basis of the advertising business, although primarily he's not in it so much as he is in the soap, or breakfast cereal, or automobile business. But to him, the advertising is vital.

—*Advertising Age,*
November 21, 1973

THE NEED FOR BUSINESS INPUT

A book of this nature would be incomplete without input from the very group of people that would benefit most from it. Although not intended to be empirical, the information gathered from these interviews is important in tracking the rationale behind the media buying decisions made on the local and regional level every day.

Media planners who buy advertising and promote their corporate goals within the various markets of free, capitalistic countries have enormous responsibilities. They may be handling the budget for a midsize regional corporation with multiple retail outlets. They may be store managers, handling not only advertising but the hiring and firing of employees and the ordering and receiving of inventory shipments. As chief executives of that business, they deal with the administration of the business and may even be business owners.

Overall, such people are enormously qualified with abundant retail knowledge. Yet they need help in the areas of advertising, marketing, and promoting. They, as a rule, do not have college or advanced degrees in advertising or marketing and like any other generalists, need specialized assistance to properly and effectively promote their businesses.

Unfortunately, in many markets, these business retailers do not have the professional resources in their markets to call on for the very type of assistance that would make them successful in the long run. The many media salespeople who call on businesses each day are likely to employ high-pressure sales tactics, invoking retailers to buy because "we're number one" with no regard for explaining the kinds of information in this volume and others devoted to the understanding of advertising.

As a result, when advertising buying decisions are made, they are most often made to favor newspaper with the highest percentage of the total budget. This, of course, is a sound decision if the goals of the business are to reach the 2 percent of "now" buyers or even the 8 percent of the warm market exclusively.

If, however, the business wishes to create a marketplace impression that will implant an image with the remaining 90 percent to 98 percent of the area population, understanding the electronic media is nothing short of mandatory.

Since few media planners really do understand the electronic media and fewer media representatives truly explain how radio and television actually work within the cornucopia of advertising, newspaper gets the biggest slice of the pie, simply because it always has.

The decision to buy newspaper on a near-exclusive basis over the past several decades, despite the inroads of radio and television into the everyday lifestyles of consumers at the great expense of print, is somewhat knee-jerk in nature.

Although these misconceptions have been addressed in this book, it is important to note the comfort and security factor that buying newspaper seems to bring. "If others are doing it, it must be right for me" appears to be an operating factor in buying print. The herd mentality always gives comfort to the individual, even if that herd is stampeding over the edge of a cliff.

Business Thinking in America Today

The current status of business thinking in America on the topic of advertising is a driving force behind this book. What media planners believe in one area of the country seems to be similar to what they believe in other geographic locations. The homogenization of America includes the way in which we think, feel, act, and buy media for advertising purposes.

It seems apparent that the lack of information available to the retail community or possibly the lack of inclination to pursue such available information, clearly demonstrates the need for education within that community. Businesspeople do not need to be sold any more advertising, print or electronic, until they are properly educated on how advertising and the various forms of such advertising work or should work within their chosen community of operation. When businesspeople understand advertising, they can then make more informed decisions without relying on what each individual advertising sales representative recommends. This book should serve as one source for that education or reeducation.

Interview Methodology

The decision to interview those who make advertising decisions on the regional and local level every day was a direct result of wanting to know what such media planners were thinking and how they viewed the media in their indigenous markets. Many of the previous thoughts expressed in this chapter are a result of those interviews.

At this juncture, it was time to employ plain common sense. Rather than to engage in a methodological survey that would provide quantitative numbers that could be verified empirically, it seemed more useful to just interview those who make daily media decisions and report those findings. By randomly selecting businesses in various states and of varying market sizes, a cross-section of opinion could be counted on to provide useful information for both those who sell media advertising and those who buy it.

The exact methodology was the telephone interview, choosing businesses and corporations of all types, from department store retailers and grocery stores to automobile dealers and furniture stores in small, medium, and larger markets from states in the East, the Midwest/West, and the far West.

All businesses/corporations were large enough to have a substantial advertising budget. Many had multiple retail outlets in several states and although central advertising planning occurred, such advertising was conducted in multiple markets. A total of fifty interviews were conducted. Questions were asked with the understanding that responses would be kept anonymous. This approach ensured the accuracy and honesty of the answers.

The questions asked were simple, but broad enough to elicit in-depth response:

- Where do you spend the majority of your advertising budget?
- What do you like or dislike about your newspaper advertising?
- What do you like or dislike about your radio or television advertising?

RESEARCH RESULTS

One very interesting discovery was the uniformity of answers in each region and in each market, regardless of size. The variables of geography, market size, or type of business did not seem to affect widely held beliefs about the media and the reasons for preferring one medium over another.

Another item of note was the passion interviewees displayed in explaining or defending what they believed worked well for them. Advertisers naturally want to feel that the decisions they make for their business are, indeed, the best for that business, much as a parent believes that the choices made for a child are in the best interests of that offspring.

Whether they are, in fact, right or whether they just want to be right is a matter for discussion. Retailers do want to be correct in the decisions they make for their businesses and they want these decisions to be understood by their superiors as well as their peers. We do not normally believe that we are irresponsible, and we all defend what we perceive to be the best course of action for our employers as well as ourselves.

Interviewee responses will be discussed, question by question, coupled with anecdotal observations on the collective responses. Although it will not be necessary to repeat previously given information, some reference will be made to information presented and points made in earlier chapters.

Question #1: Where Do You Spend the Majority of Your Advertising Budget?

There was virtually no variance in the answers given to this question. Forty-eight of fifty respondents claimed that the majority of their advertising budget went to the local newspaper in the market or markets in which their businesses were located. The two exceptions (a car dealer and a discounter) spent the majority of their budgets with television and radio/television, respectively.

Although many, especially the car dealers, invested heavily in radio and television, over 50 percent of the total budget of forty-eight advertisers was always allotted for newspaper advertising. A selected listing of responses to this question and the reasons why a particular answer was given is listed, along with the business category of the respondent.

It should also be noted that an attempt was made to interview similar business categories in all markets, again, usually the largest players in that market and hence, those most likely to have a sizable advertising budget.

As well, giving individual (50) responses in this text would be more time consuming than necessary. And many similar answers to the same question make it possible to effectively list selected responses without diluting the greater message from the group as a whole.

- Grocery Store: "Most of our ad dollars go to newspaper because people read it. It's tangible and people will look back at it."
- Large market with thirty-six stores in four states: "We see newspaper as a tangible."
- Department Store: "Seventy percent of our budget goes to newspaper. We feel we can target our market better with newspaper."
- Discount Store: "The newspaper is the major source of advertising in this region."
- Sporting Goods Store: "We use mostly newspaper because it traditionally reaches a lot of people."
- Car Dealer: "We use all the media, but mostly newspaper because it just works."

- Discount Store: "The majority of our budget goes to print because of the type of business we are. A newspaper ad is like a shopping list that displays a variety of items."
- Department Store: "Retailers are print-oriented out of habit and history. Print is the merchant's comfort zone."

The responses to this question were expected and are understandable, leaving several general conclusions that can be drawn from the given information.

First, it is apparent that business media planners, in general, buy newspaper out of habit and tradition. Newspaper is likely to be what their parents used and what they grew up feeling that businesses do—mainly, run newspaper ads. They feel comfortable with the tangibility factor and believe that consumers refer back to printed ads for reference.

What appears as the tip of the iceberg is the great amount of education that needs to take place and the lack of media and advertising understanding displayed by well-intentioned buyers of local and regional advertising. Businesses have always had a love-affair with tradition and tangibility, assuming that because a written record of their products and prices exists, everyone will see it and be motivated to visit the store.

Of course, this is not true. Only 2 percent of people in the marketplace who are in the market for whatever the business sells will be motivated enough to even note the newspaper ad. That written record does no good if it is not noticed. The wise course of action would be to trim down the size of the ad, which will still be noted by the "now" buyer, and place the savings from the scaleback plus the majority of the advertising budget into an intrusive medium that has a chance of making an impression on the majority of those in the intended demographic.

Buying newspaper because of tradition is not logical either. Because something once worked in a different era does not mean it will work in the same way today. A lifestyle change has occurred; most Americans obtain their daily information from radio and/or television, with little time left for reading.

Those who consume newspapers do so for information, not advertising (coupon-clippers are a very small minority of buyers) and will only be motivated to note an ad if they are in the market for whatever the ad is about and are attracted by the listed price. If businesses want to reach the consumers of the 1990s, the majority of the ad budget must necessarily be directed toward the electronic media.

Since most respondents did indicate a preference for newspaper over other available forms of advertising, it seems appropriate at this point to list the top twenty-five newspaper advertisers according to the September 25, 1991 issue of *Advertising Age*. Some of those interviewed, indeed, represented several of the companies listed. Table 7.1 shows figures for 1989 spending and 1990 spending with the percentage change noted. Dollar figures are in the millions.

The first half figures available for 1991 show a continuing drop in the total

Table 7.1
Newspaper Spending

Rank	Advertiser	1990	1989	% change
1.	May Dept. Stores	$ 218.2	$ 208.2	4.8%
2.	R.H. Macy & Co.	160.1	183.6	(12.8)
3.	Sears Roebuck & Co.	136.8	154.9	(11.7)
4.	Federated Dept. Stores	134.5	144.0	(6.6)
5.	Dayton Hudson	106.2	107.5	(1.2)
6.	Montgomery Ward	82.1	67.2	22.1
7.	Kmart	80.1	58.6	36.7
8.	Carter Hawley Hale	72.8	66.9	8.9
9.	J.C. Penney	70.6	81.4	(13.2)
10.	American Stores Co.	69.6	81.9	(15.1)
11.	AMR Corp.	60.7	41.0	48.1
12.	Highland Superstores	49.0	36.2	35.3
13.	General Motors	46.6	55.7	(16.3)
14.	Time Warner	46.2	43.1	7.2
15.	AT&T	43.8	39.7	10.2
16.	Tengleman Group	42.8	20.9	104.3
17.	Circuit City	41.3	37.6	9.7
18.	Tandy Corp.	40.5	37.6	7.7
19.	Woodward & Lothrup	38.1	39.8	(4.2)
20.	Walt Disney Co.	36.7	24.6	49.1
21.	Sony Corp.	36.1	30.3	19.3
22.	Matsushita Electric	33.0	28.9	14.2
23.	Delta Air Lines	32.9	28.5	15.5
24.	Dillard Dept. Stores	32.9	30.3	8.6
25.	Ahold International	31.0	27.6	12.2

Source: Advertising Age, September 25, 1991.

dollars allocated to newspaper, with the May Company down 23 percent, Dayton Hudson down 53 percent, Ward down 37 percent, K-Mart down 45 percent, and Penney down nearly 50 percent. Newspaper spending is down because of poor performance. The question, then, is: Does there exist a correlation between newspaper spending and the resultant poor performance?

Although difficult to answer with available data, many department retailers, either in bankruptcy or closed down altogether, have begun to realize that reaching a mobile market with traditional newspaper advertising is not as easy as reaching an earlier generation in the same manner.

Competition, far greater today in the retail arena, means that consumers no longer have to go to a department store to find the soft goods that they need. What used to be the domain of the larger "dry goods" store can now be bought at dozens of other stores and at lower prices. Creating a sense of value to today's consumer is increasingly more difficult in the print media that do not offer the creative, surgical strike capability of the electronic media.

An anecdotal observation would then be that, yes, poor corporate performance can be indirectly tied to high newspaper spending that does not produce the intended results common in past years. The paradigm has changed and with this change must come a new era of advertisers who understand the implications of a wired (and nonwired), high-tech society whose main consumer group has been reared on color television, rock and roll radio, and blockbuster megamovies that can be brought home on video to watch again at leisure.

Question #2: What Do You Like or Dislike About Your Newspaper Advertising?

Again, a very positive and warm feeling swelled up in favor of print advertisement. Newspapers show themselves to be the "Linus blanket" of advertising, although some deep insecurities begin to emerge about the great amounts of money traditionally directed toward the local newspapers, even in large metro markets. Most respondents used a media mix of radio, television, and newspaper, but print usually received the lion's share of the budget.

- Department Store: "We are a visual industry and newspaper allows us to illustrate and show our merchandise, to describe it in greater detail. You can't present visually on the radio."

- Department Store (different from above): "We really don't have a feel if newspapers work for us anymore. I think retailers are in a learning process today. We don't know how to talk to our customers anymore in this new age of the working woman and the mobile population."

- Specialty Clothing Retailer: "Newspaper is the cheapest way to get mass exposure. We want quick results and quick merchandise turnaround. As a result, we no longer use direct mail or catalogs."

- Electronics Store: "We look for those who have decided to buy (from our radio and television advertising) and will use the newspaper as a shopping guide for them, because they will compare prices. We have to be in the newspaper because our competition will be."

- Department Store: "The coverage and circulation of the newspaper is good, but we're not totally satisfied with it."

- Department Store: "We're going to change our strategy. The newspaper rates are too high. We can't keep creating impressions by sticking with the newspaper. Those who continue to buy newspaper as they have in the past are merely trying to maintain historical impressions."

- Auto Dealer: "We sell a lot of used cars. Used car buyers are comparison shoppers. They compare prices and features and can best do that in newspaper."

- Appliance Dealer: "Newspaper reaches a lot of people and provides measurable results."

- Grocery Chain: "Newspaper covers the entire market and it's tangible. Besides, we have to show the prices because we get paid, in the form of advertising allowances, for running specials like on Pepsi."

- Discount Store: "Newspapers reach more people than any other medium. It's credible because it caters to everybody."

- Furniture Store: "The newspaper color is outstanding! It's gorgeous! And everybody gets the newspaper."

- Hardware Store: "With fifty thousand items in stock, people want to know what is available at what price. Newspaper ads are a shortened version of a Sears-type catalog. We run four pages weekly in every market we're in."

- Auto Dealer: "Newspaper circulation hits eight out of every ten people."

- Furniture Store: "We were heavy into print several years ago, but that's beginning to change. Although most of our budget still goes to print, we're using a media mix of radio and television."

- All-purpose Discount Store: "Running a newspaper ad is like putting together a shopping list that displays a variety of items."

- Auto Dealer: "We use print as support to radio and television here. Newspaper for us is a car catalog with prices."

- Upscale Gift (china, silverware, etc.) Store: "We use newspapers for preprinted inserts."

- Electronics Store: "Print is the shopper's medium. People use it when they're in the market."

The interesting trend here is the beginning of a shift toward the electronic media and away from a traditional newspaper orientation that somehow no longer seems fulfilling. Respondents were concerned about the high costs of newspaper advertisement and were beginning to see the advantages of a media mix.

The very honest response of the media planner for a large department store chain, who stated that retailers "are in a learning process" and may not fully understand today's working woman and new, mobile customer, is telling of the frustration that exists within the retail business community in defining and reaching their intended demographic. This is nothing short of a request for assistance, for further education on how the media can help businesses survive the 1990s. It also indicates the open mind of a planner who is willing to forego tradition in favor of new approaches that will produce evident results.

There is also a strong, competitive feeling that many advertisers have, telling them that if the competition is there (in the newspaper), they had better be there too. Maybe. Maybe not. Are the goals of the competitor the same? The inventory? The intended demographic? Is the access to capital the same? Be very careful here. If you imitate, you are not different. Thousands of businesses go under each year using newspaper alone. Be sure you know who your Pied Piper is.

Much advertising and media misunderstanding still exists as evidenced by many of the reasons given for making the newspaper choice. Merchants are so print-oriented, they actually believe that they cannot present visually on the radio. Radio as the theater of the imagination, however, is the most visual of all the advertising forms.

What a consumer hears is immediately transferred to a vivid canvas of the mind where a picture is painted using his or her own brush. No black and white line drawing is presented, but a recreation of what the consumer desires. This translates to a longer memory store than viewing someone else's interpretation of what the consumer ought to want or be buying.

Several respondents were quick to tell of the large circulation their local newspaper provided. This represents a common mistake made by advertisers, that of assuming that there is a correlation between circulation and readership. No correlation exists. If a newspaper has a daily circulation of 25,000, do 25,000 households read the paper? Many will, but many will not. But the rates suggest that everybody will and you pay for the entire circulation.

Look at your own newspaper reading habits. Unless you are a businessperson looking for your ad, do you read the paper each day? What if you get home late, or you go to a movie that night? You probably will not get to the newspaper (but the television set was probably on when you got home from work in your car with the radio on). By tomorrow, it is yesterday's news and you will not pick it up at all. But the advertiser paid for the privilege of a written, tangible ad in your home that will be recycled without note. Rates based on circulation and not on actual consumers (as radio and television are) are always too high.

On the "MacNeil-Lehrer News Hour" (PBS) on June 11, 1992, the panel was discussing the presidential candidacy of Ross Perot with host Judy Woodruff. One of the guest panelists, print journalist Jonathan Alter, a *Newsweek* correspondent, mentioned that virtually no one reads the newspaper for daily information and that "people receive their information today exclusively from television."

This was one of the reasons these political analysts agreed that Ross Perot was a successful although unannounced candidate at the time. He was making the rounds of the talk shows that, together, have ratings larger than those of the combined network evening newscasts. It was no coincidence that he announced his willingness to serve in the nation's highest office on the Larry King show. And it may have been no coincidence that his star fell as quickly as it did, for it was indeed the electronic media that carried the message of a new Democratic party solidarity to the American people during the July convention, convincing Perot that he could not win by fighting two strongly entrenched political parties. Of course, Perot changed his mind about dropping out and reentered the race—by once again using television to bypass the political process and going directly to the American people.

Numerous respondents mentioned the catalog value of newspapers, mentioning the need to list varying prices from an inventory of fifty thousand items in one case. Although there is no particular problem with this approach, most readers will not be motivated to read such a catalog listing to discover if there is anything there they might be interested in purchasing.

A business that uses newspapers as a "Sears catalog" ought to consider a unique image positioning in the electronic media that can franchise consumers' minds with a positive, service-oriented campaign or other such theme. Doing this will ensure that consumers will enter the store when they need practically anything, not just when they happen to notice a newspaper price listing.

Several advertisers interviewed mentioned that they wanted quick results, correctly understanding that they can get them from the small number of today's buyers by using regular newspaper advertising. This strategy is successful as long as the advertiser is *the* business that consumers will come to when they wish to make their purchases.

On the consumer preference level scale, if a business with this strategy is at the number one position, even with strong competition, it will do well. If it is not, it is sacrificing what short-term success is available for long-term customer awareness, which can only be built over time with an intrusive electronic media campaign.

The advertisers who liked newspaper for price comparison purposes are probably using it in the best way. Those in the "now" market will use print to compare listed prices of what they have already decided to purchase.

Although newspaper ad lineage is down and, overall, they are suffering more than the electronic media from advertiser cutbacks, the infrastructure remains and, in many areas of the country, newspaper growth is actually occurring.

Following is a listing of the top ten newspapers by percentage in weekday circulation, as shown in the August 12 edition of *Advertising Age*. Such growth, of course, is to be expected in high-growth regions of the country where overall population does not decrease. Circulation gain, however, is no indicator of the same percentage of increased readership or of increased revenues for the newspaper.

1. *New York Post,* 27.7 percent

2. *Newsday* (New York City), 16.1 percent

3. *Asbury Park* (N.J.) *Press,* 8.7 percent

4. *Bergen County* (N.J.) *Record,* 6.9 percent

5. *Orange County* (Calif.) *Register,* 6.8 percent

6. *Atlanta Constitution,* 6.2 percent

7. *Dallas Morning News,* 6.0 percent

8. *The New York Times,* 5.2 percent

9. *Columbus* (Ohio) *Dispatch,* 4.6 percent

10. *Tulsa World,* 4.5 percent

Also remember, too, that more readers of a particular newspaper do not necessarily mean more readers of the newspaper's advertisements. The 2 percent "hot" market and the 8 percent in the "warm" or replacement market, who will be motivated to read the ads, are relative constants within the market, although a higher population will mean these figures, too, should be higher.

Question #3: What Do You Like or Dislike About Your Radio or Television Advertising?

Some vivid impressions are left from reviewing the responses to this probing question. Although many appreciated the strengths of radio and television as discussed in this book and were using radio in the proper way, there seems to be great misunderstanding about how radio in particular works and even greater confusion about how to select the proper station from among the dozens or so that may exist within the regional or local market.

The confusion about which station to use is so great that advertisers felt the easiest course of action was to just buy the newspaper. Dealing with one media salesperson was viewed as far less hassle than dealing with numerous radio representatives, all claiming that their station was either "number one" or one of many targeting the same adult demographic.

By buying newspaper advertising, the interviewed media planners felt they were covering the entire market and somewhere in that coverage lay the demographic they needed to reach. The approach may not be efficient but it is convenient.

Certainly, it is difficult to argue with the frustrations these advertisers feel. Radio in particular has been shooting itself in the foot for years by launching legions of gung-ho but untrained salespeople into the retail arena. This provides youth and exuberance but little professional consulting, further adding to advertiser confusion.

Another factor is the market fragmentation policies of the FCC in particular. By approving the number of radio licenses on both the AM as well as FM bands over the years, markets have become oversaturated with radio signals. The prime beneficiary of this questionable policy has been the newspapers, as seen from the responses these advertising buyers are giving.

Each market has a finite economic base that can support "x" number of media outlets. When that particular number is exceeded or grossly exceeded, a shakedown occurs and stations are sold or go dark (off the air without a buyer). This is happening now and will continue to occur throughout the 1990s as radio struggles for identity in a questionably healthy economy.

Let us now turn our attention to the specific responses given by the interviewees to the question of what they liked or did not like about radio or television advertising.

- Discount Store: "Radio is priced right, but there are too many stations to choose from. I do use it regularly, though, to target specific demographics, along with television."

- Grocery Store: "Radio works only so-so. It's a background medium, so people don't really pay attention to it. There are a lot of stations and it's confusing."

- Larger County Market: "Radio is diluted. There are too many stations. Five stations are after the same demographic. I can't judge effectiveness."

- Hardware Store: "Radio works well, but there is little budget left to buy it after newspaper. Television is used to introduce new stores or new concepts."

- Off-Price Retailer: "Television works the best for us, but we do use all three major media for specific buys."

- Upscale Department Store: "The electronic media is becoming more important to us as people's lifestyles change. People now get most of their information from radio and television and don't have time to read the newspaper.

  "About half the radio salespeople are helpful and try to build relationships and rapport. They should help make me more knowledgeable. Actually, the radio reps are humorous because there's such a wide spectrum of them available. They should come to me with specific ideas on what I can do . . . that's their job. But too often they come in and ask me what *I* want to do to get the attention of *their* audience."

- Grocer: "We can target better with radio, for example, the older demographics. Radio is better for advertising certain departments like the video shop. We use thirty-five to forty different radio stations overall in this region to target specific demos. . . . Our stores cater to the highest income profile to the very lowest."

- Auto Dealer: "Almost half our budget goes to radio and television. We have sixteen radio stations. . . . I use three or four regularly to target 25–49-year-old women. Radio is flexible and easy to buy, but since it's so fragmented, I use radio to target demographics and television for overall reach. I'm also beginning to use a lot of cable."

- Discounter: "We like radio. We buy the stations that match the demos of our main customers in each of our stores. We have stores in various areas that cater to upper ago demos, some to younger buyers, and some to minorities."

- Furniture Store: "Radio is cost-efficient. The top four stations in our market deliver 55 percent of the females in my target group. . . . I have good success in radio outside of our metro area, in areas not served by Arbitron, or else no station buys a major survey. Some buy lesser surveys that are meaningless. I could use a dart board when buying radio here and be just as successful. I like the affordability of television and can get good numbers, a 25 rating, at 10:00 P.M."

- Furniture Store: "Television is too expensive, radio is hard to measure but more affordable."

- Appliance Dealer: "We use radio for big sales only. It's too fragmented for regular advertising. Each station has a much smaller group than the number who would see a newspaper ad."

- Discount Store: "Radio is too much of a hassle, trying to decide which stations to buy."

- Furniture Store: "We like radio best in the smaller markets. The larger markets are too fragmented."

- Department Store: "Before buying radio, I first decide on the demographics or lifestyle of the group likely to buy what is being advertised and then buy the station that best suits what is being promoted."

- Department Store: "We buy radio as a media mix with newspapers."

- Grocery Store: "Radio limits the message. Newspaper is best for price, image, and detail. Besides, there's too many stations that are too difficult to buy."

- Upscale Specialty Store: "Radio is good for advertising an event, but it is too fragmented with too many stations. It's unbelievably broad and too difficult to buy. The stations that have the large shares have premium prices."

- Department Store Chain: "Radio is much better for impact than newspaper."

- Bank: "We cut radio out. People don't listen to radio. Well . . . we do buy two spots daily on the top station. And television? No one ever sees our television ad."

- Grocery Chain: "We have very funny ads on radio, but people don't comment that they have heard them. They don't comment on television either, but they always have their newspaper ad with them."

- Auto Dealer: "We don't get enough immediate results from the electronic media."

- Auto Dealer: "Radio does keep awareness up because the copy was excellent, but we spent a lot last year when the market was flat with poor return. When the market is back, maybe it will work better. We'll probably use it for special promotions. We're buying a lot of cable because it's cheaper."

Advertisers certainly do not hold back their feelings concerning the electronic media. That their understanding of this most powerful of all forms of advertising is not more advanced is a discredit to the broadcasting industry that has been more interested in reaching monthly quotas than attempting to educate clients for long-term success with radio or television advertising.

Fortunately, this profit-for-now approach of telling local advertisers whatever is needed to get the sale is slowly changing, state by state, as more professionally trained broadcast consultants are indeed educating their clients by explaining to them how advertising works and how to use the various forms of the mass media to get the biggest return for the required investment.

General advertiser confusion, however, is readily apparent from the tabulated responses to all three questions, even though many do understand the lifestyle changes occurring, the rejection of newspaper as an information source, and the necessity of targeting an audience who matches the lifestyle of the product being sold.

One apparent misunderstanding has to do with radio as a background medium. This is one of the major misconceptions of radio, that it is background to whatever is being done at home or in the office. Although radio is used in this manner, the intrusive nature of the medium still allows the message to register, much as a soundtrack is background to the dialogue of a film — never consciously registered but no less important.

Radio itself is an intensely personal medium that speaks directly and only the listener, something no other medium can do. A high percentage of any station's audience is involved "up close and personal" and listens intently to the programming, be it music, talk, sports, or the personality who is the announcer.

That markets are diluted with too many signals aimed at a similar demographic cannot be denied. The sense of frustration shown by these advertisers is understandable as they are absolutely correct. Given the nearly ten thousand radio stations in operation in the United States alone, with many of the larger markets covered by more than seventy clear signals, it becomes even more difficult to choose the proper station for any particular product or store.

The best recommendation in this situation is not to reject the electronic media as major sources of advertising, but to find a station that is represented by a true consultant who is more interested in helping you solve your business inventory and marketing problems than in selling you for the sake of a commission.

These people are out there. They will ask questions about your business, will show you if their audience profile matches the profiles of your main customers, and will not attempt to sell you until they have devised an advertising solution for your needs that you agree will address the concerns you have.

Keep these people close at hand. They are your business consultants. And you do not have to pay them, their stations do. Throw the others out. As with any other product available in large quantities, some of that number are not going to be as good as others.

Consider any business that stocks multiple products. Within that product line, there will be a product leader and there will be others that seem to perform like the leader, but will be considerably cheaper to the consumer. In many instances, the consumer who purchases the less expensive product finds that it does not perform as well as the leading product, will not last as long, and does not have the same service after the sale the leading product has. In many comparable ways, the cheaper product is likely to be deficient when compared with the leading product.

The same situation exists within the advertising field. Some stations, as are many businesses, will not be run as well. Their programming within the market will be weak and their audience numbers low, as fewer listeners consider the station to be attractive. And their salespeople will not be professionally trained, probably being pushed by an autocratic manager who is more interested in quotas than in taking the time to meet customer needs.

With the capability of each station's management to set the rates for advertising time based on total audience reached or other factors the station feels important, the advertising buyer must make a decision on which purchase will deliver the correct audience, will have the best cost-benefit ratio, and is the overall best buy for the business.

Advertisers who claim that no money remains in the budget after buying newspaper need to understand the importance of reversing their planned budget to buy the electronic media first and then back up that purchase with the newspaper. Newspaper and all print advertising should represent 30 percent to 40 percent of the budget with 60 percent to 70 percent allocated to the electronic media, if advertisers wish to achieve the kinds of results possible from tapping into the information thus far presented in the previous chapters.

It is certainly true that each radio or television station delivers a smaller group than the circulation of the newspaper. But remember that newspaper circulation is no guarantee of readership, and that the successful advertiser wants to target a message to a smaller group representing the proper target customer.

Newspaper advertising represents waste. An advertiser needs to buy the entire circulation just to place one ad in a certain section, most of which is advertising. Advertising clutter does not just exist on America's highways with its multiplex of billboards and neon signs. Overcommercialization exists within every advertising medium, including radio and television, but nowhere is it more pronounced than in newspaper.

Clutter is synonymous with newspaper advertising, which any enterprising advertiser or media salesperson could discover by referencing an edition or two of the local newspaper and analyzing the content on the basis of advertising versus news and all other nonadvertising content.

An analysis of a recent daily newspaper for a city of approximately 50,000 population showed that section A had an average of 15 pages with 1,890 column inches available. Of that total, 933 column inches were advertising or 49.3 percent of the available space. Section B had 16 pages and 2,016 column inches, of which 1,340 column inches (66.5 percent) were devoted to advertising. The two sections combined had 3,906 column inches available: 58.2 percent of the combined total was advertising; 41.3 percent was used for news, editorial page, entertainment page, columns, comics, and the like; and 0.5 percent was used for the newspaper's own promotion.[1]

In addition, not counted in the above figures were three multipage, multicolor inserts. If this edition were bound, it would look like a large book. Somewhere in that edition would be the advertiser's message. What percentage of those in the "now" market will see this ad?

If a particular radio station schedules 18 minutes of commercials per hour, which is usually the maximum saturation for the heaviest commercial station, can that compare with newspaper percentages? Eighteen minutes is 30 percent of 60 minutes. Television's normal maximum is 16 minutes or 26.7 percent of the hour.

As well, both radio and television are directing their scheduled commercials to a well-defined audience that is clearly identified for advertisers before the commercial is even run. Newspaper sandwiches a printed message to a mass audience somewhere in an encyclopedic volume for readers to randomly find.

That people do not listen to radio is, again, another myth. Radio is such a deeply ingrained part of our culture that it is often taken for granted and not noticed. The analogy is the question once posed to a college science class by the professor who asked the students to list everything they needed to survive a normal day. Correctly, the students noted food, shelter, and other college necessities like "beer and babes," but they neglected the most important element of all that would ensure their survival, simply because it was so obvious that no one thought about it: oxygen.

And so it goes with radio in our culture.

CONCLUSIONS

The confusion, misunderstanding, and lack of media education that exist, within the business community are products of the broadcasting industry and the unwillingness of advertisers to change traditional buying patterns in response to mounting evidence of lifestyle changes in an electronic society that displays little inclination to revert back to newspapers as the main source of information or entertainment.

Newspapers

That better information has to be available for advertisers is evident from the respondents to these series of interviews who essentially harbor traditional views of the newspaper: that the tangibility of the medium allows the advertiser to flip through the pages until the firm's advertisement is found and that everyone reads it since it stays around for days as a written reference, with readers looking first to the newspaper to find whatever it is they are looking for.

First, finding one's ad within the newspaper is psychological stroking. The advertiser who is looking for the ad and eventually finds it assumes that every other reader of the paper has also found and read the ad just as carefully. The newspaper also delivers a tearsheet to the large volume, regular advertisers before the ad is actually run in the paper. The advertiser can then sit back, hold this ad in hand, and admire it even before it appears in print. It then usually ends up on the bulletin board to admire for days to come, thus reinforcing the feeling that everyone else is also admiring and seeing the very same ad.

Second, advertisers who feel newspapers lie around for days, serving as a ready reference for all who care to view their ad, are no doubt reassured by the audited circulation figures that show how many newspapers are bought and that readership is several times greater than these figures, thus giving a massive audience for the printed advertisement.

Newspapers like to think that their editions stay around for days, waiting for those who missed reading the issue to pick it up and read through it, page by page. Certainly a newspaper does stay around for days—but usually in a pile awaiting recycling, simply because it has been replaced by a more current issue. Consumers do not go back and read old news. The newspaper, like most other advertising media, has its greatest impact when it is current and that currency is quickly lost.

Of course, there is some truth to the circulation figures and the observation that audiences are greater than those figures. If businesses did not advertise in newspapers, they would have died long ago, but few people read yesterday's news. An ad missed today is an ad missed; a new edition is only a day away. And circulation is never a guarantee of readership—it is only a circulation figure and nothing else.

Also, as we have been discussing, newspaper's slice of the advertising pie has decreased over the years with the advent of radio and television. The number of daily newspapers published decreases steadily each year as costs continue to put under even the most established of the traditional dailies.

We have also seen that not everybody reads the newspaper, an assumption that causes advertisers to continue to buy large amounts of space in local papers. However, circulation figures show that most newspapers do not reach even 50 percent of the local population.

Figure 7.1 shows the total time spent by women and men on a daily basis with the major media. As expected, television receives the most attention, followed by radio, with newspaper receiving the least amount of daily attention by both men and women in all age groups. This should send a more than clear message to advertisers.

Of those who do receive a newspaper, either by subscription or from a newsstand, do all of them read the volume? Contrast your own newspaper-reading

Figure 7.1
Time Spent per Day with Major Media (in Minutes)

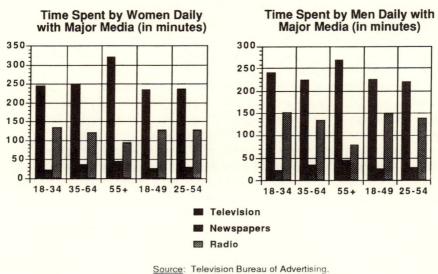

Source: Television Bureau of Advertising,
from Bruskin Associates data.

habits or ask your business associates about their newspaper-reading habits. Generally, a fair percentage miss reading the paper on any given day for any number of reasons; others who said they read the newspaper that day or the night before meant that they *skimmed* the newspaper, flipping from the front page, to the local news page, to the editorial page, to the sports page, to the comics. If you asked anyone who said they read the whole paper, "Did you see the ad for the dry cleaners or the florist shop on page 12?" the likely response would be, "Well, no. I wasn't interested in dry cleaning . . . or flowers." Of course. Only 2 percent of readers will be in the "now" market.

The Audit Bureau of Circulation provides county by county audited circulation figures that show how many households subscribe to the newspaper and how many total people or families are exposed to or had the opportunity to read the newspaper. These figures in no way can determine how many readers read any particular ad. Nor can they tell an advertiser what percentage of the market segment they are interested in reaching is penetrated by the newspaper.

Again, circulation is no guarantee of readership. Contrast your own newspaper reading habits. How often do you read parts of the paper in which you are interested, without noting the ads contained within that section? The truth is, you will not notice the ads unless you are in the immediate market. You want to finish your area of interest and move on to the next section. You are not unique in your ability to ignore ads, even full-page and double-trucks (double-page ads), as you read parts of the paper of interest to you. Millions of people do it every day.

Most people, coupon-clippers possibly excluded, do not buy a newspaper for the advertisements. Nor does one listen to the radio or watch television for the advertisements. At least in the electronic media, the commercials are intrusive. In newspaper, the advertisements are a hindrance to skip unless the reader is indeed one of the 2 percent in the immediate market.

The Media Mix Approach

The implication here is not nor has it been one of claiming that newspaper advertising is wasted money. It is imperative to reach that immediate market of "now" buyers. What is not imperative is to spend the vast majority of the budget in doing so. That majority percentage should be reserved for the electronic media, with newspaper serving an appropriate back-up role. Many companies, for example, give strong, up-front electronic media support for a product to create brand awareness. Once brand awareness has been established through frequency, newspaper advertising is then used to sell the product. Price-item print advertising works best when attempting to motivate a consumer toward a familiar product. Radio and television schedules are than maintained to keep brand-awareness levels high and newspapers regularly promote competitive prices to keep comparative "now" shoppers motivated.

This media mix approach will best serve the advertiser, as no medium is the only workable medium for advertising despite the claims of partisan salespeople. No single advertising medium can accomplish the ultimate results for every advertising need.

However, even the thought of switching to a media mix strategy encompassing more than one type of advertising medium to get a message across to a targeted audience makes some advertising managers uncomfortable. Those with smaller budgets who feel they cannot afford a wide variety of media will feel the least comfortable, while the larger stores with corresponding budgets understand the necessity of utilizing various media to accomplish their company's advertising goals. Just remember—all advertising is probably measurably effective. However, not all is equally efficient. The electronic media provides this efficiency, thus reducing overall waste.

The natural inclination of media planners, which must necessarily be reevaluated, is most often to buy newspaper first and oftentimes solely. For companies or stores that have been in business for generations, newspaper advertising is the traditional advertising medium even though radio or television may have been experimented with from time to time. Such a company or store that has found success over the years, is profitable, and uses newspaper advertising almost exclusively, tends to assume that newspaper advertising has had something to do with the success of the business.

And arguably so. Wherever the budget is spent is where success will be found. No businessperson wants to tinker with something that is working, even if the feeling is that it might be made to work better or more efficiently. There is a certain comfort with tradition. Traditional decisions ease the fear that working on something or changing it in some way might make the situation even worse.

This feeling is understandable. Radio and television are infants compared to the print media. Most businesses are astute enough to recognize that these new nonprint media do work for advertising purposes, but the fear is that they do not know how to use them properly. They therefore make token use of the electronic media, never unleashing their true potential for their businesses, while retaining the comfort of using the familiar newspaper medium as the major advertising source.

Most advertising failures result from the incorrect use of the media and the lack of understanding of how advertising works, rather than from the ineffectiveness of the media themselves. Like any other tool, advertising must be used properly to produce the intended and desired results.

Cable Television

Cable television is a player that is here to stay and will be a huge growth factor in the coming decade and into the twenty-first century. According to *Broadcasting* magazine, as of the summer of 1992, 61 percent of the 93.1 million television households were subscribers to cable television service.

More specifically, 92,040,450 were passed, meaning the actual cable wiring had been strung by their homes and service was available if desired. Of this number, 55,786,390 homes had elected to subscribe to the cable service offered by the 11,254 systems offering such services nationwide.

Most customers subscribe to the basic cable service and pay from $15 to $30 per month for this service. Additionally, premium or pay services like HBO and Showtime may be purchased for an added on monthly fee of approximately $10 per channel chosen. About half of this fee is paid by the local cable operator to the vendor company (HBO, Showtime, etc.) for the service.

Even though cable service in all markets represents the ultimate in market fragmentation, like television, it can also serve as an effective surgical strike tool. Unlike the electronic media, which receive over 90 percent of revenues from advertising, in cable less than 10 percent of total revenues from advertising. Ninety percent, or the bulk of cable revenue, comes from subscriber fees.

The more subscribers, the higher the revenue but also the higher the expense of operation. Local cable systems acquire programming by paying a per subscriber fee to the network or service being offered. The fee is based on the overall popularity of the network or station and may range from five cents per subscriber for Cable NBC (CNBC—the network for financial news) to twenty-five cents per subscriber for services like CNN or ESPN.

The growth spurt of the cable advertising industry occurred in the 1980s. At the beginning of the decade, total advertising volume (just over $60 million) represented less than one percent of total broadcast industry revenues. By the end of the decade, total cable advertising revenue was approaching $2 billion. The vast percentage of this figure represents national ad dollars that flow to the larger cable operators with the highest percentage of viewers, stations like CNN and ESPN. Of the $2 billion total, over half is spent by the top thirty spenders on cable television, as shown in Table 7.2.

Table 7.2

Leading Advertisers on Cable Television (in Millions of Dollars)

	1991	1990	% change
1. Procter & Gamble Co.	$ 67.8	$ 57.9	17.1 %
2. General Motors Corp.	32.4	26.0	24.6
3. General Mills	31.8	27.4	16.1
4. Anheuser-Busch Cos.	31.4	26.8	17.2
5. Time Warner	29.3	50.9	- 42.4
6. Philip Morris Cos.	24.1	26.6	- 9.4
7. Sears Roebuck & Co.	20.3	19.8	2.5
8. AT&T Co.	19.3	15.3	26.1
9. Eastman Kodak Co.	19.1	12.6	51.6
10. American Home Products Corp.	19.1	10.8	76.9
11. RJR Nabisco	17.8	21.7	- 18.0
12. Mars Inc.	16.6	10.4	59.6
13. McDonald's Corp.	16.2	8.8	84.1
14. Hasbro Inc.	15.6	7.8	100.0
15. PepsiCo	15.1	13.1	15.2
16. Ford Motor Co.	14.0	9.5	47.4
17. Wm. Wrigley Jr. Co.	13.9	10.2	36.3
18. Chrysler Corp.	12.9	9.2	40.2
19. Levi Strauss & Co.	12.5	12.7	- 1.6
20. Grand Metropolitan	11.4	10.3	10.7
21. Ralston Purina Co.	10.7	7.6	40.8
22. Nestle Foods Corp.	10.4	8.4	25.0
23. Kellogg Co.	9.5	3.6	163.9
24. Johnson & Johnson	9.5	8.3	14.5
25. Clorox Co.	9.0	10.8	- 16.7
26. Nintendo of America	8.9	5.8	53.4
27. Sony Corp.	8.4	9.7	- 13.4
28. Toyota Motor Sales USA	8.1	5.8	39.7
29. Coca-Cola Co.	8.1	2.9	179.3
30. Unilever U.S.	8.1	6.7	20.9
Total cable TV spending	$1,211.6	$1,110.2	9.1 %

Reprinted with permission from the May 11 issue of Advertising Age. Copyright, Crain Communications Inc., 1992.

Local systems that have an advertising sales staff in place bill a combined total of just over $500 million, scheduling advertising inserts within the total availabilities of stations like CNN.

Although an impressive growth spurt, the younger cable offspring is still a stepchild to its television parent whose total revenues are nearly ten times as great as cable. However, cable will continue to remain attractive to local advertisers throughout the remainder of the 1990s as audiences become better defined and the prospect of surgically striking a smaller, more precise demographic becomes an important part of overall advertising planning.

The attractiveness of cable to many advertisers is its overall affordability that opens the opportunity of getting the message onto the television screen itself. In many markets, the price per commercial is even less expensive than radio, from $3 to $5 per scheduled announcement.

Advertisers should understand the advantages and the disadvantages of this type of market advertising. Used properly, cable can be a big addition to the overall marketing efforts of the advertiser. Used improperly, as with a vanity buy, it can be a waste of money that could and probably should go to an identified target audience more directly related to marketing needs and available on either the proper radio or conventional television station.

The average cable system offers a total of 36 channels to its subscribers. Some offer less; many have up to 54 selections; and a few, like New York City franchises, have 150 channels. The issue of market fragmentation has certainly been addressed in this book and, as was stated, cable represents the epitome of market fragmentation.

The most popular of the cable offerings, channels like CNN, ESPN, WTNT, Lifetime, and the so-called independent superstations like WTBS (Atlanta) and WGN (Chicago) that offer their local major league baseball and basketball teams on a regular basis, have only 2 percent to 3 percent (5 percent at most) of the available market as viewers. Of this percentage of cable viewers, who watches what in which region of the country, their household size and income can be seen in Table 7.3.

An advertiser who markets a specific line of goods like sporting equipment could have success on a channel like ESPN, as the defined demographic can be assumed to be those who enjoy sports programming. However, most advertisers who offer a less specific line of goods may have difficulty choosing a channel with the desired target demographics.

Even if this can be done, as with ESPN, an advertiser will have to run a tremendous amount of frequency (commercials per week) to have an impact on that audience. Since fewer viewers are watching, with many of them "zapping" in and out to catch up on the latest sports update or watch portions of a game, more commercials (frequency) will have to be programmed to reach these people the minimum threshold of three times that researchers claim is necessary to retain top-of-mind awareness.

Most advertisers cannot afford extremely high frequency targeted to a smaller audience and will opt to spend that budget on a larger medium where effective frequency can be reached and maintained at a more affordable level.

Even though the audience for cable is fragmented, cable does target specific audiences, which can be an advantage in reaching such a defined group more efficiently. Radio and conventional television will, however, attract a larger and more homogenized consumer group that may better fit the consumer profile desired by the advertiser and at a cost that is affordable for the desired results.

When new population areas were initially wired for cable, many new subscribers were anxious to watch television that they thought would be more commercial-free. What has remained commercial-free are the pay services like HBO and the competing movie channels. The basic services are advertising-based and

Table 7.3
Who's Watching What on Cable Television and Where

Territory	A&E	BET	CNN	ESPN	HBO			LIFE	TNT	VH1		MTV			USA	......
Northeast	30%	19%	21%	21%	18%	23%	23%	13%	23%	29%	21%	27%	20%	21%	24%	25%
East Central	15	15	13	14	15	14	15	15	16	14	NA*	14	14	18	15	14
West Central	14	9	17	13	14	13	16	18	14	12	15	11	18	18	12	13
Southeast	20	29	21	23	28	22	26	35	21	17	20	17	21	22	23	19
Southwest	8	20	11	12	12	9	14	15	12	11	16	12	14	9	10	10
Pacific	14	8	18	17	13	19	6	5	15	17	28	18	14	12	15	19
Household size																
1 person	20%	11%	26%	12%	14%	17%	20%	26%	14%	13%	15%	12%	13%	18%	15%	21%
2 person	40	23	40	36	35	35	28	45	33	21	38	21	22	41	36	37
3 person	40	66	34	52	52	47	52	27	53	66	47	67	66	41	48	42
4+ person	22	45	20	32	32	30	31	13	32	45	30	42	40	24	29	22
Household income																
Under $20,000	16%	46%	25%	19%	29%	19%	26%	44%	25%	17%	NA*	24%	29%	41%	33%	25%
$20,000–$30,000	16	16	16	16	17	19	14	14	16	15	15	16	13	19	18	15
$30,000–$40,000	15	13	13	17	15	16	21	12	16	15	NA*	14	15	13	15	15
$40,000–$60,000	21	17	21	23	19	21	19	11	20	24	33	18	23	13	18	23
$60,000+	26	13	25	25	20	25	20	7	23	29	27	28	20	14	16	22
Education of household																
No college	49%	66%	50%	54%	67%	60%	53%	84%	58%	53%	40%	53%	59%	69%	65%	57%
4+ years college	30	15	30	24	14	20	28	8	27	27	11	24	21	11	16	23

Source: Advertising Age, April 6, 1992.

with no FCC regulations on the number of commercials any cable station can schedule, cable viewing is often more commercial-oriented than the traditional television offerings.

So-called informercials are the best example of this. Passing for thirty- to sixty-minute, information-based news programs, the stars of these cable shows are the products being advertised. From personal self-improvement and how to sell real estate programs to space age lint removers and auto restoration products, program hosts have the opportunity to present, explain, and demonstrate each product, sometimes to a delighted audience all anxious beyond words to own whatever is being touted. "Commercial" breaks consist of an announcer representing the product, but now introducing the price (which the host never does) and the 800 toll-free number to call to order the product.

Such advertising will continue in cable because it works and is a source of income for the cable stations paid to schedule the informercials.

THE ROLE OF THE BUSINESSPERSON

It is once again important to recognize that the proper management of advertising within the greater marketing arena is but one of the many responsibilities facing a business manager. Persons designated as "advertising managers" are likely to shoulder more responsibilities than those designated by their name plate.

When situations of multiple responsibility occur within a particular business, those decision makers whose responsibility it is to make multiple daily decisions will do what any of us in similar situations would do when faced with a full plate. They will give priority to those areas that are familiar, and are a part of their background, training, or formal education.

In most cases, this will not be advertising. Those decisions are made with what is believed to be careful thought and consideration but what is actually convenience and speed. We all spend the least amount of time on the areas in which we are the least comfortable, especially when we believe we are doing the right thing—like buying newspaper advertising almost exclusively to promote our business.

Decision makers also tend, and rightly so, to put their faith in those they believe will do the best job for them in planning their advertising. With the number of radio station representatives confronting the average retailer in one day, the confusion that exists is understandable, along with the result: a newspaper buy and a "I'll think about it" for radio. If television is in the picture, it will be given consideration if the store has a large enough budget, as television is often viewed as an entity unto itself, separate from other advertising forms and not as confusing as radio due to fewer signals available in the marketplace.

Corporations, retailers, advertisers, and media planners, in order to continue business success into the 1990s, must begin a process of "paradigm thinking." Joel Arthur Barker defines a "paradigm" as a set of rules and regulations that establishes or defines boundaries and tells us how to behave within those boundaries. Or, we could use Karl Albrecht's definition that a paradigm is a mental frame of reference that dominates the way people think and act.

Indeed, many paradigms dominate human thought. Such thinking explains our behavior as we do not act inconsistently with such paradigms. Albrecht explains: "Most paradigms . . . tend to operate below the level of conscious thought. They tend to dominate a person's thinking about his or her direct awareness [and] tend to make themselves apparent only when something violates or contradicts them. For example, if homosexual men seek to get married to each other, people who accept the standard "paradigm" of marriage as a legal and sexual union between a male and a female may not view their proposed merger as appropriate."[2]

Paradigms, like values, are neither right nor wrong. They are, as Albrecht notes, handed down from one generation to the next, communicated from company to company and culture to culture by modeling and imitation. All executives from different companies in the same field read the same trade publications and management literature and migrate from one company to another, thus causing a kind of homogeneity in thinking.

A company, however, can begin its own paradigm by breaking the mold and setting its own standards for excellence. Witness the success of Apple Computer's blue jeans whiz kids Steve Jobs and Bob Wozniak, who defined new parameters in bringing the MacIntosh computer to market; or the Dana Corporation that shares all company financial information with hourly operators on the line; or Stew Leonard's supermarket, whose attempts at pleasing the customer defy anything done by anyone in any industry.

New paradigms, of course, mean new ways of thinking and change is the most difficult challenge in entrenched organizational bureaucracies whose instinct is to protect the status quo. Twenty-first-century thinking must necessarily focus on new paradigms as the Western management paradigm is certainly failing. What is preventing the West from being more competitive and what prevents any business from being more successful is "that many of the ideas, values, priorities, precepts, rules and kinds of cultures that can deliver superior value to the customer and make quality their competitive edge"[3] are simply not in place. To become successful, to be competitive, to survive means a shift to a new paradigm.

For decades, advertisers have been utilizing newspaper as their traditional form of advertising. The advertising paradigm has been one of playing the game according to the rules: go into business and spend a majority of your budget buying newspaper advertising. This is what you do despite the logic of recognizing the dominant role of the electronic media in our culture.

This is also dinosaur thinking, as the advertising paradigm is shifting rapidly. A paradigm shift necessitates changing to a new game with a new set of rules. The new advertising game is the electronic media. Ignoring this new reality and choosing to cling to the status quo simply because it feels comfortable creates a "Linus' blanket" effect. Certainly, learning new boundaries is never easy when the old environs are practiced out of habit.

However, those who will not be affected by this new paradigm shift will be the ones who are able to anticipate the changes, to see the new rules on the horizon before they become rules. Those advertisers who recognize the rule changes that are occurring in advertising and see the massive shifts to the electronic media on the horizon, will be the survivors of this last decade of the twentieth century.

WHAT EFFECTIVE ADVERTISING MUST DO

To help advertisers and businesspeople better understand the necessity for a paradigm shift in advertising thinking, it may be helpful to draw together all of the information thus far presented in this book, mix it together with other sources, and come up with a listing of exactly what good advertising of any sort ought to accomplish if it is to be successful. Constructing any type of advertisement or commercial designed to run on any media should be done with care to accomplish certain preset objectives.

An ad should not be scheduled just to "run" for the sake of having an ad or a commercial that day. It should be constructed with the understanding that the end result must necessarily move consumers from being unaware or neutral about a store or a product to actually becoming customers.

This can only occur if the advertising is able to accomplish the following objectives; otherwise it has failed in the marketplace and money has been wasted.

After reading each item, ask yourself this question: Which media can best accomplish this goal for my business? Brief comments will be offered after each observation, with the goal of assisting advertisers in understanding the new paradigm presenting itself in a post cold war economy.

Advertising must create a sense of awareness within the marketplace. Awareness is vital due to the strong correlation between name recognition and market share.

Assuming this given, how is awareness created? Simply, awareness means receiving attention. Directing attention away from the dozens or hundreds of competing messages or images cannot be effectively done in print. One print ad next to many others does not compete. The way in which awareness is created is by using and appealing to a consumer's sense of emotion and feeling. These emotions are aroused by using humor and drama.

Newspaper is not an emotional medium and a page full of ads in either the evening edition or the Yellow Pages utilizes neither drama nor humor, although there does exist a joke—which is, of course, on the advertiser.

All advertising must create consumer confidence and must build credibility. If there is no confidence, there is no store traffic. Credibility may be the single most important goal of all advertising, as the final word flashing through the consumer's thought process, right before the moment of purchase, is just that—credibility. Credibility sustains sales for years.

How is credibility conveyed in advertising? Through a print advertisement or the creative imagery of the electronic media? How would you, for example, cause an audience to remember cheese? Specifically, "Laughing Cow" cheese?

VALLEY GIRL: So like I was driving down the Freeway, ok. And this totally gorgoso highway patrolman stops me. So I said like wow, there's wheels on your motorcycle and wheels on my car. I mean, that's really Kharmoso. He said you were speeding. I said I have to get my little round Laughing Cow in the red net bag into the fridge, ok. He said, where's the cow. I said, in the trunk, ok. He said, you're not authorized to carry livestock. I said, officer that is like really heavy. The Laughing Cow isn't like a real cow, ok, it's like cheese, ok. Mild Mini Bonbel, Nippy Mini Babybel and new Mini Gouda. You know, like really awesome and naturelle. Five delicious round cheeses in little net bags. Each one wrapped like in wax with a cute little zip thing. He said, open the trunk. I said ok. He said you need a key. I mean like this guy was totally brilliant, ok. I said you want a little Laughing Cow? So he said ok. So I said ok. So we said ok, ok. So then he asked me for my license. And I said when can I see you again. He was so totally freaked like he dropped the cheese and bit the ticket. So now it's two weeks and he never called.

This commercial from Joy Golden at Joy Radio in New York won a Clio. But, how can you develop or even recognize a creative sense? Robert Fearon, president of the Creative Zone in New York City, explains:

Remember, trust your own creative sense. You can and must make some subjective appraisals of the work you'll be seeing. . . . Keep in mind that you shouldn't get blown away by the outrageous. Being outrageous . . . for the sake of being different . . . is not . . . creative advertising. Being creative is finding the right balance of appeal and presence that will help produce sales. . . . The most important thing to look for is a message that is understandable, persuasive and clearly identifiable as yours.[4]

And who could forget our friends Jake and Clint from Wrangler? We bring them back for an encore, this time at a wedding.

SFX: Bridal march. (Jake and Clint whisper to each other.)

CLINT: Jake?

JAKE: Yeah, Clint.

CLINT: She sure makes a pretty bride.

JAKE: She sure does.

CLINT: You nervous?

JAKE: My stomach feels like that time I rode Tornado in the finals.

CLINT: It looks like every cowboy on the circuit showed up.

JAKE: Well, I guess this is it.

CLINT: There's no turning back now.

JAKE: Boy, Clint, it isn't easy being ushers at a wedding.

VO: Wrangler, the official jeans and shirts of pro rodeo. And other PRCA events.

Advertising must establish a consistent reputation within the minds of consumers. No store or merchant has all the business within any marketplace, but each has a reputation that far exceeds the customer base. That reputation is closely tied to the credibility factor. When that product or service is needed by the consumer, whether tomorrow or next quarter, which store will get the business? Where will that consumer go to make the purchase? To the business with the "best" reputation.

Reputation, as well, sustains sales into the future, but also allows a business to take on new product lines successfully or to open stores in other markets with less risk.

How best to establish "reputation" with advertising? Via a black and white "one time" impression or via the intrusive nature of a creative radio or television commercial?

Advertising must offset or combat the competitive claims of advertisers who are also competing for "share of mind" and consumer time within the marketplace. The most effective method to offset competing claims or to position a business apart from its competition is to explain. Bottom line: explanation is best done on radio and television, not with newspaper.

Advertising must paint a familiar image in the minds of consumers. Image, reputation, credibility—they all swim together on the same canvas and must be painted with the same electronic media brush. A familiar image simply means easy recognition of the business and its product line. Easy recognition means floor traffic, which means sales.

Advertising must sell the benefits of the business or the product line(s). Consumers do not always buy the lowest-priced item, nor do they all gravitate to the low-price leaders in the market. There are many other reasons besides price that motivate consumers to make a buying decision, as any businessperson well knows. These reasons are the benefits offered by the store, be they service, quality of merchandise, or convenience of location. These benefits can best be explained on an intrusive medium, not printed away in the evening newspaper.

Advertising must help a business build demand for its products or services. Demand is the cumulative result of credibility, reputation, and benefit-explanation. Consumers want what other consumers have and what they see others enjoying on television or talking about on the radio. Once a consumer has a positive experience with a business, demand begins to build as that consumer will want to come back again to buy either the same or additional goods.

In short, a business with demand for its goods and services has successfully moved numerous consumers into the top preference level or the top-of-mind awareness category. This can only be done intrusively over time, not with a printed message that will not be noted by over 90 percent of the target market.

Good advertising is a reminder to consumers that the business is still here and still offering unexcelled quality and service. The top businesses and product categories continue to advertise. They are consistent. Coke is always there, constantly reminding consumers not to forget. McDonald's is ever-present. The more established the business, the more it seems to remind consumers not to forget. Not doing so results in rapid erosion of market share.

Advertising that is effective is not only noticed by marketplace consumers, but is noted and appreciated by the employees of the business doing the advertising. Morale is always better within a store that has an effective media presence in the marketplace. Morale is unsteady at best in a business that does little to no advertising.

Intrusive campaigns on radio and television are noted more readily by employees than the accepted and expected norm of a printed ad. Radio and television imply something special and create conversations like, "Did you see or did you hear . . . ?"

Finally, as noted by Brian Mullen and Craig Johnson, *nothing much in advertising makes sense unless it is able to make people feel good about the advertised store or product.* Feeling good sums up everything to this point. If a consumer does not feel good about entering a store or buying a particular product, it will not happen.

We have considered a number of distinct possible determinants of emotional responses toward products. . . . One common element in all of these mechanisms should be emphasized. In each case, the issue is not whether consumers believe or accept the message (cognition); and the issue is not whether consumers remember the product information (memory); the issue is not even whether consumers can report awareness of the product (perception). The issue that underlies the determinants of emotional response is, simply, whether the consumers feel good about the product.[5]

Making people feel good is the prime objective of the entertainment media of radio and television. This is done quite simply through repetition. Even if consumers do not use a particular product or enter a particular store, they can still feel good about that product or store by being exposed to intrusive advertising. How does this help a business? Good feelings eventually make good customers.

TOP TWENTY-FIVE MEGABRANDS BY 1991 AD SPENDING

It is always interesting, whether planning local, regional, or national advertising campaigns, to see who spends the most overall to promote which product or products. Table 7.4 presents the 1991 top twenty-five brands according to the total amount spent on all forms of advertising.

Closing the Gap

Two avenues are available for closing the gap that exists between what the advertiser knows and what that person should know to make effective advertising decisions: self-education or finding a media sales representative who will serve as a mentor and educator in helping the advertiser to better understand advertising and how it works in the marketplace of the 1990s.

This book will hopefully be one source for self-education and, as well, will

Table 7.4
Ad Spending on Megabrands, 1991

Total Measured Ad Spending

Rank 1991	1990	Brand & Product	1991	1990	% change
1.	1.	AT&T / phone services	$ 388,926.9	$ 463,848.8	-16.2 %
2.	2.	McDonald's	387,326.5	426,422.9	-9.2
3.	5.	Ford / cars, trucks,vans	373,052.4	341,701.7	9.2
4.	4.	Kellogg / cereals	351,109.1	381,149.0	-7.9
5.	3.	Sears /stores	330,665.7	416,103.5	-20.5
6.	7.	Toyota / cars & trucks	315,274.4	307,304.8	2.6
7.	6.	Chevrolet / cars, trucks	268,239.0	307,711.2	-12.8
8.	13.	Miller beer	233,719.4	181,398.1	28.8
9.	12.	Budweiser beer	212,145.6	184,074.2	15.3
10.	25.	Dodge / cars, trucks, vans	174,601.4	128,138.7	36.3
11.	8.	Nissan / cars & trucks	163,791.2	235,909.8	-30.6
12.	10.	Kmart / stores	159,264.6	193,215.9	-17.6
13.	9.	General Motors	158,751.3	204,359.2	-22.3
14.	14.	Mazda / cars & trucks	156,773.9	180,981.9	-13.4
15.	11.	Kraft Foods	156,128.4	187,700.2	-16.8
16.	17.	Buick / cars	155,213.7	158,695.6	-2.2
17.	30.	Disney shows / parks, cable	151,926.1	115,355.7	31.7
18.	16.	Coca-Cola & Diet Coke	149,904.9	159,647.3	-6.1
19.	23.	Tylenol / remedies	148,168.5	134,288.8	10.3
20.	20.	Macy's / stores	147,415.4	144,857.0	1.8
21.	24.	Honda cars / cycles	142,152.0	130,132.0	9.2
22.	18.	Pepsi & Diet Pepsi	139,263.6	155,905.7	-10.7
23.	21.	American Express	136,005.3	142,307.2	-4.4
24.	15.	Burger King	133,589.1	177,677.8	-24.8
25.	46.	Circuit City	128,156.7	91,796.6	39.6

help in the "selection" process involved in identifying a professional media consultant within the broadcast marketplace who can serve as an educational resource and advertising and marketing consultant. Such an advertising consultant will know what advertising needs to accomplish to be effective and how to handle the creative thinking that goes into developing advertising that can accomplish the "Big Ten" just discussed.

The responsibility for better decision making within the business community lies with the advertiser; the responsibility for improved consulting to that advertiser lies with the media sales representatives who call on these advertisers on a daily basis.

The resources for improvement are available. Let us waste no time in utilizing them.

Know Thy Competition

Many retailers and advertisers feel it is not important to bother about the competition. Fear is certainly a factor in not wanting to know why someone else may be better and certainly no one wants their ego deflated by knowing or feeling their store or business may be second or third best. However, knowing a competitor well may be the best possible way to improve a business position within any given market. Robert H. Waterman explains:

Harvard Business School professor Andy Pearson says that when he was president of PepsiCo, looking at the competition was the company's best form of market research. "The majority of our strategic successes were ideas that we borrowed from the marketplace, usually from a small regional or local competitor. . . . In each case what we did was spot a promising new idea, improve on it, and then outexecute our competitor. To some I'm sure that sounds like copying competition. To me it amounts to finding out what's already working in the marketplace and improving on it."[6]

Know thy competition by listening to and reading their advertising. And then, be more creative in the marketplace when it's your time to promote, execute and advertise.

NOTES

1. Barton C. White and N. Doyle Satterthwaite, *But First These Messages . . . The Selling of Broadcast Advertising* (Boston: Allyn and Bacon, 1989), p. 322.

2. Karl Albrecht, *The Only Thing That Matters* (New York: HarperBusiness, 1992), p. 45.

3. Ibid., p. 47.

4. Robert Fearon, *Advertising That Works* (Chicago: Probus, 1991), p. 149.

5. Brian Mullen and Craig Johnson, *The Psychology of Consumer Behavior* (Hillsdale, N.J.: Lawrence Erlbaum Publishers, 1990), p. 89.

6. Robert H. Waterman, Jr., *The Renewal Factor* (New York: Bantam Books, 1987), pp. 155–156.

CHAPTER 8

The Landscape of the Future
Toward New and Emerging Technologies

> Face it, we all guess wrong about the future. . . . The established experts and the big companies and their planners are wrong time and again. Even if they were once pioneers, they seem rapidly to become overly conservative about the future.
>
> — Tom Peters, *Thriving On Chaos*

THE FUTURE LANDSCAPE

In many ways, the future is already here. The global village and marketplace of today was yesterday's fantasy. In less than a century, we have evolved from the telegraph (wired communication) to the wireless communication of radio to sound with pictures (television) to today's satellite communication, fiber optics, and computers collectively providing instantaneous coverage of events from almost anywhere in the world.

As reported by Lloyd Dobyns and Clare Crawford-Mason, American newspaper columnist Jim Hoagland penned just one month before the 1991 Persian Gulf War that made CNN a worldwide entity, "CNN is a technological and journalistic marvel that transmits not only news but an illusion of meaningful interdependence around the globe to plugged-in officials and travelers. . . . People everywhere know about the same thing at the same time . . . anywhere is rapidly become everywhere."[1]

Indeed, anywhere became the Gulf War one month later whose beginnings were broadcast live by ABC's Gary Shepard. Later, with CNN's Bernard Shaw pinned down in his Baghdad hotel room while broadcasting live, Iraqi leader Saddam Hussein followed his reports and subsequent political developments on CNN while his armies occupied and raped Kuwait.

Such immediacy in communication forms would seem like science fiction to an earlier generation. Dobyns and Mason remind us of the 1812 war with Britain that "started after the main grievance had been settled and continued after the peace treaty had been signed."[2] The reason was communications. It took up to four weeks to get a message across the Atlantic.

So the war started on June 18, 1812, even though the British repealed maritime orders that had upset America on June 16. Raging for two years, it ended with the Treaty of Ghent on Christmas Eve 1814, but Andrew Jackson became somewhat of a folk hero two weeks later at the Battle of New Orleans by devastating the British who suffered two thousand casualties to the Americans' one hundred. This battle after the war was over made Jackson a two-term president.

Contrast this story to the image of Hussein watching daily developments live on CNN. Such immediacy has led to the wide usage of metaphorical terms like "global village" and "spaceship earth" to describe the planet earth.

Globalization versus Homogeneity

Even with the reality of a global economy and the emergence of CNN as the world's most watched news network, forging a global opinion in eighty-six countries with live coverage of world events such as the 1989 Chinese repression of the student protests in Tiananmen Square and the 1991 Persian Gulf War with Iraq, we are reminded that globalization is not quite the same as homogeneity. The more homogeneous we become, the more we strive for individual identity. This has been witnessed on the world stage with the failure of global marketing as a concept. We all do not want the same products precisely because we are all different.

Alvin Toffler reminds us that "Rather than homogenizing the planet, as the old Second Wave media did, the new global media system could deepen diversity instead. Globalization, therefore, is not the same as homogeneity. Instead of a single global village, as forecast by Marshall McLuhan, the late Canadian media theorist, we are likely to see a multiplicity of quite different global villages — all wired into the new media system, but all straining to retain or enhance their cultural, ethnic, national, or political individuality."[3]

Dealing with micromarkets and not the masses, as we have seen, is the message for today's advertisers. Part of micromanaging means offering choices. Toffler explains, using a media example:

Says Robert Iger, head of ABC's entertainment division, "The key words in all of this are choice and alternatives. It's what people didn't have back in 1980. It's what they do have today." But these are precisely what the main networks were designed to prevent. For CBS, ABC, and NBC were Second Wave smokestack companies, accustomed to dealing with masses, not heterogeneous micromarkets, and are having as much difficulty adapting to the post-smokestack Third Wave economy as are General Motors and Exxon.[4]

Although much has been made of the global village concept that has given us common media images and sent American manufacturing jobs overseas to cheap-labor factories, Toffler is quick to remind us that the process that makes this possible will return these jobs home to the United States. The reason? Speed — the speed of information processing, which the less developed countries do not have.

Wealth creation today is a product of instant communication — global networks of markets, banks, and production centers constantly exchanging huge flows of data, information, and knowledge. The communication infrastructures of the lesser developed countries do not provide this; implementing such a structure is a cost factor that is bringing factories and contracts back home again to American soil.

Choice, Choice, and More Choice

Whatever choice is available to either manufacturers or consumers, that choice is dependent upon an electronic society that has truly made the entire world a local neighborhood.

Choice is now what consumers have, not only with available print and electronic media, but with products and services as well. Looking at the media, from the black and white days of the early 1950s when television programmers controlled our lives with the weekly scheduling of widely popular shows at the same times each week, viewers have now wrested control from the programmers with the availability of videocassette recorders. Now viewers watch what they want when they want, regardless of when it is scheduled.

Consumer products can now be purchased twenty-four hours a day on home shopping cable channels or in countless stores that are open around the clock, even on holidays. And, of course, there is never a time when radio or television is not available.

Although 60 percent of Americans are dependent upon the wired cable television services to bring twenty-four-hour-per-day programming into the home, satellites broaden the television audience by bringing distant signals into unwired, rural areas that do not have access to wired cable television.

Signals from satellites are received by large, backyard dishes that literally open up hundreds of possible unscrambled signals to the receptor, giving owners the choice, for example, of watching the local evening news from their hometown station or from stations in cities they may have an interest in hundreds or thousands of miles away. But there are other technologies.

Advertisers and media planners, confronted with present market fragmentation (the number of FM stations has doubled since 1970) may soon, if they have not already, see sales representatives in their offices selling time for LPTV and MMDS stations, along with representatives explaining why their AM radio station is changing frequency on the kilohertz band. Much confusion can be avoided by understanding what the future is likely to bring and how it will impact the local advertising budgeting process.

AM Broadcasting

Since AM radio was the first wireless technology available to advertisers, therefore being the traditional buy for many decades until FM became widely accepted in the 1970s due to its overall interference-free, stereophonic signal, some explanation of recent FCC action may help advertisers and media planners to understand the current status of AM radio in America.

The issuance of new FCC rulings pertaining to AM, according to consulting engineers du Treil, Lundin & Rackley of Washington, D.C., culminate at least five years of effort by the commission to address the declining competitive position of the AM broadcast service. Audiences and advertising dollars have essentially flowed from AM to FM over the last twenty-five years, leaving AM with an overall audience share of under 25 percent.

Essentially, music has gone to the superior quality of the FM band while sports, news, and talk shows have been offered on AM. True, the large metro AM stations that have had the best management, top ad dollars, and biggest budgets over the years — stations like KOA in Denver, WLS in Chicago, and WHAS in Louisville — have remained top-rated and competitive. These stations have done so, despite the AM "handicap," because they could pay the best program hosts to remain with them and/or their adult format is more conducive to more talk, news, or sports and less music.

In general, however, AM stations have not been competitive. To address this concern, the FCC has adopted a plan for expanding the AM band by permitting additional frequencies from 1610 KHZ to 1700 KHZ. No new stations, however, will be allowed to apply. In keeping with the FCC's primary objective of reducing the current AM interference, the expanded band will be available only to existing licensees.

Over time, some level of interference reduction should be apparent by encouraging the most significant interference contributors to migrate to the expanded band. This means the smaller Class IV stations will not be permitted to file for a new channel, since they would not be considered significant interference contributors.

AM stations that are encouraged to migrate will be allowed to operate on both the existing band (their current AM frequency) as well as their new, expanded band frequency for a transition period of five years.

Under these new rulings, too, some daytime AM stations will be allowed to broadcast at night with reduced power.

Although no "new" stations will appear as the result of these actions, a more interference-free AM band will better serve both broadcasters and advertisers in the highly competitive media marketplace of the 1990s.

Reception Technologies

It would be fair to state that the majority of new technologies are the reception technologies or the equipment available to consumers to receive the signals sent out by the various radio, television, or cable stations. Such technologies will have no direct impact on advertisers, per se, other than possibly creating an increased desire to watch more television, thereby increasing potential available audiences. Such technologies, however, will impact the consumer market tremendously.

High-Definition Television (HDTV)

Television receivers are dramatically changing. High-definition television (HDTV) is already a reality in Japan, where Nippon transmits three hours of HDTV daily to large screens set up in public areas. The picture is even sharper than 35 mm film, made possible by 1,125 scanning lines in contrast to today's 525 line scanning system, the U.S. standard. How many years away the economic reality of this new technology is, is anyone's guess, but likely not before the next century.

Special receiver sets (new television sets) will be needed to receive the signal. Even in Japan, the price of HDTV sets ranges from $9,000 to $27,000 (U.S. currency), putting these sets outside of the budget of most homes in a weakening economy. Analysts had predicted the price in Japan to be closer to $4,000 with a one million set penetration by 1992.[5]

Homes using HDTV actually number in the neighborhood of three thousand, mostly due to cost but also because of the size of a six-square-foot object weighing three hundred pounds. In the typically small Japanese home, that would be like putting a Sumo wrestler in one corner of the livingroom. Even if the technology were available in the United States, such limitations would also eliminate most consumers from the market.

To make HDTV viable in the United States, existing television stations would need to convert in order to be able to send out the HDTV signals, a cost of upwards of $50 million per station. Not until worldwide consumer acceptance demands change will broadcasters invest this amount of money in new equipment and technologies.

Advanced Compatible Television (ACTV)

Advanced compatible television (ACTV), a compromise between current television broadcasting and HDTV with 1,025 scanning lines that can be picked up by existing sets, might be the answer. The improved picture quality provided by the additional lines would not be readily apparent, however, without an ACTV set made to receive 1,025 scanning lines. Manufacturers, though, have rushed to fill this gap in anticipation of consumer demand. More than two dozen models are currently available, waiting for the signals to be broadcast from local stations. When this will occur is still a fortune teller's prediction.

Other New Reception Technologies

Other new reception technologies include flat screen televisions that can be hung on walls like pictures and 3-D television without glasses, already unveiled at the National Association of Broadcasters meetings in 1991 and 1992. Playback technologies include a new version of the CD player that can play video as well as audio discs and a new generation of computers that will house massive amounts of information on a five-inch disc.

Some of these new technologies may take the consumer away from traditional forms of media, and thus away from the advertiser's message altogether. This, of course, would be a worst-case scenario as, to date, new technologies such as satellite and cable have not eroded the total time spent with media. What has occurred is a shifting away of the audience from network dependence to cable and satellite dependence that are advertiser-supported. For the foreseeable future, advertisers will still be in the game of trying to identify where their consumers can be found and reached most efficiently. That game of chasing the consumer—trying to identify the many fragments behind which the right consumer group can be found—certainly will not get any easier.

Nonreception Technologies

Low-Power Television (LPTV)

Since 1980 many smaller communities that could never have their own television service now have low-power television (LPTV) stations that broadcast on both VHF and UHF frequencies that reach fifteen to twenty-five miles in any direction. With only ten watts of assigned power on VHF and one thousand on UHF, these stations are truly local in nature and will not interfere with the higher-powered stations assigned to the larger population centers.

The genesis of these stations has its roots in giving individuals, particularly minority groups, an opportunity to enter the broadcast arena since very few television stations are minority-owned or -controlled. And, with the FCC essentially adopting a hands-off regulatory policy toward LPTV, their programming and sales efforts can take many forms.

"The FCC has made few regulations in terms of programming, finances, or ownership. . . . LPTV stations have no regulations concerning how they obtain their money. They can sell ads, operate on a subscription TV basis, ask for public donations, or gather money in other creative ways. . . . Neither does any limit exist on the number of stations any particular group or individual can own."[6]

The likely rationale behind the looser restrictions may rest with the limited influence such smaller stations are likely to exert within their programming area and the fact that when these stations were approved in 1980, Mark Fowler was the chairman of the FCC, successfully courting an era of deregulation where the marketplace was seen as the regulator, not the federal government.

Although not as established as the traditional media, LPTV stations can be a less expensive avenue for television advertising, since rates are similar to local cable television and radio stations. However, advertisers themselves must decide how much of their target audience can be reached via LPTV advertising.

Audiences are still small and the name "low-power" has given a certain stigma to the industry that implies a service of lesser status. Lesser budgets, too, mean older programming that is not necessarily competitive with today's syndicated offerings, which can cost tens of thousands of dollars per episode and are picked up by the larger stations in the metro markets.

The LPTV niche may lie with local news coverage. Most stations offer the local evening news twice nightly, as do their larger cousins, giving celebrity status to the talent and a presence in the market that otherwise would not be apparent. Audiences for the local news are probably the largest of the day and a good value for advertisers who otherwise could not afford the expense of television.

Multichannel Multipoint Distribution Service (MMDS)

One of the least established of the newer television delivery systems, MMDS is a technology that offers cable service without wires to rural areas that have not been wired with traditional cable services. Referred to as "wireless cable," MMDS uses short-range microwave transmissions that are sent to subscriber homes and decoded by means of a downconverter.

As a new technology with investor potential, the FCC became logjammed in 1992 with applications from potential owners of MMDS stations to the extent that a freeze was imposed on the submission of additional applications until the backlog could be cleared up.

Much of the jam was caused by unscrupulous companies or application mills that sold application services with little to no profit potential to investors wishing to capitalize on a new, investor-driven television technology. Because of this and other factors, MMDS has been slow to develop and remains uncompetitive with the wired cable services. However, the potential still remains.

When these systems do come on-line within a given service area, they will, for all practical purposes, be no different from wired cable services with the exception of fewer channels being offered. Stations will have sales staffs who will sell local availabilities on the offered channels to willing advertisers wishing to reach subscribers of the basic services.

The same caveat applies here as with wired cable. Large frequency will be required to reach an extremely fragmented audience; that fragmented audience, however, will likely be even smaller than the wired cable potential, raising serious questions as to whether operators can garner enough business to remain in business.

Advertisers considering this option should ask for validation of the exact number of wired homes, the channels offered to those homes, and any audience measurement studies pertaining to the offered channels.

Beyond the Hype: A Warning to Advertisers

As Howard Gross of Hofstra University points out, "Nearly 80 percent of all technological forecasts turn out to be wrong (Schnaars, 1989)."[7] Therefore, much of the information in this chapter may be all wrong—or, completely right. Or, what is contained herein maybe should not be here at all.

Gross helps us clear the air a bit: "With broadcasters, cable operators, telephone and computer companies contending for the same audiences, it is unlikely that one institution or industry will dominate. It is now a viewer's market and how companies get into the home will no longer be as important as what they bring."[8]

Gross correctly observes that the acceptance of any medium is based upon its capacity to meet the needs of users. Such needs themselves will be based on variable social and economic factors (J. Carey 1989).

Demographics

The younger consumers (under age 50) are the most likely to embrace new technologies, yet their lack of economic resources may price them out of the market. Better educated consumers are also logical prospects and may be able to afford the expense, although discretionary spending among Americans has been falling in recent years due to lack of faith in the economy.

Various segments of the population, then, embrace new technologies differently. Older consumers will not want to change and they will be the most plentiful market. Fewer younger consumers may want new technologies, but cannot afford them as shown by consumer electronics sales statistics for 1991. Overall sales growth, once in the double-digit range, was a paltry one percent, with Sony experiencing a $160 million operating loss.

Cost

As indicated above, new technologies are costly and must find consumer groups willing to pay initially high prices. Prices must then fall, as was the case with digital watches and personal home computers, in order to be acceptable to the broad population. Any new product must eventually fail if not embraced by the masses at a cost that will sustain margins for the manufacturing company.

Benefits

New products must necessarily offer improvements over and above what the consumer already enjoys. This brings us back to price related to benefit. If the resulting benefits are not significantly better than what the consumer is currently using, the price will then not be worth the benefits of ownership.

Design

Consumers logically expect to see differences between old and new technologies but do not adapt well to products that compel them to make significant changes. If something new requires a whole new set of skills, it may not compete well in the consumer marketplace of tomorrow. Adults have a difficult enough time today programming their VCRs and with children the only humans capable of removing the flashing "12" from the set, tomorrow's technology must necessarily be user-friendly.

Individuality

Consumers today want products that serve particular, individual needs. One model does not fit all. Products are increasingly ordered to fit the needs of consumers rather than trying to make each consumer fit into a particular shoe.

The Silver Lining

Despite the difficulties of catering to a new generation and continuing to appeal to the current generational group of consumers who grew up with standard television, companies that today offer new technologies to either consumers or advertisers are beginning to realize that service and quality of product are the only ways to attract and maintain customers for the long term.

"Manufacturers who long ignored the design problems of their products have begun to heed the frustration of consumers. VCR owners, computer operators and facsimile customers once daunted by a plethora of buttons and keys, are now encountering more user-friendly machines."[9]

The Future of the Mass Media

That the mass media will continue to play a role in the information era of the future is beyond question. The need for quick and selective information will only increase with time, meaning that electronic deliverance will only increase in importance.

Whether consumers retrieve this information at will from their computers or television screens or whether the information will be delivered over the air or telephone lines will bring about new questions of power and control in the media marketplace and most certainly the role of federal regulation, as the FCC attempts to ascertain what is best for the consumer as well as the media conglomerates behind the message.

Regardless of how consumers receive their information in the next century, however, what will not change is the retail and business communities' collective need to identify and effectively reach the very group of people that will sustain their businesses. The landscape of retailing itself will likely be transformed by the winds of change, even more so than the topography of the mass media.

The malling of America that began in earnest in the 1970s and boomed in the 1980s is already falling victim to smaller strip centers where merchants can operate with much more favorable leases and overhead, or to shopping experiences like the Home Shopping Club on cable television where consumers do not even have to leave their homes to go into major credit card debt. Of course, consumers usually buy on impulse from this service. Few would watch around the clock to wait for what they need to be offered so they could call in an order.

Soon computer services and other companies destined to cut out the middle-man from retailing will allow consumers to buy anything they want and when they want from their own homes with just the touch of a button. One large fiber-optic trunk line will carry all information services into the family room. That line will be connected to a large television modem that will serve as telephone and computer as well as television. Whatever the consumer wants can be immediately accessed—movies, stock quotes, high-speed access to databases in libraries and museums, software controlled by remote control. The family room will be a communications central reminiscent of the control deck on the starship *Enterprise*.

The interesting thing is, the technology is here to do all of this now. It is just that no one is quite sure how to put all of the pieces together yet. Local telephone companies have already received the necessary FCC go-aheads to carry information/television signals on their telephone lines, via a "video dialtone," which can be accessed on television or computer screens. Congress must still repeal the 1984 Cable Act's telco-cable cross-ownership restriction to allow phone companies to provide video programming directly to subscribers, but these hurdles will soon be past history as video broadcasters make strategic alliances with telephone companies that will usher in a new era of consumer access to fiber optic-based programming.

In fact, the Clinton administration may be leading the way. In the February 19 issue of *USA Today,* it was noted that a $200 billion fiber optic network was being pushed to assist businesses, educators, and researchers. "President Clinton and Vice President Gore have been pushing hard for what they call the 'information superhighway'—a high-tech, fiber-optic network that carries massive amounts of digital information. The network would get $54 million in seed money in 1994 in Clinton's proposed budget; $150 million in 1995."

Consumers will need to be educated to the possibilities and then demand these services for the companies involved to have the economic incentive to proceed, as an enormous cost will be involved in the implementation of a national fiber optic-based video network. It will therefore take quite a few years before that fiber-optic trunk line reaches your home, but reach it it will, and likely sooner than was thought due to the present administration's plan for financial backing.

The impact this will have on shopping districts is unknown. A barren, desolate landscape could be created by homebound consumers no longer dependent on retail services away from the home.

Or merchants could find that shopping from home is only an infrequent convenience—that what consumers really enjoy is the social experience of getting out to the mall or the shopping district, having lunch or dinner with family or friends, and dealing with real people in real stores where merchandise can be seen, touched, tried on, and generally appreciated before purchase.

Part of how the consumer reacts to the already changing retail landscape will be manifested by the business community and how it approaches overall advertising and promotional efforts in the years to come. It is no longer true in opening and sustaining new businesses that "if you build it, they will come."

Consumers are an independent lot. They do not have to do anything. And when money is tight and the manufacturing and industrial sectors of the economy are shrinking in response to the shifting of America to a service-oriented economy, many consumers are losing jobs and are uncertain about future employment. These types of uncertainties mean saving for the future, not spending today. And those who do spend will do so judiciously.

Advertisers cannot assume traffic, customers, and retail sales without needed and proper promotion or advertising. And, when advertising, the assumption cannot be made that such advertising is responsible for the acceptance of the product or the service within the marketplace. Advertising does not make or break a product—only total quality and service from the business can do that.

Nor can advertisers afford the waste that comes from placing a majority of an advertising budget in newspapers or in any other print media that are designed to appeal to everybody and to nobody. Advertising must surgically strike at the right group at the right time. Radio and television are the ultimate surgical strike weapons. To not make them the major part of an advertising budget is the type of dinosaur thinking that is designed for obsolescence. Tradition be damned! It is time for a new paradigm in advertising. Survival is the operative word the remainder of this decade.

SUMMARY

That technological landscape of the future, although unpredictable at best, should serve advertisers as well as consumers well. Although the majority of new technologies seem to be the reception wonders like HDTV and 3D television without glasses, businesspeople can expect new advertiser-driven technologies to compete for the ad dollars in their respective markets. Even the accessed programming on the fiber-optic trunk line that will reach all homes early in the next century will likely have business sponsorship of some sort.

Whether the new telecommunications products and services on the market in the coming decade will meet consumer needs is a matter of conjecture, rooted within demographic profiles and the variables of cost, benefit, design, and individual appeal. That there will be social impact is beyond dispute.

Consumers will be the ones to tell us whether these new forms within a telecommunications infrastructure will increase the flow of information in a positive sense or whether they will make life even more complicated, thus widening the information gap between consumers and their markets.

The advertiser will need to decide what is legitimate and what has no relevance to the long-range goals of the business, but the proper selection of advertising vehicles will be mandatory as the business faces a changing retail landscape that does not ensure consumers will continue to shop away from home as they have traditionally done in the past.

Whichever vehicle is chosen for reaching the ultimate consumer or the end-user, advertising must be placed in proper perspective. It cannot cause a product to succeed any more than it can be held responsible for failure in the market-place. Total overall quality and unparalleled service to the customer are the only variables that ultimately will keep customers from doing their business else-where.

Whatever we do end up seeing on the landscape of the future in terms of new technologies and electronic wonders, however, one thing is for certain. We "ain't seen nothin' yet!"

REPLAY

As with any work done in an area like advertising, where creative forces combine to form as many opinions as there are observers and pundits, there exists much information and/or opinion that could have been included in this book. That the script does not contain all that is available or that some would deem necessary is a tribute to its nonencyclopedic nature; alas, such is also its short-coming.

NOTES

1. From *Quality or Else,* by Lloyd Dobyns and Clare Crawford-Mason. Copyright © 1991 by Lloyd Dobyns and Clare Crawford-Mason. Reprinted by permission of Houghton Mifflin Co. All rights reserved.
2. Ibid., p. 235.
3. Alvin Toffler, *Power Shift* (New York: Bantam Books, 1990), p. 341.
4. Ibid., p. 337.
5. Howard Gross, "Beyond the Hype," *Feedback* 33/2 (Spring 1992): 12.
6. Lynne Schafer Gross, *The New Television Technologies* (Dubuque, Iowa: Wm. C. Brown, 1990), pp. 105–106.
7. Gross, "Beyond the Hype," p. 10.
8. Ibid., p. 11.
9. Ibid., p. 12.

OTHER WORKS CITED

Carey, J. "Consumer Adoption of New Consumer Technologies." Paper presented to the Gannet Center for Media Studies' Technology Studies Seminar, October 23, 1989.

Bibliography

Aaker, David A. and John G. Myers. *Advertising Management*. Englewood Cliffs, New Jersey: Prentice-Hall, 1987.

Albrecht, Karl. *The Only Thing That Matters*. New York: HarperBusiness, 1992.

Ambrey, Margaret K. *1990–1991 Almanac of Consumer Markets*. New York: American Demographic Press, 1989.

Balon, Robert E. *Radio in the 90's*. Washington, D.C.: National Association of Broadcasters, 1990.

Bargh, J. A., R. N. Bond, W. J. Lombardi, and M. E. Tota. "The Additive Nature of Chronic and Temporary Sources of Construct Accessibility." *Journal of Personality and Social Psychology, 50* (1986): 869–878.

Barker, Joel Arthur. *Future Edge*. New York: William Morrow and Company, 1992.

Bolen, William H. *Advertising*. New York: John Wiley & Sons, 1984.

Buchholz, Laura M. and Robert E. Smith. "The Role of Consumer Involvement in Determining Cognitive Response to Broadcast Advertising." *Journal of Advertising, 20* (1991): 4–17.

Burnette, John J. *Promotion Management*. St. Paul: West Publishing Company, 1984.

Burt, Alfred LeRoy. *The British Empire and Commonwealth*. Boston: D.C. Heath and Company, 1965.

Calder, Bobby J. and Brian Sternthal. "Television Commercial Wearout: An Information Processing View." *Journal of Marketing Research, 17*(2) (1980): 173–186.

Carey, J. "Consumer Adoption of New Consumer Technologies." Paper presented to the Gannet Center for Media Studies' Technology Studies Seminar, October 23, 1989.

Clancy, Kevin J. and Robert S. Shulman. *The Marketing Revolution*. New York: HarperBusiness, 1991.

Cornish, Edward, ed. *The 1990's & Beyond*. Bethesda, Maryland: World Future Society, 1990.

Craig, Samuel C., Brian Sternthal, and Clark Leavitt. "Advertising Wearout: An Experimental Analysis." *Journal of Marketing Research* (November, 1976): 371.

Davis, Kenneth C. *Don't Know Much About History.* New York: Crown Publishers, 1990.

DeFleur, Melvin L. and Sandra Ball-Rokeach. *Theories of Mass Communication.* New York: David McKay Company, Inc., 1975.

Dobyns, Lloyd and Clare Crawford-Mason. *Quality or Else.* Boston: Houghton Mifflin Company, 1991.

Dominick, Joseph, Barry L. Sherman, and Gary Copeland. *Broadcasting/Cable and Beyond.* New York: McGraw-Hill Publishing Company, 1990.

Edell, Julie A. and Kevin L. Keller. "The Information Processing of Coordinated Media Campaigns." *Journal of Marketing Research,* (May, 1989): 149–163.

Fearon, Robert. *Advertising That Works.* Chicago: Probus Publishing Company, 1991.

Finn, David W. "The Integrated Information Response Model." *Journal of Advertising, 1* (1984): 28.

Greenwald, A. G. and C. Leavitt. "Audience Involvement in Advertising: Four Levels." *Journal on Consumer Research* (June, 1984): 581–592.

Gross, Howard. "Beyond the Hype: Determining the Success of Future Media Technologies. *Feedback* (Spring, 1992): 10–13.

Gross, Lynne Schafer. *The New Television Technologies.* Dubuque, Iowa: Wm. C. Brown Publishers, 1990.

Hansen, C. H. "Priming Sex-Role Stereotypic Event Schemas with Rock Music Videos: Effects on Impression Favorability, Trait Inferences and Recall of a Subsequent Male-Female Interaction." *Basic and Applied Social Psychology, 10* (1989): 371–391.

Hansen, Christine Hall and Ronald D. Hansen. "Constructing Personality and Social Reality Through Music: Individual Differences Among Fans of Punk and Heavy Metal Music." *Journal of Broadcasting and Electronic Media* (1991): 337.

Head, Sydney W. with Christopher H. Sterling. *Broadcasting in America.* Boston: Houghton Mifflin Company, 1982.

Hofstadter, Richard, William Miller, and Daniel Aaron. *The American Republic.* Englewood Cliffs, New Jersey: Prentice-Hall, 1959.

Holbrook, Morris B. "Situation-specific Ideal Points and Usage of Multiple Dissimilar Brands." *Research in Marketing, 7* (1984): 93–131.

Hughes, David G. "Realtime Response Measures Redefine Advertising Wearout." *Journal of Advertising Research* (May–June, 1992): 61–77.

Jones, John Philip. *How Much Is Enough . . . Getting the Most From Your Advertising Dollar.* New York: Lexington Books, 1992.

Kehrer, Daniel. *Doing Business Boldly.* New York: Times Books, 1989.

King, Edith W. and August Kerber. *The Sociology of Early Childhood Education.* New York: American Book Company, 1968.

Kotler, Philip. *Marketing Management.* Englewood Cliffs, New Jersey: Prentice-Hall, 1976.

Kover, A. J. "Models of Men as Defined by Marketing Research." *Journal of Marketing Research, 4* (1967): 129–132.

Krugman, Herbert E. "The Impact of Television Advertising: Learning Without Involvement." *Public Opinion Quarterly* (Fall, 1965): 349–356.

Margan, Anthony I. "Point of View: Who's Killing the Great Advertising Campaigns of America?" *Journal of Advertising Research* (December, 1984): 34.

Marquardt, R. A. and G. W. Murdock. "The Sales/Advertising Relationship: On Investigation of Correlations and Consistency in Supermarkets and Department Stores." *Journal of Advertising Research* (October–November, 1984): 55–60.

Martin, David N. *Romancing the Brand.* New York: Amacom, 1989.

Martineau, Pierre. "Social Classes and Spending Behavior." *Journal of Marketing* (October, 1958): 130.

Marx, Steven and Pierre Bouvard. *Radio Advertising's Missing Ingredient: The Optimum Effective Scheduling System.* Washington, D.C.: National Association of Broadcasters, 1990.

Miller, Eric, ed. *Future Vision.* Naperville, Illinois: Sourcebooks Trade, 1991.

Mullen, Brian and Craig Johnson. *The Psychology of Consumer Behavior.* Hillsdale, New Jersey: Lawrence Erlbaum Associates, 1990.

Murdock, B. B., Jr. "Auditory and Visual Stores in Short Term Memory." *Acta Psychologica, 27* (1967): 316–324.

Murray, George B. and John R. G. Jenkins. "The Concept of Effective Reach in Advertising." *Journal of Advertising Research* (May–June, 1992): 34–35.

Nickels, William G. *Marketing Communication and Promotion.* New York: John Wiley & Sons, 1984.

Ogilvy, David. *Ogilvy on Advertising.* New York: Vintage Books, 1985.

Ostheimer, R. H. "Frequency Effects Over Times." *Journal of Advertising Research* (February, 1970): 19–22.

Ostrow, Joseph W. "Setting Frequency Levels: An Art or a Science?" *Journal of Advertising Research* (August–September, 1984): 10–11.

Pauk, Walter. "Forgetting and Remembering." *How To Study in College.* Boston: Houghton Mifflin Co., 1984.

Peters, Tom. *Thriving On Chaos.* New York: Alfred A. Knopf, 1987.

Peters, Tom and Robert H. Waterman. *In Search of Excellence.* New York: Harper & Row, 1982.

Pfeffer, Jeffrey. *Managing With Power.* Boston: Harvard Business School Press, 1992.

Ray, Michael, A. G. Sawyer, and E. C. Strong. "Frequency Effects Revisited." *Journal of Advertising Research* (February, 1971): 14–20.

Ries, Al and Jack Trout. *Positioning: The Battle For Your Mind.* New York: Warner Books, 1981.

Schumann, David W., Richard E. Petty, and D. Scott Clemons. "Predicting the Effectiveness of Different Strategies of Advertising Variation: A Test of the Repetition-Variation Hypotheses." *Journal of Consumer Research* (September, 1990): 192–202.

Seiden, Hank. *Advertising Pure and Simple.* New York: Amacom, 1976.

Singleton, Loy. *Telecommunications in the Information Age.* Cambridge, Massachusetts: Ballinger Publishing Company, 1983.

Smith, Frank. "Learning to Read." *Phi Delta Kappa* (February, 1992): 432, 434.

Toffler, Alvin. *Power Shift.* New York: Bantam Books, 1990.

Washburn, Stewart. *Managing the Marketing Functions.* New York: McGraw-Hill, 1988.

Waterman, Robert. *The Renewal Factor.* New York: Bantam Books, 1987.

Wells, H. G. *The Outline of History.* Garden City, New York: Doubleday & Co., 1984.

Wheeler, Keith. *The Townsmen.* New York: Time-Life Books, 1975.

White, Barton C. and N. Doyle Satterthwaite. *But First These Messages . . . The Selling of Broadcast Advertising.* Boston: Allyn and Bacon, 1989.

Young, Daniel R. and Francis S. Bellezza. "Encoding Variability, Memory Organization, and the Repetition Effect." *Journal of Experimental Psychology: Learning, Memory and Cognition, 8*(6) (1982): 545–559.

Zajonc, Robert B. "Attitudinal Effects of Mere Exposure." *Journal of Personality and Social Psychology Monographs, 9*(2) (1968): 1–28.

Index

About the Author

BARTON C. WHITE is Associate Professor of Communication and Broadcasting at Western Kentucky University and a national speaker/trainer in the areas of advertising and marketing. He has co-authored a book on broadcast selling and is a former radio station manager, salesman and announcer. He addresses hundreds of media salespeople and retail business owners and managers each year on the topic of effective retail advertising.